Big Sam

Baseball's Greatest Clutch Hitter

ROY KERR

McFarland & Company, Inc., Publishers

Jefferson, North Carolina

ISBN 978-0-7864-9708-9 (softcover : acid free paper) ∞
ISBN 978-1-4766-1949-1 (ebook)

LIBRARY OF CONGRESS CATALOGUING DATA ARE AVAILABLE

BRITISH LIBRARY CATALOGUING DATA ARE AVAILABLE

On the cover: Detail of Sam Thompson from the 1886 Detroit
Wolverine team photograph (National Baseball Hall of
Fame Library, Cooperstown, New York); *background image*
Recreation Park, circa 1880 (courtesy Burton Historical
Collection, Detroit Public Library)

Printed in the United States of America

*McFarland & Company, Inc., Publishers
Box 611, Jefferson, North Carolina 28640
www.mcfarlandpub.com*

For the Thompson family,
whose members kept the flame alive

Table of Contents

Acknowledgments

Many people helped make this book possible. Margaret Lyday, Leon Lyday and Ed Borsoi reviewed and critiqued each chapter with care and insight, as did baseball historian Bill Jenkinson, who also allowed me full access to his Sam Thompson files. Nora Galbraith at Florida Southern College's Roux Library patiently responded to all my microfilm requests. Steve DeHoff provided important details on early baseball in Danville, Indiana, and unearthed crucial information on the origin of the Danville Browns, Sam Thompson's first team. Betty Jackson graciously shared her research on Big Sam and on Ida Thompson's family. Joe Gonsowski's expertise on Thompson baseball photos and the Detroit Wolverines was invaluable.

The late Victor B. Meyer's research that led to his 1970s campaign to have Sam Thompson elected to the Hall of Fame, as well as his impassioned letters of support for Big Sam, proved to be required (and entertaining) reading. Ken Voyles, editor of the *DAC News,* kindly granted permission to use Detroit Athletic Club photos of Sam in the book.

Don Thompson, a descendant of Sam's brother, William, was my first Thompson family contact. Don's SABR essay on Sam, and his genealogical materials, family photos and newspaper clippings, proved to be indispensable elements for this study. The late David Thompson, a descendant of Sam's brother Nathan, spent most of his life investigating Sam's career, and though he did not live to complete his work, his groundbreaking efforts serve as the bedrock for this study. Keith Thompson, David's brother, generously allowed me full access to David's voluminous records and granted me permission to use clippings and photos from his own extensive collection. Keith Thompson's son, Dr. Nathan Thompson, supplied photos and encouragement during the last phase of this project.

To these friends and colleagues, and to all others who assisted in the completion of this study, I express my deepest thanks and appreciation.

Preface

"Sam took the breath away from the crowds, both in batting and fielding."—Charley Bennett, *Detroit News*, November 8, 1922

Sam Thompson's feats on the diamond have faded from public memory for all but the few who still study and discuss baseball's early years. Even among this group, however, the notion persists that Thompson's greatness lies only in his hitting ability. This misconception is not surprising, given the fact that with the exception of historian Jerrold Casway's perceptive essays, most modern summaries of Sam Thompson's career pay little attention to his brilliant defensive skills.

There is, of course, no doubt that the Danville Slugger was one of baseball's greatest hitters. In 11 full and three partial seasons, he compiled a .331 lifetime batting average, including a .415 mark in 1894, the eighth highest in history. He was the first man to reach the 200-hit plateau in a season (in only 127 games), and he would twice repeat this feat. He scored 100 runs in ten seasons, drove in more than 100 in eight seasons, led the league once in triples, extra base hits and batting average, and in multiple seasons led the league in doubles, hits, home runs and total bases. His RBI per-game ratio, .923, is the highest of any man who ever played the game. Thompson's 126 career home runs rank second among hitters of his era, and many of his four baggers can vie with those hit by his contemporary, Dan Brouthers, for the title of the longest hit in the 19th century. On the base paths, the 6'2", 200-pound Thompson ran well and aggressively, averaged 25 steals per season from 1889 to 1895, and routinely used any perceived hesitation on the part of an opposing outfielder to take an extra base after making a hit.

Forgotten today, however, is the fact that Thompson was as accomplished in the field as he was at the plate and while running the bases. Using a primitive form-fitting fielding glove with no pocket or webbing

1

to help trap the ball, he compiled the highest fielding average of any outfielder who played 1,000 games and whose career concluded before the 20th century. His 283 outfield assists rank twelfth all time, and among all outfielders who played more than 1,000 games, his assist-per-game ratio (one every 4.9 games) is the highest in history. Depending on the reporting source, Thompson in 1895 became either the first of four men to record three outfielder-to-catcher assists in a game, or the only man ever to record four in a game.

After his major league career ended, Sam Thompson played amateur ball for nearly a decade, and in 1906, at age 46, ten years after his last full big league season, he came out of retirement to play eight games for an injury-plagued Detroit Tigers team, winning one of those contests by a timely hit, and saving several others by spectacular outfield catches.

In addition to correcting errors that have crept into the literature about Sam Thompson, the present study provides a comprehensive review of his life and career from his childhood in Danville, Indiana, to his last years working as a U.S. Deputy Marshal in Detroit. It concludes by reaffirming what Sam's contemporaries knew: far from being just an outstanding hitter, Thompson was a true "five skills" player who hit for power and average, routinely stole bases and took extra bases on hits, made spectacular outfield catches seem commonplace, and regularly threw out advancing runners from anywhere in the outfield.

Sam Thompson, the complete ballplayer, ranks among the very best who ever played the game.

A Note on Spelling, Punctuation, Usage and Syntax

Nineteenth century spelling, punctuation, usage and syntax varied greatly from today's norms. Baseball was usually spelled as two words—base ball—until the early 20th century. Center field was almost invariably spelled *centre* field. Some nouns that normally are capitalized today, e.g., the Huntingdon Street Grounds, were not during that era (Huntingdon Street grounds). Comma placement, particularly in newspaper articles, was frequently haphazard. Player nicknames, such as *Charley* (or *Char–*

lie) Bennett, were often spelled one way on one day, and another way the next.

In all press accounts recorded in this volume, the original spelling, punctuation and usage has been maintained except in cases in which clarification was deemed necessary.

CHAPTER ONE

Son of the Heartland: 1860–1884

"Knock the leather off it," someone shouted to Thompson as he went to the bat…. "I'll try," said Sammy, and bif! bang! boof! The ball went sailing over the fence.—*Evansville Daily Journal*, August 18, 1884

In the late 18th century, the state known today as Indiana was part of an enormous expanse of land called the Northwest Territory, which stretched from the Appalachian Mountains to the Mississippi River. In 1800, a large portion of this area officially was designated the Indiana Territory, and in 1816 it became the nineteenth state of the Union. Attracted by the region's rich soil and inexpensive farm land, hardy pioneers from the east and south soon crossed the Appalachians and settled in what would come to be known informally as the Hoosier State.

The Thompsons and the McPheeters were two pioneer families that put down roots near the small town of Danville, 20 miles west of Indianapolis. Kentuckian Samuel McPheeters' father was a Revolutionary War veteran who had received a land grant in Washington County, Indiana, in the early 1800s. In 1829, McPheeters moved with his wife Eliza to a farm northwest of Danville. Their six children were born there. James Thompson, a North Carolina farmer, arrived in the area with his wife Martha and four children in 1838. Another five Thompson children were born in the family's new home state.

The Thompsons and the McPheeters worked the land on neighboring farms, and in 1849 the families were united by the marriage of 20-year-old Jesse Thompson to the McPheeters' third child, Rebecca, who was just 16. The young couple settled on the Thompson family farm, and while Jesse perfected his woodworking skills as a cabinet maker, Rebecca was busy having babies. Six Thompson sons were born to the couple between 1850 and 1860, although the fifth, John, died before his first birthday. Another son and three daughters would arrive in ensuing years.

Like all Americans, the lives of the Thompsons and the McPheeters were irrevocably altered by the Civil War. Southern-born Jesse joined the Union cause and was absent from home for three years. Two of Rebecca's brothers, Joseph and William, were among the more than 24,000 Union dead from the Hoosier state.

The traditional rhythms of Midwestern country life gradually returned after the war. Rebecca and Jesse moved their growing family from the farm to Danville proper in 1868. First settled in 1824, Danville was the seat of Hendricks County government, and by 1850 boasted a population of 500. Thanks to nearby Indianapolis's status as the state's railroad hub, Danville soon was a stop on the rail line from the capital

Left: Jesse Thompson, Sam Thompson's father. A Civil War veteran, Jesse was a cabinet maker whose fine walnut and cherry furniture pieces were highly praised in Central Indiana. *Right:* Rebecca Thompson, Sam Thompson's mother. Rebecca's grandfather, James McPheeters, fought in the Revolutionary War from the Battle of Cowpens, January 1781 to the Battle of Yorktown, October 1881, and was rewarded a grant of land in Indiana for his service (courtesy Don Thompson).

Sam Thompson and his five brothers. Standing, from left to right: Arthur, Sam and Cyrus. Seated, from left to right: William, Nathan and Lawrence. Cyrus, William and Sam all played on their hometown baseball team, the Danville Browns (courtesy Don Thompson).

west to Terre Haute. By the early 1880s, the town's business community, while lively, was still operating on a modest scale. A state business directory of the era noted that its major industries were limited to two saw mills, a flour mill, a tannery, a brick yard and a tile factory.[1] A neighboring village's newspaper of the era described the town admiringly as "quite a pretty little city, with five business blocks and residences, and [it] is strictly a temperance town."[2]

Amid the din and clamor of the second Industrial Revolution that was taking place in America's big cities and towns during the post–Civil War era, change arrived more slowly in rustic Danville, where pioneer values of hard work, independence and devotion to family and religion still held sway. They were values the Thompsons never abandoned.

While Jesse Thompson's finely made cherry and walnut furniture was prized in and about Danville, he often supplemented his earnings by making coffins for the recently departed, and for this practice he was humorously dubbed "the undertaker" by the town newspaper. According to family legend, he walked the town's streets carrying a large staff, into which a series of regularly-spaced notches had been carved. Placing the staff next to any citizens that he would encounter, he was able to get a good estimate of the coffin size they would need for their final journey.

Eight of the nine surviving Thompson children spent their entire lives in Indiana. Two daughters, Annie and Julia, married and raised families in Indianapolis. The third girl, Jessie Mae, a spinster, ran a millinery shop in Danville. Elder sons Lawrence and Arthur took up their father's cabinet-making trade, while third-born Nathan followed in his grandfather's footsteps and worked the land on the family farm. William (also known as Humphrey) became Danville's baker, and Cyrus became the town druggist.

The life of the remaining Thompson child, Samuel Luther, born in 1860, took a decidedly different direction. He would earn his living as a professional baseball player and become a nationally-known star. His abilities on the diamond were of such high caliber that they eventually earned him a place in the Baseball Hall of Fame.

The Thompson children received a rudimentary education at the local school house, and by their late teens began their work careers. All six of the slender Thompson boys were more than six feet tall, but they divided into two different camps with regard to personality. The three oldest, perhaps as befitting the nature of their professions of carpenter and farmer, were quiet, reserved and circumspect. Two younger siblings, William and Cyrus, were more outgoing and fun-loving. Although fourth-born son Samuel's eventual occupation, like those of the other younger Thompson boys, brought him into constant contact with the public, he was by nature quiet and retiring, and like his older brothers showed little emotion. These traits later earned him nicknames like "Silent Sam" or the "Silent Outfielder" in baseball circles.

The younger Thompson boys, particularly Cyrus and Samuel, were famous in their youth for "wandering with loose terms [unsupervised] in the highways and woodlands in and around Danville,"[3] which they knew as well "as a spider knows its web."[4] A writer from the town newspaper once recalled an incident from their youth that could easily have appeared in Mark Twain's The Adventures of Tom Sawyer.

Cyrus and Samuel "knew where blackberries grew thickest; knew which watermelon patches were unguarded in the dark of the moon; where hickory nuts, walnuts and paw paws grew; where swimming holes were deepest and fishing was best. They were the first Danville boys to go barefoot in spring and the last to put on their shoes in autumn."[5] One spring when the mulberry crop was particularly bountiful, the two Thompsons eagerly visited their favorite such tree north of Danville when the crop was ripe. Along with the mulberries that year came clouds of a pest known as "Lady Betty" bugs that "stung the cherries, grapes, peaches and mulberries to drink of the delicious juices."[6] Many local residents incorrectly believed that Lady Betty bugs left an injection of poison in the fruit as they bored into it.

The Thompson boys, however, had not heard of the alleged poisoning power of Lady Betty bugs. They only knew that the mulberries were ripe, and they shinnied up their favorite tree one afternoon and ate their fill. A passing farmer then predicted their demise: "Did you know them mulberries was stung and poisoned by Lady Betty bugs?"[7] His face turning pale at the thought, he continued, "Your Dad is an undertaker and you better hurry home and give him an order for two coffins."[8] That evening around the supper table, "the two mulberry eaters secretly and sorrowfully wondered if it was to be the last supper the family would have as a complete unit. Early next morning the family breakfasted together as it had supped the evening before. Nothing uncommon had happened between the two meals. There were no after-effects from the mulberries which Lady Betty had not poisoned with her sting. There were still nine [children] in the Thompson family."[9]

The two coffins were not ordered. "Instead, soon after breakfast the same two Thompson boys hustled back to the mulberry tree north of Danville and stripped it clean of its fruit, even to the mulberries in the topmost branches."[10]

Young "Sammy" Thompson, as he was known around Danville, was a good student who "excelled in reading and geography,"[11] and a budding outdoorsman who loved to hunt and to fish the local streams. Unlike his brothers, who settled on professions early in life, Sam by his late teens still seemed to have no traditional career in mind. The 1880 Census lists the then 19-year-old's occupation using the generic term "laborer."[12] A year later he was clerking in a Danville restaurant and confectionary shop. "Sammy Thompson ... is doling out peanuts and caramel at McCurdy's."[13]

Despite his slow professional start, Sammy possessed enormous baseball talent, and found that performing occasional odd-jobs instead of dedicating himself to a traditional full-time profession gave him more time to devote to the sport. It did not take long to discover the wisdom of his decision.

Some accounts of Sam Thompson's life and career suggest that his father Jesse discovered baseball while serving in the Union army during the Civil War and then taught the game to his sons upon his return home.[14] While it is likely that Jesse witnessed and even played ball games during his service, early forms of baseball were already popular in nearby Indianapolis decades earlier. In 1837, the *Indianapolis Journal* reported that a city ordinance had been passed that provided for a fine of one dollar upon conviction of "any person who shall on the Sabbath day play at ... bandy [bandy ball], town ball, corner ball, or any other game of ball."[15]

While Jesse Thompson was off to war in 1862, an amateur adult baseball nine, the Summit City Base Ball Club of Fort Wayne, Indiana, was founded. Although it was a short-lived endeavor, many of the club's members were transplants from New York and Pennsylvania, and they continued to spread interest in the game throughout the state. Several Midwest clubs, including the Buckeyes of Cincinnati (1856), the Unions of Chicago (1856) and the Cyclones of St. Louis (1859) were active before the start of the war.

By the time Sammy Thompson reached his tenth birthday in 1870, a group of Cincinnati businessmen had recruited and hired the first recognized fully-professional team, the Red Stockings, and sent them on a two-year tour across the nation to represent the Queen City. The Reds took on all comers, won more than 90 percent of their games, drew national attention to the sport, and hastened both the rise of professional leagues and the demise of amateur baseball organizations.

In 1871, the first professional league, the National Association, was founded, and an Indiana club, the Fort Wayne Kekiongas, was among its teams during its inaugural season. The Kekiongas made baseball history on May 4, when they defeated the Cleveland Forest Citys, 2–0, in the first major league game ever played. Fort Wayne pitcher Bobby Mathews struck out six in a five-hit shutout for the win, and would go on to collect 296 more victories over an 18-year major league career. Three of Cleveland's five hits were made by catcher Jim "Deacon" White, and his leadoff double off Mathews in the first inning of the game was the first hit made in major league history. White was still in the game sixteen years later, and became Sam Thompson's teammate on the Detroit Wolverines. Both men would eventually be enshrined at Cooperstown, an honor that would only arrive posthumously, more than a half-century after their deaths.

Players on the financially weak Kekiongas were paid from game gate receipts instead of by standard salaries, and the team folded on August 29, 1871, after several players, including star pitcher Bobby Mathews, left the club in protest over not being paid. Despite this brief stay by an Indiana team in the first professional league, by the time Sam Thompson entered his teen-age years, numerous other professional leagues in the Midwest and across the country had formed, improving the odds for talented, aspiring young ball players to make a career in baseball.

After Sam Thompson became an established national star, sportswriters became interested in how he got his start in the game. Since records of his play prior to 1883 were lacking, contemporary sources improbably concluded that he did not play baseball at all until that year, when he already was in his early twenties. "Imagine an American boy reaching the age of 23 before discovering he could play ball—and within three years becoming one of the greatest batters the game ever produced. Such is the history of Samuel A.[*sic*] Thompson."[16]

The myth of Thompson's late start in the game persisted even after his death. In 1923 sportswriter Fred Lieb, longtime contributor to *The Sporting News* and inductee as a Sportswriter to the Baseball Hall of Fame, asserted that Sam's introduction to baseball did not occur until he was 20. "An odd thing about Thompson's career is that he never played any baseball until he was 20 years of age. He took to the game quickly, for three years later he landed a baseball job with Evanston [i.e., Evansville]."[17]

Others with a greater familiarity with Sam's early life in Danville offered a more likely account. "It was in the commons near the town that he first learned to pick up 'daisy cutters' [hard hit ground balls] and wield the willow [bat]."[18]

Sam and his brothers Cyrus and William all eventually played for Danville's top amateur team, the Browns, and while growing up they undoubtedly served as each others' practice partners. After they moved from the family farm north of Danville into town in 1868, when Sam was eight years old, greater opportunities for team play with other boys became available for all the Thompsons. In addition to the Danville Browns, local historian Steve DeHoff's research[19] has uncovered the names of nearly a dozen town squads of the era, most of them christened with colorful nicknames such as the Blues, the Paralyzers, the Sluggers, the Cool Heads and the Comets. Their numbers even included two "old timer" squads, the West Side Choctaws and the North Side Cyclones. It was humorously noted after one of their contests that the "participants have been so sore ever since that they can be easily told [identified] by their daily walk, which would admit them to the third degree of the order of the Limps, and no questions asked."[20]

The Browns were Danville's premier club, and even boasted a reserve or second-tier nine, whose members substituted when a first team starter was injured or otherwise unable to play. The reserves occasionally played morning games against weaker opponents or other clubs' second teams before the Browns' regularly scheduled afternoon contests.

The only extant reference to Sam's baseball career prior to his start with the Browns in 1883 suggests that he was not always a star player. After he had retired from big league play the *Hendricks County Republican* noted that while Sam at the time had been furnishing sportswriters with reminiscences of his career, "he failed to tell them about the time his brother Cy chased him off the old 'Paragon' team at Lagoda [a nearby town] because he couldn't either bat or field."[21]

By 1883, however, 23-year-old Sam Thompson had earned a spot on the Browns, hitting fourth and playing first base. Brother Cy hit seventh and played right field or occasionally third base. The Thompson boys were the best hitters on the team. "The fashion the Thompson boys have of knocking balls over into Washington Township should not prove popular [to their opponents] during the summer months. If they keep it up the boys will be ruled in the fast ring."[22]

Cy may have possessed as much talent as younger brother Sam, but at 26, married, and with a young daughter and a full-time job as the town druggist, he gave no thought to becoming a professional. Sam, 23, single, and not tied down to a steady job, clearly was attracted to a career in baseball. Years later he recalled the thrill he experienced when he saw his first professional contest:

> The first professional game of ball I ever saw was in Indianapolis in '82 between that club and the Philadelphias. Among the players of the Phillies I remember were John Manning, Warner and Sid Farrar, and the Indianapolis nine was composed of such players as James Keenan, Larry McKeon, Dan O'Leary, Jerry Dorgan, Patty Callahan and Al Buckenberger. The game ran along very smoothly, with the Indianapolis club in the lead, 11 to 8, until the eighth inning when the Phillies got three men on base and Warner came to the bat. He hit the ball over Dan O'Leary's head for a home run, clearing the bases and winning the game, 12 to 11.[23]

With the exception of the year in which it was played, Sam's memory appears to be precise with regard to the details of this game. It must have taken place during Sam's tenure with the Danville Browns in 1883, however, since some players mentioned as being on both clubs in 1882 were not then on the respective teams.

The first of two contests played between the Browns and the Plainfield Crescents in the summer of 1883, described years later as "the most important game ever in Hendricks County,"[24] was of particular significance for the town of Danville and for Sam Thompson.

> The game was the result of weeks of bantering between the two teams. That spring, the Danville Browns and the Plainfield Crescents were organized, and from the first both played fine ball. But it appeared that each side had a wholesome respect for the other, and it was not until July 9 that they finally clashed, and then only after weeks of jockeying. In some manner it developed into a betting game, and every day for a week or more, Danville sent men to Plainfield and Plainfield sent men to Danville with rolls of money to wager on the result.[25]

As game day approached, Danville resorted to trickery to attempt to assure a victory. "They sent to Indianapolis and hired a [professional] pitcher named 'Dickerson' to do mound duty for them in that one game, for it was their intention to rob Plainfield and then disband [the Browns team] and put in the rest of the summer spending the money."[26] Feeling assured of victory, Danville's residents then added to their original bets on the game, and then headed to Plainfield. That town's newspaper, the *Friday Caller*, offered a description of the trip that was worthy of an O. Henry or a Mark Twain short story.

For days prior to the game, every mode of transportation in Danville had been engaged, and it was impossible to find anything in the driving line. Some few fellows who had bet all their money actually walked to Plainfield, for they knew they would have money enough after the game to go to Indianapolis on the train and either stay all night or go home on the midnight train. Buggies, carriages, hacks, even farm wagons were chartered for the trip, and the livery stables reaped a harvest. And it seemed that in spite of the money which had been wagered, every fellow had a few dollars in his pockets to put up after reaching the grounds. In the hacks had gathered a number of those who were willing to take a crack at most any kind of game of chance, and poker games, craps, seven-up at a dollar a corner, and other games were played on the trip. Some of the sports lost all their remaining money before they reached Plainfield.[27]

The Browns hit first, and scored two runs, but Plainfield responded by tying the score, and then gradually increased their lead, thanks to a clever strategy.

By this time the Crescents had learned that while Dickerson [the professional] was some pitcher, the Browns had no catcher who could hold him. This was before the days of the catcher's mit[t] and mask and chest protector, and these catchers were doing their work bare handed and completely unprotected…. The Crescents had found out that while the catcher was standing back by the backstop, which was the play at that time, they could not touch "Dickerson's" balls, so they struck at two, and then when the catcher came up "behind the bat" and "Dickerson" had to ease up, they could hit him. And these tactics they played throughout the rest of the game.[28]

Plainfield won the game, 14–9, and "it was a sorry crowd which wended its way homeward to Danville that evening."[29] The Browns played two more games against Plainfield, one in August and another in September, winning both, with Sam Thompson contributing a home run in the first contest. Nevertheless, even two decades later, "when a Danville man begins to talk baseball with a crowd of Plainfield fellows, one of the latter is sure to smile and ask: 'Do you remember when we licked you and won all your money?'"[30]

Contrary to what one might expect, Sam Thompson declared that the Plainfield game was the luckiest thing that ever happened to him. "For … while I lost every cent I had on earth, if we had won that game the Browns would have disbanded and the chances are I would never have been heard of instead of working my way to the top."[31]

"Dickerson," the imported Danville Browns pitcher in the first

Danville/Plainfield game of 1883, was in reality Indianapolis native Al McCauly, a pitcher/first baseman who spent two seasons with the American Association Indianapolis Hoosiers, and who became Sam Thompson's teammate again in 1890, when he put in 116 games at first base for the Philadelphia Phillies.

Not all amateur games between local rivals were as hotly contested as the Browns/Crescents matchup. In fact, the ritual pleasantries associated with adult amateur baseball that had developed in the 1850s and 1860s were still practiced among some small town Central Indiana rivals in the 1880s, even though such customs had long since disappeared in the emerging professional ranks.

Upon arrival at an opponent's home town, rival teams often were warmly welcomed and afforded the respect usually due visiting dignitaries. Ball games served as major social events for the amusement-starved rural populace, and a festive holiday mood prevailed. This air of excitement was captured in an account of the arrival of the nearby community of Thorntown's team to Danville for a game scheduled with Sam Thompson's Browns on August 13, 1883.

> The Thorntowns arrived here at ten o'clock in the morning, having driven through in carriage, and to the delight and surprise of everybody, brought with them one of the best bands it has been the pleasure of our citizens to listen to for a long time. When the procession filed in town and the band struck a stirring air, the square assumed a wonderful appearance of life and people issued from everywhere.... The band proceeded to take in [explore] the town during the next few hours. They infused more life into the town than has been exhibited for weeks.[32]

In the game that followed, the Thorntowns were demolished, 26–0, by the powerful Browns, with Sam Thompson contributing a home run, his first recorded four-bagger, and brother Cy collecting three hits and scoring three runs. The festivities concluded with a show of good sportsmanship. After the contest, the Thorntown band led both teams back to Danville from the ballpark located just east of town.

The Browns most powerful adversary in 1883 was the Indianapolis Hoosier team, the same independent professional nine whose game against Philadelphia Sam had witnessed that year. Historically, the Hoosiers were the third professional team that had been organized in the state capital. In 1876, the Indianapolis Westerners competed in the

International League, a short-lived rival of the National League. Two years later, the Indianapolis Blues joined the National League and finished fifth in the then six-team circuit.

The first 1883 contest between the amateur Browns and the independent professional Hoosiers took place in Indianapolis on August 25. Sixty Danville residents lent moral support to the Browns by accompanying them to the game in the capital, but the amateurs were pounded by the Hoosiers, 14–4. Both Sam and Cy Thompson took the collar that day, going a collective 0–8, with Sam making an error at first base. Despite the loss, "the Indianapolis boys paid the Browns the compliment of saying they are the best amateur club they have played thus far."[33]

The second meeting between the two teams took place in Danville on September 21, and this time the Hoosiers barely escaped with their dignity intact. Regarded as the premier professional team outside the two national leagues, they had already beaten the Philadelphia and New York League clubs, and the New York Metropolitans, Columbus and Baltimore of the American Association during the season, an accomplishment that virtually assured them an invitation to join the Association in 1884. A loss to a small town amateur team at this juncture would have dealt a serious blow to the team's national aspirations.

The Hoosiers avoided disaster by narrowly defeating the Browns, 13–10, in their second meeting. Batting second in the Browns' lineup, Sam Thompson connected for three hits, including a double, the only extra-base hit of the game. He also scored two runs and registered an error and an assist at first base. Breathing a sigh of relief, the *Indianapolis Times* provided some details of the game: "The O'Learyites [the Hoosiers were managed by Dan O'Leary] barely escaped a crushing defeat at Danville yesterday, their antagonists being the Browns of that village, who battered [pitchers] Murphy and Veach at will, and kept well in the lead until the sixth inning, when they lost the game by a succession of costly errors. Downing of the home [Indianapolis] team and [Sam] Thompson of the Browns, excelled with the stick."[34]

Coverage of 12 Browns games appears in extant copies of Danville's newspaper, the *Hendricks County Republican*, in 1883, and it includes ten box scores (but only the first of the two games against Indianapolis) and two line scores. In these games the team compiled a 9–3 record, losing only to Indianapolis, Terre Haute and Plainfield, but managing to avenge losses to the latter two clubs in a second meeting. In the ten games for which complete statistics are available, Sam Thompson recorded 16 hits, including three doubles, a triple and two home runs. Playing first base with little or no protection for his hands, he made eight errors, but had two assists and one unassisted double play.

While there is no existing record of the Danville Browns competing against a team from Evansville, Indiana, in 1883, baseball enthusiasts there had heard of Sam Thompson's heavy hitting with the Browns. A professional team was organized in that city for the 1884 season, and in February Sam Thompson was listed as "under contract with the Evansville club."[35]

Although he spent the entire 1884 season traveling the Midwest with the Evansville nine, later accounts of Thompson's transition from amateur to professional baseball (including one of his own) almost unanimously overlook this formative year in his career, focusing rather on a dubious story about the future Hall of Famer's alleged discovery while he was still playing for Danville by a well-known baseball promoter of the era. Viewed collectively, these accounts reveal how the repeated retelling of an undocumented baseball story can conceal the truth behind a fascinating but false facade.

The originator of these stories was "Hustling Dan" O'Leary, an average minor league player who had brief stints in the major leagues (45 games in five seasons, while playing for five teams) before turning to managing and sports promoting. O'Leary, born in Detroit in 1856, had a long-established reputation for spinning self-ingratiating stories that often bore no resemblance to the truth. His major baseball achievement was assembling the outstanding independent professional team in Indianapolis in 1883, leading to the club's admission to the American Association the following year. Slated to manage the Indianapolis nine in the Association, O'Leary had a falling out with the club owners and moved on to Saint Louis, where he managed that city's entry in the short-lived Union League. Afterward, O'Leary's trajectory was "progressively downward in the baseball pecking order, although he would occasionally succeed in planting stories that he was about to be hired here, there, and everywhere."[36]

Out of baseball by the mid 1890s, "Hustling Dan" spent his last years in trouble with the law for running illegal gaming houses. His biographer summed up his life by suggesting that "if God had not created Hustling Dan O'Leary, Damon Runyon would have."[37]

In 1897, at the end of Sam Thompson's illustrious career, O'Leary, perhaps grasping for one last attempt to get back into baseball, boasted to *Sporting Life* that he had been responsible for signing Sam to his first pro contract after the second meeting between the Browns and Indianapolis in 1883, a game whose details have been discussed above. "Perhaps everybody don't know it, but Sam Thompson is a crack first baseman as well as outfielder. He was playing for the 'Danville Browns' when the irrepressible Dan O'Leary discovered him. However, Dan says that when he afterward came here [to Danville] to sign him for his famous aggregation [the Indianapolis Hoosiers] he found him away up in the country, seated on top of a barn nailing on shingles."[38]

A few months later, O'Leary repeated his story for the *Indianapolis Sun*, once again claiming credit for getting Thompson started on his professional career. This revised and expanded version, rich in humor and detail, and recounted in O'Leary's own words, soon captured the imagination of the baseball world:

> Do you know how I got Sam Thompson? The Danville club in Indiana wanted a date [opportunity to play the Indianapolis club] and I gave it to 'em in Indianapolis, and then to turn the compliment, I took the [team] to Danville. After I got there the president of the Danvilles told me there was a pretty strong player named Sam Thompson 'round there. Sam, he said, was out a mile, building a house. I thought I'd go and see Sam.... I met Sam coming along home ... with his Hamlet countenance, and I said to him, "Do you play ball?" He says, "Yes, I play a little ball ... I used to play in the Danville." "Will you play this afternoon?" "Yes, I guess so." He did play. The grounds were country, the grand stand cost $10, and half of it fell down before the first inning was over.... I put Murphy in to pitch ... [and] when Thompson came up with the willow, he hit Murphy over into the corn field and out of sight; the ball was never found, and I guess it is going yet. He repeated the dose in the sixth inning.... Sam played first base and played it well ... we had a rough time to beat them but we managed it. After that it wasn't long before I signed Sam Thompson, you bet. And look at him now. Isn't he great?[39]

Eight years later, sportswriter Hugh Fullerton retold O'Leary's now well-known tale in the *Chicago Daily Tribune*. Although Fullerton later gained national recognition for being the first to suggest that the 1919 World Series between the Chicago White Stockings and the Cincinnati

Reds was fixed, he was just ten years old at the time of O'Leary's alleged signing of Sam Thompson. Nevertheless, his revised version of the story adds elements that do not appear in the O'Leary original, details that must be considered to have proceeded from Fullerton's imagination.

According to Fullerton, the Danville Browns' manager was "in distress because his star player [Thompson] had to work that day and could not play."[40] Sam Thompson, described here as a "tall, awkward-looking man"[41] was working to earn a day's wage of $3 by "clap boarding a house three miles down the state pike."[42] Arriving on the scene, O'Leary purportedly offered Thompson five dollars to play against Indianapolis. Sam agreed to the offer, and during the game was reported to have slammed the ball over the center field fence. "That night, Thompson signed an Indianapolis contract. He demanded $75 a month, and O'Leary filled in the contract for $150."[43]

There are several problems both with O'Leary's original story and Fullerton's elaboration. First, O'Leary had already seen Sam play a month earlier in the first game between Danville and Indianapolis, when the Browns lost 14–4. In that game, Thompson went 0–4 and committed an error at first base. It is possible, but highly unlikely, that O'Leary, whose Indianapolis nine that year had already defeated powerful National League and Association teams, would go out of his way to seek out and sign an untried amateur like Thompson, who had gone hitless and committed an error in his team's first game against the Hoosiers. Second, in O'Leary's account, Sam says that he "used to play" for the Browns, when in fact he was still a team member and played every game for them both before and after the Indianapolis games. Third, as we shall see, although Sam performed much better in his club's second game against O'Leary's team, collecting a double and two singles, he did not slug two home runs "into the cornfield" as claimed by O'Leary. Fourth, Sam Thompson did not receive a contract offer from Indianapolis shortly after the game, as suggested by O'Leary. Rather, he signed with Evansville for the 1884 campaign. Finally, O'Leary himself was no longer with the Indianapolis club in 1884, having taken a position of player/manager for the new Union League's Saint Louis team.

The inconsistencies in O'Leary's original story and Fullerton's elaboration did not prevent a third version of the tale from surfacing in 1907. This one, which strayed even further from the original, was published in various newspapers, including the *Salt Lake Herald*. It left out O'Leary as a protagonist, retained the story of coaxing Sam away from a carpentry job to play ball, incorrectly identified the Indianapolis team as a National League club, and inaccurately claimed that Danville's amateurs had defeated the Hoosiers.

In this version, when it was discovered that the Danville Browns were shy a man on their team, Sam, who purportedly was shingling a house a mile outside town, was hunted down and offered $5 to play. "Sam just fell off his ladder, so eager was he to get into the game. He hit the ball all over the lot and it was his terrific batting that caused Danville to beat Indianapolis. The manager of the Indianapolis team signed him before he left the grounds."[44]

A few years later (1910), Sam Thompson himself added to the confusion over the details of his transition from amateur to professional when he unaccountably omitted his Evansville year from an oral summary of his career that he gave to the press. "I had gone from Danville to Indianapolis to play center field for the short-lived Northwest League team."[45] Sam did play center field for a half year for an Indianapolis team of the Western League in 1885, but between his Danville days and his stint with Indianapolis, he put in a full season in 1884 with Evansville. Additionally, it was Evansville, not Indianapolis, which briefly was a member of the Northwest League.

In 1913, the *Indianapolis Sun* offered a new version of the story, now including Sam's erroneous assertion that he went directly from Danville to Indianapolis, and reinstating Dan O'Leary as a participant in the story.[46] A decade later, Sam Crane, a major-league-infielder-turned-sportswriter, and Sam Thompson's teammate for two years in Detroit (1885–1886), offered a fifth version of the O'Leary story, this time including an imagined Thompson dialogue presented in rustic language. According to Crane, after O'Leary offered Sam a contract, Sam responded, "You see, I have never been away from home further than five miles, and I am sort of skeered about going to such a big city as Indianapolis, but I reckon when I tell paw and maw 'bout them five dollars per day they will be willing to let me go."[47]

Both hustling Dan O'Leary and Sam Thompson died a few months after Sam Crane's version of the story appeared in print in 1922, and modern sports historians still include further-altered versions of O'Leary's tale of the tall slugger being coaxed down from his carpentry job to play ball in their brief Thompson biographies. A 1996 portrait, for example, incorrectly suggested that the contract offer came from Detroit's National League club: "Legend has it that a scout for the Detroit Wolverines coaxed Thompson down from a roof he was repairing with an offer to play baseball for the same $2.50 per day he was earning as a carpenter."[48] More recently, a 2007 version offers some more twists to the original tale. The scout is now claimed to be from Evansville and not Indianapolis, and he purportedly comes to Danville to see Sam's brother Cy play. Cy recommends that he look up Sam, who is allegedly doing carpentry work nearby with his father. Offered $2.50 per game to play for Evansville, Sam accepts the contract.[49]

While the complete and accurate account of Sam Thompson's transition to professional ball may never be known, most of the details of original Dan O'Leary version of the story, and almost all the details in the story's numerous extrapolations over the years have no basis in fact. Time and repetition, however, have done their jobs well, for the story of the young amateur slugger lured away from a carpentry job to play ball and then offered a professional contract is now inextricably, if incorrectly, associated with Sam Thompson's career.

In a final ironic twist to the story, Sam's 1884 Evans-

Sam Thompson in his Evansville uniform, 1884, his first year as a professional. This is the earliest known photograph of Sam in a baseball uniform (courtesy Keith Thompson).

ville team got a new manager for the last two weeks of the season. He was Dan O'Leary—the inventor of the Thompson tall tale. As we shall see, this would not be the only time that sportswriters would indulge in fantasy rather than fact in detailing Sam Thompson's life and career.

Sam turned 24 a month after signing with Evansville—a late age to begin a professional career in any sport. Fair complexioned, with blue-gray eyes and regular features, he sported a splendid Victorian handlebar moustache that made him look older, but which a modern observer, unschooled in late–19th-century popular culture, declared made him look "like a wounded moose charging a hunter."[50]

Tall and lean, Thompson carried 200 pounds on a 6'2" frame. Thanks to a rigorous off-season lifestyle that included hunting, fishing, ice skating and a strenuous annual winter training routine conducted later in his career at the Detroit Athletic Club, his playing weight never varied more than ten pounds. A testament to his efforts to keep in shape came in 1906, eight years after his last major-league at-bat. Then 46, Sam filled in for an injury-plagued Detroit Tigers team in right field for eight more big league games, doing so in the same offensive and defensive style that he had in his prime.

Described as "graceful Sam"[51] off the field during his amateur years, once he transferred from first base to the outfield as a professional, Thompson's loping, long-legged strides enabled him to reach balls that most could not, and his long arms could snare sinking line drives and snatch balls out of the air that were headed for the bleachers. He considered no ball uncatchable, and made the spectacular catch a commonplace event.

Sam possessed the most powerful and consistently accurate outfield throwing arm of his era, and he ranks twelfth all-time in outfield assists. Among outfielders who played in at least 1,000 games and completed their careers in the 19th century, he ranks first in fielding (.934; one of only six from this category to reach the .900 mark) and first in the ratio of assists to games played (one assist every 4.9 games).

Thanks to his long strides, Thompson was no lumbering giant on the base paths. He averaged 20 steals a season in his 12 full major league seasons, stole three bases in a game in 1889, and stole five in a game in a pre-season exhibition contest in 1892.

Although traditionally classified as a left-handed hitter and thrower, some evidence, as we shall see, suggests that he might have thrown right-handed. His left-handed hitting style was considered highly unorthodox by some of his contemporaries. "'Sam Thompson' ... says [future Hall of Famer] Hughie Jennings, 'is the only ball player I ever saw in my life who would hit a ball stepping away from it. Sam was a left-handed hitter. He would stand well up to the plate, and when he saw one coming that he liked he would shove his left foot back and bring his bat against the ball. And how he could hit them! There was one of the greatest batsmen the game produced and probably the only one who stepped away to hit.'"[52]

An anonymous author writing two decades after Thompson retired agreed with Hughie Jennings' assessment. "Sam Thompson, a great hitter, stepped back with his rear foot as he hit. This is a terrible handicap. Thompson overcame it."[53] Sportswriter John B. Foster, editor of the *Spalding Official Baseball Guide*, also recalled that while at the plate, Sam "hung [raised] one foot and leg."[54]

What was perceived as a step backward and a "hung foot and leg" was actually a weight shift onto Sam's back (left) leg, accompanied by a slight rise of the right leg—in modified Mel Ott–style—before he exploded into the ball. Sam crouched "low at the plate, his weight planted on his left foot. When the pitch was released, he would spring out of his crouch and lash at the ball. As the first lefty hitter to successfully use his left foot as his pivot foot, he produced tremendous topspin when he made solid contact."[55] Sam's .331 lifetime batting average, his second-place ranking among 19th-century home run hitters, and his first-place ranking all-time in RBIs per game testifies to the effectiveness of his unusual hitting method.

By natural inclination, Thompson was a low ball hitter, but when an 1887 rule change ended the ability of the hitter to request either a high or low pitch and extended the strike zone from the top of the shoulders to the bottom of the knees, the change had no negative effect on the great slugger. In fact, his greatest offensive years occurred after the rule change. The topspin created by Sam's swing not only resulted in balls being hit a great distance, but in their climbing to a great height—the classic "high and deep" combination associated with many of the great power hitters of the game. His "moon shots" prompted Irish-born pitcher and some-time outfielder Tony Mullane to observe humorously that

Thompson of the Detroits can knock a ball higher than any man I know of. Out here [Cincinnati] last spring when the Detroits played us, Thompson got a cracking hit at the ball and sent it up in the air. I tell you, it nearly went out of sight. I was playing centre field and both Corkhill and myself started for it. It seemed to me to take about ten minutes to come down. "Do you want it?" I asked John. "No, you take it," he replied. And ... that ball had snow on it when it reached me. I believe it traveled clean to the North pole and back.[56]

As we have seen, the ex-ball player-turned sportswriter Sam Crane contributed to the popularity of Dan O'Leary's tall tale about Sam Thompson's discovery. In another of his versions of the story, he added a comment on Thompson's choice of bats that also has the flavor of a tall tale. "Sam Thompson, one of the longest drivers of a base ball, is said to have been engaged for the Indianapolis club in 1884 through Dan O'Leary's seeing him wallop a ball a mile or so by picking up and using an old wheel spoke, the only other bat having been broken."[57]

While no known record exists of the specific length or weight of Thompson's bats, photographic evidence suggests that they were typical war clubs of the era—longer and heavier in comparison with their modern counterparts, and with a thicker taper from the barrel to the knob-end. An 1895 account from *Sporting Life* indicates that Thompson's preferred lumber was still sturdy enough to be usable in a game after having been broken and then repaired:

Sam Thompson, the big right fielder of "dem Phillies," is happy again over coming into possession of a heavy wagon-tongue [a long, heavy piece of wood used to guide a wagon] bat which he wielded to good effect all last season [1894]. While the team was in practice at Hagerstown, Md., Sam split the long bat, and believing its days to be over, reluctantly threw it away. Catcher Buckley, however, picked it up, put a screw or two in it, wound it with twine, and made it comparatively as good as ever. Thompson did not know what became of the bat until about a week ago, when he found it in the club's collection, just as he was about to step to the plate. "Seems to me I've seen that bat somewhere," he remarked. Explanations followed, and Sam decided to try the mended stick once again "just for luck." The first ball that came over the plate was lined out over the right field fence for a home run, and the stick did good service in helping Sam make 11 hits out of 14 times at bat in the Baltimore series.[58]

As an amateur first baseman playing for the Danville Browns, Thompson may have played the field barehanded, used either a skintight glove on one hand, or padded fingerless gloves on two. Although it has been asserted that as a major league outfielder he played "most of the time without a glove,"[59] by 1890 his name appears among those of dozens of other players in ads promoting the use of a new fielder's glove developed by Art Irwin. After injuring his fingers in a game while playing for the Providence Grays in 1885, Irwin added padding to the palm

Modern-day replica of an early version of the Art Irwin fielder's glove, the first full finger glove used in the big leagues. Sam Thompson used a similar glove from 1889 to 1898 (author's photograph).

and fingertips of a leather driving glove and created the first full-fingered leather fielding glove. The following year it went into mass production, and soon became standard issue for the remainder of the 19th century.

Sam's shy, quiet and undemonstrative nature was initially construed and humorously represented in the press as a rustic's awed reaction to the big city. Dan O'Leary's previously-mentioned description of Sam's unchanging "Hamlet countenance," for example, was mirrored in *Sporting News'* observation that he "wore a stereotypical expression of countenance which never changed under any condition."[60]

Thompson's unfailingly "mild and inoffensive"[61] on-field behavior, exhibited during baseball's most violent and aggressive era, soon was praised as "model deportment,"[62] since he was never fined or ejected from a game. Late in his career, his uncharacteristic decision to man the coaching box and cheer on his teammates prompted *Sporting Life* to observe that "it looks funny to see Sam Thompson in the coach's box. One thing is certain—the umpire will never remove him for making unnecessary noise."[63]

Billy Shetsline, longtime Philadelphia Phillies club secretary and manager, recalled an incident involving Sam that suggests that the slugger's on-field comportment was not only motivated by politeness.

> Sam Thompson was as mild and inoffensive as a sick kitten on the ball field, and in the whole of his long career was never fined…. The nearest approach that Sam ever came to the fining business happened in a game between the Phillies and the Giants with Tim Hurst as the umpire. The Phillies wanted about three runs to tie, and in the last inning Sam walloped one of Joe [Jouet] Meekin's slants [curves] for a homer over the right field wall. The ball was safe [fair] by 20 feet, but somehow Tim's orbs contracted a case of foggy lamps, as Dan Clarke calls it. Delehanty, Lajoie and the entire Quaker troup flocked to the plate, indulged in a flight of rhetoric in which dub, lobster and stiff were starred in the conversation. "Get out of here and get back to the bench, you dubs, or I'll fine the whole bunch," roared Hurst. After Tim had consumed ten minutes in benching the irate ball tossers, he turned on Sam Thompson and said, "Here, Sam Thompson, you big rube, if you haven't had your say, just spiel. Come on with it, I want you to say it before my face." "Well, Mr. Umpire," faltered Sam, "I have an idea that the ball was fair. That's all I have to say." "And it's a good thing you haven't any more to say, I would just cop a 25 dollar wad out of that sock full of coin you have soaked [*sic*] away on the farm," said Tim. "All right, Mr. Umpire. All right. I ain't saying a word, sir," returned Sam. Sam was a saver, and the first dollar he ever earned is framed on the wall of his parlor, I have heard. After the game, Sam said to

me, "Shet, what would I have done if he had fined me $25? Why that amount keeps me three weeks in the winter."[64]

Thompson's characteristic thriftiness noted here was another aspect of his nature that was often highlighted humorously in the press, both during and after his career. "There's that Sam Thompson now. He's the worst [spendthrift] of all. Why Sam has been playing twenty sivin years and he has the first dollar he ever got for playing ball nailed upon his wall alongside his 'God Bless Our Home' motto."[65]

One of many players in the game with small-town backgrounds, Sam's Hoosier roots at times made him the butt of jokes and uncomplimentary tall tales. Although for most the term "hoosier" today simply signifies a native of Indiana, it was a negative term in Thompson's era. Originally, "hoosier" was an expression "of contempt and opprobrium common in the upland South, and [was] used to denote a rustic, a bumpkin, a countryman, a roughneck, a hick or an awkward, uncouth, unskilled fellow."[66]

Southerners migrating to Indiana first applied the term to "the presumably unsophisticated in Southern Indiana," but later, "it was expanded to include all residents of the state."[67] The negative aspects of the term were given a visual counterpart in a caricature that appeared in a number of *Harper's Weekly* in 1867. The magazine featured eight cartoon characters purportedly depicting "Citizens of the United States," and among them appeared the image of a "Hoosier"—portrayed as a slouching, bearded, uncouth man pushing a plow.[68]

One 1886 story about Sam Thompson, which contains an echo of Dan O'Leary's famous Thompson discovery tale, praised the hitting of the "Backwoods Giant," but ridiculed his rustic speech and clothing:

Sam is born "hoosier." He was raised near Evansville [actually, Danville is 172 miles distant] and he first entered that town three years ago. He was then dressed in a suit of home spun and looked like a real hoosier. Calling on the manager of the Evansville club, he said, "Be you wanting ball players?" The manager said he guessed he did, thereupon Thompson astonished him by saying, "I kin play a little bit and can knock the stuffin out of a low ball." Just for fun, the manager gave him a trial that day. The Louisvilles happened in Evansville that day [the actual game was in Louisville] and Hecker was their pitcher.... The boss tailor of Evansville had offered a new suit to anyone who would hit the first ball over the fence.... It was early in the season [actually the first game of the season] and the feat up to that time had not been accomplished. When Thompson went to the bat he created no furore, and it was generally believed that he was a regular duffer. He however sized up Hecker in short order, and the first ball that crossed the plate was lifted several feet over the fence. It was the longest hit that had ever been seen in Evansville and it made the Hoosier's reputation for all time. That night Sam called on the boss tailor of the town, put in a claim for that suit of togs and blossomed out as a real dude.[69]

On one occasion after his retirement from baseball, Thompson himself provided evidence that at least a few of the tales about his country-boy naive nature may have had some basis in fact. In a 1910 *Washington Post* interview, he revealed that while playing for the Indianapolis Hoosiers early in his pre-major-league career, he was fooled by Tom Taggart, a restaurant operator at Indianapolis's Union Train Depot who eventually became the city's mayor.

One afternoon, just after the game, we left the lot [field] supperless, to catch a train. Leaving the bus, I hurried into a dirty little fly-specked lunchroom and spotted a heap of fried chicken. Taggart ... was behind the counter. "What will you have?" he asked. "Couple of pieces of fried chicken," I answered, tossing a quarter on the counter. Taggart picked up the tempting looking fowl, which he took to a concealed counter. A moment later he handed me a package wrapped in coarse brown paper, the string tied in a hard knot. I grabbed it and rushed for the train. A few miles out of town, with a longing for that chicken, I unwrapped the package—and disclosed two pieces of pigs' feet, dripping in brine.[70]

Some stories purporting to recount descriptions of Sam's "backwoods" childhood, however, were as vicious and unkind as they were untrue. Their purpose may have been humorous, but their effect was tasteless.

Big Sam was an agriculturalist to the extent that he occasionally ran away to his grandfather's, who lived a couple of miles in the country, and in whose neighborhood rural entertainments often occurred. Although it happened many year ago, the inhabitants are still telling, as they rest on dry goods boxes on the shady side of a house in Danville and whittle, of the time when Sam made his debut in country society. His coming-out party was a dance. It was about three miles from town and some say Sam went to it bare footed. He skipped cross country and as he neared a field where the corn had been recently cut ... he gathered up a quantity of stalks as he passed and trudged along trailing the end ... on the ground behind him. Sam was early for the dance. No one had arrived before him and the [sponsoring] family were in the kitchen at supper. The long hitter of the National League entered the back door and announced his presence by dragging the corn stalks over the table, cleaning it of everything save the cloth, which had been tacked on. He threw his stalks in the back log of the fireplace and without a greeting of any kind, made his way through the house and out the front door. In that part of the country some of the farmers sink a barrel at a convenient place until the top of it is buried to the level of the lawn, and in this is deposited the dish water and table leavings. As Sam left the house, he gathered up the but-along [stone slab] which served as a step to the front door. It was a large slab and it strained his muscles to carry it. But he got it in the swill barrel, raised the stone as high as he could, and let it fall with a long deep ker-ching into the barrel. Farmers say it rained slop in that neighborhood for days. Sam Thompson, Hendricks County history says, has been barred from back county society from that day to this.[71]

By the end of Thompson's career, such portraits of him as an uncouth Hoosier rube were replaced by praise for him as "the grand old man of baseball."[72]

Evansville fielded its first professional team in 1877 as part of the League Alliance, a pact between the National League and a loosely-organized group of nearly three dozen teams spread across the country from New York State to Illinois. These teams' sole purpose for joining the Alliance was self-preservation, since membership insured that the National League would honor their contracts and not sign away any of their players. The Alliance lasted only a year, but is regarded today as the "first step toward National League control over commercial baseball,"[73] and the beginning of the distinction between "major" and "minor" leagues. This distinction would be formalized in 1903 between the National League and the fledgling American League.

The 1877 Evansville squad folded at the end of the year, but a new team was organized there in 1884, and its primary goal for the season was to achieve membership in the Northwestern League. In the decade that followed the establishment of the National League (1876–1886), professional teams like Evansville sprang up in dozens of cities and towns across the country, although few endured for long. Joining a regional league was a team's best chance for survival. League play guaranteed predictably-scheduled games against known opponents, and it offered at least the possibility of a reliable revenue source. The leagues themselves, however, were dependent upon a stable fan base in each franchise and a level of competition between all teams that was sufficient to maintain interest among fans of every club.

As an independent, Evansville's biggest problem was locating and scheduling opponents to play. Consequently, they took on all comers, playing 40 different clubs in an 84-game schedule, including major league teams and their reserve clubs (second stringers who would fill in for regulars on the big league squad in the event of injury), Northwestern League teams, other independents, and amateurs.

Scheduling was daunting under these circumstances, since hoped-for engagements often were cancelled if the proposed opponent got a more lucrative offer. On May 1, the *Evansville Daily Courier* hopefully announced that "it is probable that game will be arranged for next Saturday and Sunday in this city with the Golden Eagles of Indianapolis."[74] The next day brought the bad news that the games were cancelled by Indianapolis, and Evansville had to settle for a contest against a local amateur nine, the Shamrocks.

Evansville scored a coup for its season opener, however, when the American Association Louisville Eclipse agreed to begin their home season against them on April 6. The Eclipse had finished fifth in the six-team Association the previous year, and thanks to the hard hitting (.336) of hard-drinking infielder Pete Browning and pitcher Guy Hecker's career-best season (52 wins, 1.80 ERA, both tops in the Association) the team would rise to third place in the Association in 1884.

Resplendent in their new uniforms, consisting of "white shirts and pants with wine-colored belts, caps stockings,"[75] the Eclipse took the field, confident of an easy win in their first game over the newly-minted Evansville nine. Two hours later they had gone down to defeat, largely because of their thirteen errors, every player on the squad having committed at least one. "A very large crowd assembled at Eclipse Park yesterday for the ostensible purpose of seeing the Louisvilles wipe up the earth with the little club from Evansville, and they left the park a sadder and wiser lot."[76]

Hitting third and playing left field, Sam Thompson collected two hits and scored a run against Louisville's ace, Guy Hecker, and made a "brilliant running catch"[77] in his first Evansville game. His debut still held special meaning for him a decade later, when he recalled his performance for the press, although his recollection adds an extra run and hit to his accomplishments that do not appear in the box score.

> The first professional game I ever took part in was in Louisville, Ky., on Sunday, April 6, 1884. I was playing with the Evansville, Ind., Club. I played left

field, and we had about 8500 people out to see the game. That was about 6500 more than I had ever seen at a game before. I was frightened so badly that I did not know where the left field was. After I did find it I was unable to get near any ball that was hit out to me in practice. I was scared so much that I was almost sick. The crowd hooted at me for the exhibition.... The game started with Louisville at the bat. The third man hit a fly ball out to me, which of course I did not see until it hit the ground at my side. We got them out after they had made three runs. Then it came our turn to bat; I was fourth batter to face Guy Hecker with two on base. The first ball he pitched almost took what little breath I had away, it came so near me. But the next one was just my speed; I hit it to right field for two bases, bringing in the two men who were on bases. That hit braced me up, and I played a very good game for the rest of the afternoon, making three hits and two runs, and having three put-outs. We won the game, 11–9.[78]

Playing in 75 games for Evansville, rookie Thompson got an extended introduction to professional ball. He was moved from first base to the outfield, adjusted to better-quality pitching, and got his first taste of the rigors of minor-league travel, riding the rails with the team through Illinois, Indiana, Ohio, Michigan, Minnesota and Wisconsin from April to October. Evansville proved to be a formidable franchise, winning 63 of its 84 league and non-league contests.

In a remarkable display of athletic ability, Sam made a seamless transition from the amateur to the professional level both offensively and defensively. Unofficial statistics gathered from available accounts of Evansville's games reveal that in the 75 games Sam played, he collected 116 hits, including 14 doubles, 11 triples and five home runs. His first four-bagger came on August 11 in a game against an amateur "picked nine." He hit his first two home runs against a professional team six days later in a 19–2 blowout of the Union Association Saint Louis Blues.

The feature of the game ... was Thompson's work with the stick—five times at bat and four hits.... In the third inning with two balls and a strike on him, he nipped a ball just above the knee and sent a line hit over the right field fence. It was a rising ball going seven feet over the fence. In the seventh inning he secured a double past short and in the same inning again sent the ball over the fence in almost the same spot, the ball being a sky scraper, dropping over the fence thirty feet above it. Both hits were the longest ever made on the grounds.[79]

The Evansville press was captivated by the shy Thompson's reaction after hitting the first of these two blasts. "Thompson bore his honors yesterday like a young lady receiving her first lesson in love. His gentle blush must be seen to be appreciated."[80]

There was nothing gentle in the manner in which Sam clubbed the ball in a 16–12 victory over the same team the next day: "Thompson made another home run in the first inning on a line hit over the right field fence, almost exactly where the other went over [on] Sunday. Then again in the fifth he cracked a hard ball to the right field fence which hit the top of the brace [for a triple]."[81]

Balls hit over outfield fences for "clean home runs" were rare events in the era; even rarer were home runs hit on successive days by a player. Thompson's power display prompted a local haberdasher to present him with a reward: "Messers Stroun and Bro. have presented Thompson with half a dozen fine shirts for his recent performance in knocking the ball over the fence."[82]

Sam's final four-bagger of the season came on September 14 in an 8–4 win against another Union League team, Cincinnati. "Thompson played great ball both in the field and at the bat. His home run, as the saying goes, 'brought down the house.'"[83]

Sam's transition from amateur first baseman to professional outfielder was even more remarkable than his hitting in 1884. The "brilliant" fielding noted earlier in the season opener against Louisville was repeated in a return engagement against the Eclipse. "Pete Browning ... raised a long fly which seemed good for three bases, but Thompson reached it and nabbed it."[84] A few days later against Terre Haute, "Thompson ... made four neat fly catches,"[85] and in a close 4–3 contest against the same opponent a week later, "Thompson made the last out ... by a beautiful running fly catch. A muff would have tied the score."[86]

By mid-season, such efforts were drawing high praise from the Evansville fans and press: "Thompson is playing a great left field. His hands, when spread and Sammy on a dead run, look as though they were a yard long."[87] This report also seems to suggest that at this early stage of his career Sam was playing the outfield barehanded.

Thompson was the recipient of similar accolades for his outfield throws that cut down runners at home, third and first.: "[A] pretty assist was also made in a long throw of Thompson home"[88]; "A fine double play from Thompson to Veach [at first base] was one of the particularly fine features"[89]; "Thompson made two beautiful throws from left field to home plate, by which [catcher] Decker put out two men."[90]

Besides Sam Thompson, several other members of the 1884 Evansville team eventually played big league ball, although none had the success and longevity of the team's tall left fielder. One of these players, Harry Decker—the catcher who put the tag on runners who ill-advisedly attempted to beat Sam Thompson's throws from left field to home plate— deserves special mention, although not for his ball-playing abilities.

Born in Chicago in 1864, Decker is known today primarily for having invented the first catcher's mitt. Although the popular mitt was often termed a "decker" in the era, its inventor was too impatient to wait for the patent to be approved, turning over his interest in the glove to a business partner, who in turn sold the patent rights to the Spalding Sporting Goods company. During his baseball career he played briefly for five different major league teams, and was blacklisted for contract jumping and accepting advances from multiple teams for which he never played.

Out of baseball by his late twenties, Decker was successively accused of or prosecuted for a host of different crimes, including larceny, check-forging, fraud, bigamy, seduction of a minor and counterfeiting, and twice was committed to hospitals for the insane. He spent a total of fifteen years behind bars for his crimes in three different states. Released from San Quentin prison in October 1915, Decker disappeared, and afterward, despite the efforts of numerous baseball historians, "not a trace of his whereabouts ... has been discovered."[91] For baseball historian David Nemec, Decker's bizarre life of crime qualifies him as "one of the worst rogues, scoundrels and scamps to don major league threads in the nineteenth century."[92]

While Evansville was working diligently to earn a place in the Northwest League during the 1884 season, the league itself was floundering. Its cumbersome twelve-team composition required grueling, expensive rail commutes through five states, and the widely varying levels of performance among the teams took their toll in low home attendance among the weaker clubs. In rapid-fire succession in early August, the Stillwater, Terre Haute, Grand Rapids and Muskegon clubs disbanded. At this low point, Evansville was finally admitted to what remained of the League, but only after posting a $500 bond to insure that it would play the season out against the remaining teams—Quincy, Saginaw, Milwaukee, Minneapolis and Saint Paul.

After Quincy withdrew a week later, the *Evansville Daily Chronicle* reported that "the next game is somewhat indefinite, as nearly all the Northwestern League games have been cancelled, there being a strong probability that the organization will exist but a short time longer."[93] The "short time" mentioned here turned out to be five games for the Evansville team, during which Sam Thompson collected nine hits, including two doubles and a triple, for a .391 batting average. The league had died, but young Thompson had firmly established himself as a player of note.

With the demise of the Northwestern League, a familiar figure, Dan O'Leary, was named manager of the Evansville team for the rest of the season, largely for his promise to recoup some of the team's losses by closing out the year on a barnstorming trip through the South, with games scheduled in Atlanta, Chattanooga and Nashville. There are no extant accounts of the results of these games, but it was on this barnstorming tour that O'Leary acquired first-hand knowledge of Sam Thompson's baseball prowess.

Several other players from the defunct Northwestern League, including pitchers Bob Caruthers (Minneapolis), Dave Foutz (Bay City), and Charley Getzien [alternately spelled Getzein] (Grand Rapids) went on to enjoy long careers in the Major Leagues (a combined 29 years and 449 wins). Getzien spent four years as Sam Thompson's teammate in Detroit, where his 29 wins in 1887 helped the Wolverines to secure the National League pennant. None of these other Northwestern League alumni, however, would achieve the status of the organization's most famous participant, Sam Thompson.

With the dissolution of both the Evansville nine and the Northwestern League, Sam Thompson's services were immediately sought after and acquired by the Indianapolis Hoosiers in September. After a disastrous 1884 season in the American Association (29 wins and 78 losses; twelfth place), Indianapolis had joined a new organization, the Western League, in 1885.

The *Evansville Argus*, anxious to keep Sam Thompson in the city in the hopes of reviving the now moribund Evansville franchise, offered a tongue-in-cheek summary of what they told an Indianapolis team director about Sam in an attempt to keep him in town. Thompson, according to a report in the *Argus*, "couldn't throw and he couldn't hit a brick house. He was cross-eyed, walked bow-legged ... and swore like a sailor. Of course we told him [the Indianapolis director] that Thompson hated the Indianapolis club and was anxious to see it come out at the end of the season at the tail end of the association."[94] Big Sam's transfer to the Indianapolis club was another step up for him in the baseball hierarchy, and one that also enabled him to be closer to his family in Danville during the Hoosiers' home stands.

The Western League's 1885 season is perhaps best known today for the brief participation of two African American players on league teams. Moses "Fleet" Walker, who as a catcher for the Toledo Blues of the American Association the previous year became the first African-American to play major league ball, appeared in 18 games for the Western League's Cleveland entry in 1885 until the team went bankrupt.

James "Bud" Fowler, who as a pitcher for the 1878 Lynn, Massachusetts, Live Oaks of the International Association became the first African American to participate in organized baseball, played eight games as an infielder for the Western League's Keokuk, Iowa, club before transferring to the Colorado State League. By 1889, African Americans were banned from organized baseball until Jackie Robinson broke the color line in 1947.

The Western League Indianapolis Hoosiers were managed by Bill Watkins, a weak-hitting substitute infielder for the 1884 Association Hoosiers who became the team's skipper late in the season. Watkins, a strict disciplinarian, was hired to curb "the carousals ... of the whiskey element"[95] that had plagued the team in 1884. Watkins, rookie outfielder Gene Moriarty, pitcher Larry McKeon and infielder Chubb Collins were the only holdovers from the previous year's team. Watkins and Moriarty would later play significant roles in Sam Thompson's rise to stardom in the major leagues.

Most of the remaining members of this predominately youthful Indianapolis squad were transfers who had spent their rookie year in the now defunct Union League. The team veteran was thirty-one-year-old Sam Crane, a weak-hitting infielder who would play with Sam Thompson in Detroit, and who, as a sportswriter in later years, collaborated with Dan O'Leary in inventing tall tales about the great slugger.

Sam Thompson was the only member of the 1885 Hoosiers who had no prior major league experience.

Like Thompson's Evansville squad of the previous year, Western League teams filled out their season schedule by playing major league teams on off days. The 1885 Indianapolis Hoosiers mirrored Evansville's experience the previous year by opening their season with a victory against the same big league opponent—Louisville, which for the 1885 campaign had changed its nickname from the Eclipse to the Colonels.

Hitting third in the lineup and playing center field, which was still described in game accounts as "mid-field," Sam made his debut with Indianapolis in the season home opener at Seventh Street Park against Louisville on April 6. The Hoosiers were victorious, 7–4, and Sam went 0–4 and committed one error, but he received a favorable review from the *Indianapolis Daily Journal.* "Thompson both hit and played in hard luck, but is evidently a capable player."[96]

Two days later against the same team, he recorded his first extra-base hit, a double. His defense at his new position would continue to be shaky, but his batting remained strong and consistent. In another non-league contest against Cincinnati that was played in very cold weather on April 11, Sam's hitting and base running won the game for Indianapolis: "Thompson was first to bat in the ninth inning, and led off with a hit, got to second on Collins's sacrifice, stole third, and came home on a passed ball by Snyder."[97] A few days later, with cold weather still a factor, he collected two hits and scored two runs in an 8–0 win against Detroit's National League club. "In the third Thompson made a three-base hit to right and was brought home by Collins's single."[98]

When official Western League play began, Indianapolis took three of four games from Milwaukee in quick order, outscoring the Brewers 28–8 in the process. Thompson collected three hits, including a double, and registered his first outfield assist in the final contest of the series. The local press described his fielding as "brilliant,"[99] and *Sporting Life* declared that "Thompson, in center, is already a great favorite."[100]

The Hoosiers' quick league start, coupled with four pre-season victories against National League and American Association teams, was now the talk of the baseball world, and on April 22 they received a formal invitation to join the Association. Surprising many, the club's owners declined the offer. They did so with good reason. As a Western League team, they would receive half of the receipts for away games, while the Association only offered them $65 for such contests.

After notching three more successive road victories against two league rivals and one independent, Indianapolis returned home and beat Cincinnati again, with Sam connecting for his first home run of the season. It was a tremendous blast that left the game's spectators awe-struck. "Thompson made, in all probability, the longest hit that has ever been made on the grounds. He came to bat with the bases clear, and sent the second ball that was pitched whistling over the right field fence, and it would be going yet had not a small boy stopped it in its arrival at Tennessee and Eighth Streets."[101]

In the club's next outing against league rival Toledo (managed by Dan O'Leary), he collected three hits, including a double and a triple, and scored two runs. His hitting was now drawing regular notice in the local press. "In the last four games in which he has played in Indianapolis, Thompson has made six singles, two two-base hits, one three-base hit and a home run—ten hits with a total of seventeen bases."[102]

In May the red-hot Hoosiers won 15, lost three, and tied one. Sam continued his heavy hitting, singling out Omaha's pitchers for special damage. He collected nine hits in three games against the crudely-nicknamed "Omahogs," and then had a four-hit effort against Kansas City on May 12, including his second home run of the season. Taking note of Thompson's whereabouts on an off-day at the end of the month, the *Indianapolis Daily Journal* coined a new nickname for the tall slugger: "Big Sam Thompson, the center fielder, is visiting Danville today, his native heath."[103] It was the nickname by which he would be best known for the remainder of his career.

As the season progressed into June, so did Sam's hot hitting, including four triples (two in one game) in a three-game series versus Toledo, and four hits, including a triple and two record-breaking home runs, in a double-header against Milwaukee: "The principal feature of the game was Thompson's two home runs on phenomenal drives over the right field fence, the last being the highest and longest hit ever made on the local [Indianapolis] grounds, clearing the fence by fully fifty feet."[104]

Indianapolis's delight over its league dominance was tempered by hints that the Western League was experiencing serious difficulties. Omaha (6–21) disbanded on June 6, and was replaced by Keokuk, Iowa.

As the Hoosiers completed a home stand and headed east for a series with Toledo, the press reported that "rumors are again afloat to the effect that the Western League is doomed and will not last another month."[105] Of the six league franchises, only Indianapolis, Kansas City and Milwaukee had "furnished paying audiences,"[106] and it was believed that Cleveland and Toledo would soon disband, following Omaha's lead.

In the midst of such troubling news, "Big Sam" continued his hitting spree, collecting eleven hits in 6 games, including 3 doubles, a triple and a home run. The latter was hit against St. Louis at home, and it was described as "a tremendous drive … over the left field fence."[107] Some of Thompson's home town friends were present for the St. Louis game, and "the Danville delegation yelled themselves hoarse when big Sam Thompson knocked the ball over the fence."[108]

Sam struggled adjusting to his new outfield position, committing 13 errors in April and May. By June, however, he was beginning to replicate his Evansville habit of cutting down advancing runners on the bases. He collected two assists in a June 6 win against Toledo and picked up another a few days later against St. Louis.

By mid–June, the Western League was near collapse, and conflicting rumors about the future of the Indianapolis team surfaced. One story suggested that Indianapolis would purchase the Detroit franchise and bring National League baseball back to the Hoosier state.[109] A second story posited the opposite scenario, suggesting that "the Indianapolis club will be transferred to Detroit and will supersede the players in the present nine there."[110] The latter report proved correct, although as we shall see, league rules governing contract signings and some devious behavior on the part of Detroit's management delayed the transfer for another two weeks.

Statistics for Indianapolis's non-league games in 1885 are incomplete, but extant records suggest that Sam Thompson's offensive performance in these games (11 hits, including two doubles, three triples and two home runs in eight games) was equal to or better than his work in league contests. Officially, he hit .321 with a .478 slugging average in 30 Western League games.

For twenty-five-year-old Sam Thompson, the transfer of the Indianapolis roster to Detroit marked the culmination of a remarkable eighteen-month personal journey from his rural Indiana amateur home town team to the National League, where he would play for the next fourteen years. After participating in less than 130 professional games, the shy slugger from Danville was now a member of the Detroit Wolverines, and soon would be known around the country as one of the game's great hitters and outfielders.

Chapter Two

In the City of Straits: 1885–1888

"Thompson is the king of sluggers."—*Sporting Life*, October 14, 1885

Sam Thompson began his major league career at the approximate mid-point of a chaotic thirty-year period (1871–1901) of innovation, experimentation and evolution in both the organizational structure and the playing rules of baseball. By the end of this period, the bi-partite league structure (National and American) that we know today was in place, as was almost every important playing regulation except those that abolished the spitball and established the designated hitter.

The war for control of professional baseball had already seen some casualties by 1883, when Sam became a starter for his hometown Danville Browns. The player-controlled National Association, the first major league, expired in 1875, after five years of mismanagement and corruption. It was succeeded by the National League, run not by players, but by business men, who put up the capital to support the teams, set player salaries, and tried to make a profit. The League's monopoly was briefly challenged in 1877 by the International Association, which offered a new business model for the game—a co-operative plan in which all revenues were shared equally among the teams. It collapsed after just one year.

The American Association, a far more successful challenger to the National League, was launched in 1882. Its weapons in the baseball wars were cheaper admission prices (25 cents versus the League's 50 cents), Sunday baseball and liquor sales at the park. The Association's success forced the National League to seek a truce in 1883, when the two groups signed a peace treaty known as the National Agreement. The pact recognized each organization as an equal "national" league, established rules that ended bidding for players between clubs and leagues, and extended the Reserve Rule to cover 11 players on each team.

Initiated in 1879, the Reserve Rule stipulated that once a player signed with a team, he was bound to it until traded or released. Initially, five players from each team were reserved, and for a short time those selected viewed the rule as a positive sign of their success and importance to the team. Such satisfaction quickly disappeared when they realized that they had lost their right to set a price for their services or sell them to whomever they pleased. With the 1883 extension of the Reserve List to cover 11 players—the typical roster total for teams of the era—the entire team came under full and permanent control of the club owners.

With both the National League and the American Association vying for revenues from baseball's fans in 1884, a third league, the Union Association, attempted a new challenge to their monopoly by offering non-reserved contracts to players who would defect. It attracted just 30 League and Association players, and folded at the end of its first season. The demise of the Union Association returned the number of major league squads to sixteen in 1885, with each team composed of 11 or 12 men, for a total of less than 200 big league ball players—a very exclusive group.

The last great 19th-century battle for control of major league ball would occur in 1890, with the establishment of the Players' League. As we shall later see, Sam Thompson's actions during this conflict would come under national scrutiny and considerable criticism.

At the same time in which professional baseball was experimenting with different modes of organization and administration, it also was experimenting with the game's playing rules and regulations. Most of these actions were aimed at establishing a balance between the hitter and the pitcher.

In the early amateur years of the sport, the pitcher's sole function was to serve the ball to the batter, and his effort approximated that of a man pitching horseshoes by using a soft but stiff-wristed underhand toss, with the arm swinging below the knee. By the early 1860s, pitchers like Jim Creighton of the Brooklyn Excelsiors had upped the speed of their tosses and were varying them with change-of-pace pitches. In doing so, these innovators changed both the pitcher's role and the strategy of the game forever.

Pitchers worked on a level plane with the batter from a pitcher's box whose dimensions varied over time. Initially, the hitter stood just 45 feet away. Until 1887, the pitcher was required to throw either a high (from the waist to the top of the shoulders) or low (from the waist to the bottom of the knees) strike, according to the hitter's request.

An 1872 rule amended the pitching requirements to allow a wrist snap on the throw, leading to the development of the curve ball. The pitcher's motion now resembled that of a modern fast-pitch softball pitcher. The pitching distance was increased to 50 feet in 1881. Sidearm pitching was legalized in 1883, and overhand pitching was approved in 1884.

Standing in the batter's box in 1885, Sam Thompson could still request a high or low strike, but he could face either an underhand, sidearm or overhand-throwing opponent, all of whose release points were just fifty feet away. Over the next dozen years, the pitching distance would increase to 55'6" (1887) and then to its current distance, 60'6" (1893).

From baseball's earliest years to the mid 1880s, batters were expected to hit the ball in order to reach base. Walks were discouraged by requiring a high number of balls for a "free pass." During the National League's debut season, for example, nine balls were required for a walk. That number had been reduced to six by Sam Thompson's first season with Detroit, would be lowered to five in 1887, and finally reduced to four in 1889.

The most challenging and dangerous years for hitters in baseball history were between 1884 and 1886, when helmet-less batters faced overhand pitching from just fifty feet away. These were precisely the years in which Sam Thompson made the transition from amateur to major-league baseball. Over the course of his career, he had to adjust to four different pitching distances and the doubling of the size of the strike zone. His lifetime batting average, home run total, slugging percentage and RBI-per-game ratio demonstrate not only his great talent as a hitter, but a remarkable adaptability to the near-constant changes that were taking place in the game during his era.

The City of Detroit, Thompson's first stopping point in his major league career, acquired its French-derived name because of its unique geographic location. In the 18th century, French fur traders brought their merchandise to what was then a trading post there, traveling south from Canada through Lakes Huron and St. Clair by way of a strait, now known as the St. Clair River, that connected these bodies of water. From the southern end of Lake St. Clair, the furs were then transported through another strait to Lake Erie for sale in the East. The French called this gateway strait to Lake Erie (now known as the Detroit River) *le détroit du lac Érie*, the strait of Lake Erie. *Detroit* was later adopted as the city's name. A century before it became known as the Motor City, therefore, Detroit's most common nickname was the "City of Straits."

Several amateur baseball clubs were in existence in Detroit before the Civil War, including the Franklins (1857), the Detroit Base Ball Club (1858) and a team called the Early Risers (1859). Baseball fever soon spread throughout Michigan, which by 1867 "boasted 240 documented clubs, representing 117 cities and 36 counties."[1]

In 1879, a group of Detroit entrepreneurs hired a team of Eastern professionals to represent the city as an independent team and play at the recently-constructed Recreation Park, the city's first enclosed baseball field. Called the Hollinger Nine, the team was defeated in their first game, an exhibition contest against the National League's Troy, New York, team on May 12, 1879, but it managed a winning record for the season playing against a host of teams from across the Midwest. The Hollinger club disbanded at the end of the season, but the interest in the game that it created in Detroit prompted the city's mayor, attorney William Thompson, to team with other investors to buy the National League's Cincinnati franchise, which had been expelled from the National League for serving liquor and playing on Sunday, and to move it to the City of Straits.

Since the purchase of the Cincinnati franchise did not include any of the players on the team's roster, the new Detroit club needed to be creative in putting together a team for its debut 1881 season. Their starting nine consisted of four players released by the Worchester Ruby Legs, three seasoned veterans from the old National Association, and two rookies. Over the course of the season, a dozen substitutes, including Dan O'Leary (two games; eight at-bats, no hits), were shunted in and out of the lineup.

To everyone's surprise, the Wolverines finished a respectable fourth in the eight-team league in 1881, thanks to the hitting of rookie first-baseman Martin Powell (.338) and catcher Charley Bennett (.301), the outfield play of speedy center fielder Ned Hanlon, and the pitching of George Derby (2.20 ERA) and Stump Wiedman (1.80 ERA, best in the League). Derby and Weidman's success was brief, since both soon saw their promising careers ended by arm trouble. Powell's remarkable freshman season would be the best of his short career. He contracted tuberculosis in 1884 and died four years later at age 32.

Catcher Charley Bennett proved more durable, until a horrific accident ended his career a dozen years later. An average hitter, he was an outstanding backstop who led the league in fielding his position seven times. While on a hunting trip in 1893, he slipped as he ran to catch a train and fell under its wheels, which severed his legs. Undaunted, he gamely donned artificial limbs and crutches, and supported himself after baseball as a china painter and cigar store owner. As we shall see, Bennett and Sam Thompson became close friends during their years with the Wolverines. Both retired in Detroit, and together the pair rarely missed a Tigers home game.

Edward "Ned" Hanlon stole more than fifty bases five times in his career, and led the league twice in outfield double plays and three times in putouts. His election to the Hall of Fame, however, was more for his managerial abilities than for his on-field play. Known as "Foxy Ned" for his reliance on the hit and run, the bunt, the sacrifice and the double steal, Hanlon led the Baltimore Orioles to three consecutive pennants (1894–96) with a rowdy and aggressive player roster that included John McGraw, Hughie Jennings, Willie Keeler and Joe Kelley—all of whom would eventually be enshrined at Cooperstown with Hanlon.

Detroit's fine 1881 start in the National League was not sustained over the next three years, when the team finished sixth, seventh and eighth respectively, changed managers three times and owners twice. The team's fortunes began to improve after the 1884 season, when Frederick K. Stearns joined the ownership team.

Stearns, a Buffalo native, became a full partner in his father's then small-scale Detroit pharmaceutical company in 1875, taking charge of both the manufacturing and retail departments. Soon afterward, he implemented his "New Idea" of putting out a complete line of remedies with their contents clearly stated on the labels. These medicines quickly outsold the popular patent medicines of the day, which often consisted of secret and occasionally harmful ingredients. Within a few years,

Stearns' company went international. Among the prosperous businesses of Detroit, it was considered "certainly one of the busiest, the most successful and the most representative."[2]

Stearns' baseball knowledge was excellent. While attending the University of Michigan, he played second base and captained the school's baseball team. His strategy for building a championship professional club was simple: buy good players who would bring home the pennant. The plan initially appeared to be successful, but some of the questionable tactics that he employed in signing such players aroused the enmity of other League owners, and ultimately hastened the demise of the Detroit franchise.

A local press portrait of Frederic Stearns hinted at aspects of his character that became apparent after his purchase of the Western League Indianapolis team: "Frederick K. [Stearns] certainly has all the assurance, the force of character, and the consciousness of power necessary to dominate men ... he is argumentative, aggressive, and ... he will see to it that Frederick K. Stearns is not ignored wherever his interest lies."[3]

As soon as the sale of the Indianapolis franchise and its players to Detroit was finalized on June 15, 1885, Stearns rounded up Sam Thompson and most of the other former Hoosier players and put them on a train bound for Detroit, with the intention of using them in the next Wolverine game. Before the train arrived, he had received a wire from National League Secretary Nick Young informing him that, according to the directives of the National Agreement, ten days had to expire before released players could be signed by another team.

Stearns was aware of this regulation, but clearly was seeking to circumvent it, reasoning that once the players were signed and had appeared in Detroit games, and once the Detroit players they replaced were released, the likelihood of the new Wolverines being reassigned was slim. Two Indianapolis players, star pitcher Larry McKeon and his catcher, Jim Keenan, knew that Stearns' action was illegal under the terms of the National Agreement. The pair slipped away before the team boarded the train for Detroit, and subsequently signed contracts with Cincinnati.

With the majority of the team still under his control, Stearns then devised a stratagem to prevent other clubs from contacting them with offers. In an interview that took place 38 years after the event, Stearns, who was then retired and living in Beverly Hills, California, bragged about what he did next:

> With our 10 players in Detroit, we were afraid that other club owners would try to steal them away from us, and we decided to hide them out until the 10-day period had passed … we got a yacht, put our players aboard and sailed out into Lake St. Clair, where we cruised around for the ten days. The players were infuriated. Some of them were far from being good sailors and were sea-sick most of the time. However, we kept them practically prisoners until the time limit had expired, when we brought them back to Detroit, where they all signed their contracts.[4]

To complete his coup, Stearns fired the Wolverine's player/manager Charlie Morton and hired Indianapolis' skipper, Bill Watkins, to run his revamped Detroit nine.

Although the bulk of the Indianapolis players had been transferred to Detroit, not all of them saw immediate action, including Sam Thompson. Since ace pitcher Larry McKeon had escaped the wiles of Frederick Stearns, new Wolverines manager Watkins retained pitchers Stump Wiedman and Charley Getzien from the previous Detroit club, and acquired Charles "Lady" Baldwin from Milwaukee's Western League club. Ironically, Baldwin, whose unusual nickname was bestowed on him because he refused to drink, smoke or carouse with his teammates, only became available after Indianapolis's departure from the Western League resulted in the League's dissolution.

Watkins replaced the entire Wolverine infield and its right fielder, but the left and center field positions remained the domain of Detroit veterans George Wood and Ned Hanlon respectively. Eight-year major-league veteran Charlie Bennett remained behind the plate.

The two candidates for the right field position, Sam Thompson and Gene Moriarty, had been on equal footing offensively with the Hoosiers, hitting .321 and .325 respectively. Sam, however, as we have seen, had been shaky on defense in his first year as a center fielder. Moriarty, on the other hand, was described as a "fielding whirlwind"[5] with a superb throwing arm, and had a year of major league experience under his belt. Consequently, Watkins gave the starting right-field slot to Moriarty, and Sam Thompson, who would become the 19th-century's greatest right fielder, began his major league career as a substitute.

Mired in last place with just seven wins against 31 losses before the arrival of the Indianapolis players, Detroit's new blended nine rallied to compile a 34–36 record during the remainder of the season. The new era began inauspiciously on June 25 with a 7–0 loss to Providence. After a second game against the Grays was rained out, the Wolverines played a four-game series against New York, picking up a win on June 29 and then dropping two close contests to the Giants, 1–0 and 2–0.

Midway through the last game of the series on July 2, Gene Moriarty suffered an accident on the field. "While running for a foul fly in the fifth inning, Moriarty smashed into the low fence in front of the bank seats and came out of the collision with a broken toe and two knees that looked as if they had been sand-papered. He will be disabled for some time."[6]

Sam Thompson made his major league debut replacing Moriarty in right field to complete the inning. Then, in the seventh frame, he "made a short hit to center,"[7] his first major league hit, starting a rally that brought in two runs. For the next dozen years, he would remain a fixture in the outfield and a terror to league pitchers at the plate.

The fates were not so kind to Gene Moriarty. In a few weeks, he had recovered sufficiently from his injury to fill in a few times at shortstop and third base for Detroit, and even was asked once to try his luck in the pitcher's box. However, he would never play the outfield again for the Wolverines. He spent the next seven years playing for teams in nine different minor leagues across the country before being called up by St. Louis for 47 games in his final season (1892). Released by

Sam Thompson studio portrait, 1886, Sam's first full season with the Detroit Wolverines (courtesy Keith Thompson).

the Browns at the end of the year after hitting an anemic .175 and making 23 errors in the outfield, he dropped out of sight. It was only recently discovered (2013)[8] that he died in St. Louis in 1904, at age 41.

Several sources assert that Sam borrowed Moriarty's uniform pants in his debut, cracked out a double in first major league at bat and "split his pants running into second [base]."[9] An undated newspaper clipping in Thompson's Hall of Fame file repeats the "borrowed pants" story, but correctly states that he hit a single rather than a double, and that he also scored a run.[10]

Moriarty was 5'8" and weighed 130 pounds. It is highly unlikely that the 6'2", 200-pound Thompson would have considered wearing Moriarty's pants, let alone have been able to stretch them over his long legs.

Team owner Frederick K. Stearns, who was present at the game, offered an eyewitness account of Sam's first hit, which, while also unusual, is more likely than the torn pants scenario. "One day … Moriarty, in running for a fly ball, crashed into a fence and suffered a broken toe. Sam Thompson was called out of the grandstand, where he had been sitting, to take the injured man's place. Sam didn't have a uniform. The only thing he changed was his shoes, and he played in civilian clothes."[11]

Given a chance to play, Big Sam quickly gave notice that he had no intention of returning to the ranks of the substitutes. He collected 14 hits in his first ten games, including two doubles and two triples, scored ten runs, and recorded his first RBI/sacrifice: "Bennett hit for three bases and came home on Thompson's long fly to Manning."[12] He also made his first outfield assist and stole a base.

The steal, in the sixth inning of a closely fought game against the Phillies on July 11, was followed by more heads-up base running that allowed him to score the winning run. With Sam on second after the steal, and with Ned Hanlon on third, Charley Bennett lifted a long fly to left. Hanlon tagged up at third and beat the ball to the plate, tying the score. When Sam saw the throw going to the plate, he took off for third base. Phillies' catcher Charley Ganzel tried to nab him there, but his throw went into left field. Meanwhile, "Thompson kept right along for the plate, and got there."[13]

Playing in just 63 of Detroit's 108 games in his abbreviated rookie season, Thompson finished third in the league in home runs (7), led the

Wolverines in batting average (.303) and slugging (.500), and was second on the team in runs and triples. The outfield fence at Recreation Park, the Wolverines' home field, separated the baseball ball field from the cricket grounds, and stood 400 feet from home plate, a nearly impossible distance to clear in the dead ball era. However, batters with the power to hit a ball over an outfielder's head or hit a long fair fly ball that found its way into the spacious foul territory down the right and left field lines, had a chance for an inside-the-park home run.

Two of Sam's rookie home runs rolled to the fence after being hit over outfielders' heads. "Thompson drove the ball to the cricket fence, trotting to the plate before Buffalo's fielders in relays could get the ball to the diamond"[14]; "Thompson sent the ball over the dude's head [New York centerfielder Esterbrook's nickname was "dude"], making a home run…. Thompson was applauded vigorously, his magnificent hit being one of the hardest made at Recreation Park this year."[15]

Another pair of four baggers landed fair in deep right field and then bounded into the spacious right field foul territory, allowing Sam to reach home. Against Providence on September 29, he accomplished this by "a ferocious drive clear to the right field corner of the grounds,"[16] and then repeating the feat the next day: "Thompson landed the ball in his favorite spot in the right field corner for a home run."[17]

Although Sam was still error-prone in right field (14 in 122 chances), runners who challenged his arm on the base paths were methodically thrown out. He had four two-assist games and registered a remarkable 24 total assists—roughly one every three games—including four double plays. His throws caught runners at every base as well as home plate.

By season's end, Thompson was not only a fan favorite in Detroit, but was rapidly gaining national attention for his hitting and throwing. Referring to him as "the Backwoods Giant,"[18] *Sporting Life* also dubbed him "the king of sluggers."[19]

Sam's fine rookie record and the play of the other Indianapolis transfers pulled Detroit out of the league cellar and into sixth place, but these efforts were overshadowed later in the season by another move by owner Frederick Stearns—one that stunned the baseball world. Attendance at Wolverine home contests had been "exceedingly bad,"[20] hovering between 300 and 400 fans. In an attempt to increase attendance and win a pennant, Stearns went looking for more talent, this time not from relatively unknown players in minor leagues, but from other National League clubs. He settled his attention on the Buffalo Bisons, a team that had been in the league since 1881, and which, like Detroit, was struggling to bring fans into the park.

Stearns explained his reasoning by observing that "five great ball players like Bennett, Baldwin, Wood, Hanlon and Thompson do not make a team, so I began to look around for more material. I went to Buffalo ... this club had four good players: Dan Brouthers, Hardy Richardson, Jack Rowe and Jim White (known as Deacon White)."[21] This quartette of Bisons represented Buffalo's entire infield.

In much the same fashion as he had earlier in the season, the Detroit magnate purchased the Buffalo franchise and all its players' contracts and transported the four stars in the group, Brouthers, Richardson, Rowe and White, first to Detroit, and then "to parts unknown,"[22] in order to keep them hidden from other clubs until the required ten-day waiting period had elapsed before he could sign them.

It was later revealed that in July, two months before the actual transfer, Detroit center fielder Ned Hanlon, acting on Stearns' behalf, had met secretly with the four Buffalo players and the Wolverines' secretary, Bob Leadley, who "drew up a contract in writing binding the four men to play with Detroit next season, in case they were released from Buffalo."[23] Stearns was taking no chances, however, and as soon as he purchased their release, he transported them to a remote hunting lodge in northern Michigan, where they spent ten days before signing their new Detroit contracts, each for a hefty salary increase.

News of the secret negotiations to insure that the Buffalo quartet would sign with Detroit enraged the other League owners, who for the second time in the same season had been denied the opportunity to bid on outstanding players due to Frederick Stearns' chicanery. The New York Giants were particularly incensed. They were locked in a tight pennant battle with Chicago, and in the last two weeks of September were

Opposite: The "Big Four" (Dan Brouthers, Jack Rowe, Hardy Richardson and Jim "Deacon" White), 1886. The Big Four were the entire infield of the Buffalo Bisons. The Bison franchise and the Big Four were sold to Detroit in 1886, and the following year the Wolverines won the National League pennant and then defeated the American Association St. Louis Browns in the World's Series (Library of Congress).

BROUTHERS, 1st B. Detroits

COPYRIGHTED BY GOODWIN & CO. 1887.

GOODWIN & CO. New York.

ROWE, S. S. Detroits

COPYRIGHTED BY GOODWIN & CO. 1887.

GOODWIN & CO. New York.

RICHARDSON, L. F. Detroits

COPYRIGHTED BY GOODWIN & CO. 1887.

GOODWIN & CO. New York.

WHITE, 3d B. Detroits

COPYRIGHTED BY GOODWIN & CO. 1888.

OLD JUDGE
CIGARETTES.
GOODWIN & CO., New York.

scheduled to play a four-game series with Detroit and a five-game set with Buffalo. "If Buffalo's four star players were allowed to transfer immediately to Detroit, the Wolverines ... might prove to be much more formidable adversaries at a critical moment in the season. If, however, these players were required to remain with the weaker Buffalo team, the Giants stood a better chance of victory against them."[24]

The League ultimately resolved the issue by approving the transfer, but prohibiting the players involved from starting for Detroit until the following season. Stearns' victory would be temporary, as we shall see, for a year later the other team owners would devise a successful plan to effect their revenge. With the Buffalo players out of the lineup both in Detroit and in Buffalo, New York, in the last two weeks of the season, took seven of its eight games with the teams, but still was unable to catch Chicago for the pennant.

The sale of Buffalo's entire infield, third baseman White, second baseman Richardson, shortstop Rowe and first baseman Brouthers, to Detroit, was the first mass-transfer of major league players since the institution of the Reserve Clause, and the press dusted off a nickname, the "Big Four," which had been applied to some players from the National Association era, to refer to the new Wolverines, calling them the best infield in baseball.

Jack Rowe, a multiple-position player from Hamburg, Pennsylvania, spent time behind the plate, at second base, and in the outfield for Buffalo. His batting average usually hovered around .300, and in 1884 he led the league in outfield putouts.

Clarksboro, New Jersey, native Hardy Richardson was a seven-year major league veteran and an equally versatile player. Over the course of his career, he played every position. A lifetime .299 hitter, Richardson had his career shortened by two accidents that he suffered while sliding into bases. In 1888, he broke his ankle sliding into second base. In 1891, he broke his leg sliding home on an inside-the-park home run, an injury that effectively ended his career.

Thirty-seven-year-old Jim "Deacon" White, a tea-totaling Sunday school teacher from Caton, New York, spent his first decade in the major leagues as a catcher, and then prolonged his career another decade by switching to the infield. Arguably the best all-around player of the 1870s, he led the league in batting average, triples, hits, RBI, and runs in that decade and compiled a .312 lifetime batting average. As a catcher he led his league in fielding five times and once in assists.

Powerfully-built Dennis "Big Dan" Brouthers, who hailed from the mid–Hudson Valley village of Wappingers Falls, was baseball's first great slugger. In sixteen major league seasons, he won five batting and seven slugging titles while compiling a lifetime .342 batting average, equaling that of Babe Ruth, and hitting some of the longest home runs of the 19th century.

With the acquisition of the Big Four approved, Detroit's hopes for a pennant were high as the Wolverines began the 1886 season. The former Buffalo quartet manned the infield, with Charley Bennett behind the plate and returning pitchers Charley Getzien and Lady Baldwin in the pitcher's box. Sam Thompson was now the regular in right field, and veteran Ned Hanlon was in place in center field. The only question mark was left field, where the switch-hitting Jim Manning replaced George Wood, who was sold to Philadelphia.

Manager Watkins's preference for Manning over Wood in left is puzzling. A Canadian-born outfielder described as a "great player"[25] by Frederick Stearns, Wood was a five-year

CHAS. W. BENNETT.
ALLEN & GINTER'S
RICHMOND. Cigarett's. VIRGINIA.

Charley Bennett, Sam Thompson's teammate in Detroit and his closest friend, Allen and Ginter chromolithograph tobacco card. For more than 20 years after Bennett and Sam Thompson retired, they appeared together during Detroit Tiger Opening Day ceremonies where Bennett caught the first pitch thrown by Detroit's mayor, and Thompson served as honorary umpire (Library of Congress).

53

Detroit veteran, who in 1882 led the league in home runs (7) and in out-field double plays (8), and who had hit .290 in 1885. Traded to Philadel-phia, he thrived there, and spent another seven years in the major leagues. The switch-hitting Manning played center field for Boston and hit just .206 in 84 games in 1885, and after being sold to Detroit late in that season, hit .265 in 20 games as a Wolverine, filling in at shortstop for the remainder of the year. Starting in left for Detroit in 1886, he hit .186 until he broke his arm in a collision with shortstop Jack Rowe during a Decoration Day game. He finished his career in 1889 as a lifetime .215 hitter.

Manager-player squabbles surfaced on the Detroit team in 1886, and it is possible that the veteran Wood did not get along with new man-ager Watkins. If true, he would not be the first Wolverine, as we shall see, to tangle with the prickly Watkins, perhaps "the most detested man-ager by his own players ever to win a ML [Major League] pennant."[26]

The completely transformed Detroit team weathered several injuries to play splendid baseball in 1886, compiling an 87–36 record (.707), but they would still come up short against the Chicago White Stockings, whose remarkable 90–34 tally (.726) earned them the pennant. The positive effect of the presence of the Big Four on the team was immediate. Jack Rowe hit .303 and Deacon White averaged .289. Brouthers and Richard-son did even better. The duo tied for the home run lead with 11, Brouthers hit .370 (third in the league) and took first honors in slugging (.581). Richardson lead the league in hits (189) and figured among the top five in batting average (.351), slugging (.504), runs (125) and stolen bases (42).

Lefthander Lady Baldwin paced the Wolverine pitching staff, com-pleting 55 of 56 starts, compiling a 42–13 record, with a 2.24 ERA, and leading the league in strikeouts (323) and shutouts (7). Baldwin's curves stymied left-handed hitters, but he "also featured a nasty in-shoot and drop ball that made him just as tough on right handers."[27] German-born Charley Getzien, a right hander who mixed a drop pitch with a blazing fastball, had suffered through a 12–25 season in 1885, but rebounded in 1886 for a 30–11 record.

With much of the press's attention focused on the Big Four and Lady Baldwin's league-tying 42 victories (shared with New York's Tim Keefe), Sam Thompson's fine sophomore season in large part went unno-

Detroit Wolverines and Manager Bill Watkins, 1886. Four future Hall of Famers are seated in the middle row. Sam Thompson, first right; Jim White, to the left of Thompson; Ed (Ned) Hanlon, center; Dan Brouthers, second left (courtesy Transcendental Graphics/the ruckerarchive.com).

ticed. Playing in all but four of the team's 126 games, he hit .310, scored 100 runs for the first of ten times in his career and slugged eight home runs. Defensively, he led the league with 29 assists, and became known for his spectacular catches in the outfield. This talent helped his assist total, since his great ability to run down apparent hits caught runners off-guard while attempting to take extra bases.

From late March to mid–April, the Wolverines prepared for the upcoming season playing exhibition games, starting in the south and then working their way through the mid Atlantic states and New England. Batting fourth behind Hanlon, Brouthers and Richardson, Sam continued the steady hitting of his rookie year.

Detroit opened the 1886 season at St. Louis on April 29, and Thompson greeted the Maroons' starter Charley Sweeney with a tremendous clout over the fence. The blow was reported differently in the

Detroit and national press. According to the *Detroit Free Press*, "Thompson made the longest hit of the game. It was a high fly over the center-field fence, and he made a home run on the drive."[28] While today it seems obvious that a ball hit fair over the fence would be a home run, the Detroit newspaper's report had to add the final clause to its account, since at the time, a ball was still in play if a fielder could get over a fence to retrieve it, or if it bounced or was thrown back onto the field.

Sporting Life's account of Sam's four-bagger placed it in right-center and described it in even more impressive terms. "In this game, Thompson, the big Indianian, made the longest hit ever made on the League grounds, the ball going over the coal houses in right center."[29]

In a three-game stretch in late May—two official games against Washington and an exhibition contest at Toronto, Sam collected five triples and two doubles. By the end of June, Detroit led the league with a 34–7 record, with Chicago following close behind at 31–9. Sam's defense as well as his offense was helping to keep the team on top. On June 4 at Washington, he threw out the Nationals' left fielder Cliff Carroll at the plate in the third inning of a 13-inning contest that ended in a 1–1 tie. At St. Louis on June 14, Thompson had a magnificent game both offensively and defensively. He collected four hits, including a double, scored two runs, stole a base, and picked up two assists.

The press provided details of one of his throws in this game. "In the fourth inning, Quinn tried to stretch a single into a double, but was thrown out by Thompson to Crane [at second base].[30] During a 6–3 victory against Washington on June 30 Sam registered another assist: "Ed Crane smashed an upshoot for a base [hit], on which Larry Corcoran [on second base] tried to tally, but he was very finely thrown out by Thompson."[31]

By mid-season, injuries had sidelined left fielder Jim Manning and catcher Charley Bennett, but some judicious pickups from Philadelphia and St. Louis kept the Wolverines in first place. To relieve Bennett behind the plate, Detroit acquired Waterford, Wisconsin native Charley Ganzel, who could play the infield and outfield as well as catch. Ganzel was from a baseball family—two brothers played minor league ball, his brother John played first base for four big league teams, and his son Babe played briefly as an outfielder for Washington.[32]

The new catcher hit .272 for the 1886 Wolverines, catching 45 games and playing five games at first and seven in the outfield. He was regarded as "a steady, consistent, versatile hand who arrived at the park every day expecting to play and never was heard to complain when his name was not on the lineup card."[33]

After Jim Manning broke his arm in a collision with Jack Rowe, Hardy Richardson filled in for him in left field, leaving a gap at second base. On August 6, the Wolverines acquired Fred Dunlap from the financially troubled St. Louis Maroons. The Philadelphia native, who also was a champion handball player, was a lifetime .292 hitter who led the league in fielding in 1885. Dunlap took over at second for weak-hitting substitute Sam Crane, played steady ball for Detroit, and hit .286.

The Wolverines remained in first place through July, but a 10–13 record in August brought them perilously close to losing the league lead. The big bats of Brothers, Richardson and Thompson were providing runs, but pitchers Baldwin and Getzien were tiring. Both started three consecutive games during one stretch, and each also had to pitch in back-to-back games. In order to spell his starters, Manager Watkins picked up right-hander Pete Conway from Kansas City and then purchased a battery from the Southern League's Macon, Georgia team that included hurler Billy Smith and catcher Harry Decker. The latter, as has been indicated in Chapter One, would soon be out of baseball and spending a good deal of his time in prison instead of behind the plate. These new additions did little to help the Wolverines down the stretch. Conway and Smith combined for an 11–9 record, while Decker hit just .222 in 14 games.

By September 1, Chicago, which had equaled Detroit's 68 wins, but had lost four fewer contests, moved into first place. The White Stockings would remain there for the rest of the season.

Throughout Detroit's decline over the summer, Sam Thompson continued his steady hitting and spectacular fielding and throwing. He went on an offensive tear in mid July, collecting 12 hits in five games, including three triples and two doubles, and scoring 11 runs. The hitting streak ended on July 17, when he went 0–4 against St. Louis, but he made up for it by making a great catch and throw to complete a double play, shutting down a ninth-inning Maroons rally. "Glassock tried hard to bring in two more runs, and sent the ball like a rifle to right. Thompson made a great catch and then threw in time to double up Reardon at the plate."[34]

View of Recreation Park, Detroit's first enclosed baseball field and home of the Detroit Wolverines, from the "trotting track" in right field, circa 1880. The 50-foot wide track for harness racing began 230 feet from home plate. Beyond the outer edge of the track (280 feet) the outfield grass continued for another 120 feet, ending at the outfield fence, 400 feet away. Playing right field from 1885 to 1888 in this cavernous park, Sam Thompson averaged 26 assists per year (courtesy Burton Historical Collection, Detroit Public Library).

In a three-game series earlier in the month against Boston, Sam put on a remarkable defensive exhibition. Although Detroit lost the first game, 11–2, the *Detroit Free Press* noted that "Thompson played faultlessly,"[35] doing "some of the finest fly catching ever seen on a ball field."[36] The *Detroit Morning Times* provided more details.

Thompson was the bright and shining star of the Detroits so far as fielding went. In the third inning he made a running catch with one hand that was simply marvelous. Johnston hit a fly that started out for the vicinity where six of the seven home runs were batted that the Detroits made of Sweeney, when the St. Louis club was here. Thompson started for the ball, it must have been with scarcely a hope of reaching it. With one hand extended, and while he was going at the rate of a lightning express, the ball descended just in front of him. He made a lunge and captured it with his right hand. He held it fast, and the spectators shouted with delight, while Johnston, who nearly reached second base, walked off the field with a look of disgust on his countenance. It was the greatest catch ever seen on the ground. He caught four other flies during the game, none of which were easy ones.[37]

Such a performance prompted the *Free Press* to ponder, "Has Thompson got a patent extension arm? It certainly looked fourteen feet long when he stretched out for Johnston's liner in the third yesterday."[38]

Two days later, Sam's quick pick up of a hit and his subsequent throw back to the infield helped cut down runner Sam Wise, who was trying for an inside-the-park home run: "Wise made a magnificent hit to right center, which Thompson's sharp fielding and splendid throw to Crane [at second base], Crane's perfect throw to the plate and [catcher] Decker's quickness in touching the runner turned it into a three-base hit while it had all the symptoms of a home run."[39]

St. Louis left fielder Emmett Seery had a bad day against Sam on July 22. Thompson first robbed Seery of a hit and then threw on to complete a double play against an advancing runner. Then, later in the game, he threw Seery out at third: "Thompson did great work in right field, notably his catch of Seery's liner and effecting a double play [Thompson to Brouthers to Crane], and his fine throw from right in the eighth, catching Seery at that bag."[40]

Several other July press reports helped to keep the news of Thompson's fine fielding and throwing exploits before the public.

"Thompson made another of his marvelous catches today, getting Flint's fly after a long run when it was nearly on the ground."[41]

"Thompson made a great catch and then threw it in time to double up Reardon at the plate."[42]

"Thompson's fielding was superb. His three fly catches were difficult. His throw home on the ninth was perfect, while the manner in which he stopped three base hits in right field and held the runners on first caused some religious admirers on the home team to swear."[43]

Sam's fine defense continued in August. At Philadelphia on August 2, his throw home following a catch nipped a runner trying to tag up at third and score. A few days later at Boston, he fielded a ball and relayed it to Dan Brouthers at first, who threw on to catcher Charley Ganzel, who then tagged a runner trying to score. The following day in Boston, Sam was praised for another fine catch. "The fielding of the Detroits was remarkable ... Thompson making a one-handed catch of a long hit by Wise that looked safe for three bases. The play deserved high praise, and the big right fielder received a perfect ovation."[44] This performance prompted the *Boston Herald* to affirm that "Thompson makes more phenomenal catches than any league fielder."[45] As if to prove the point, the tall Danville native made another pair of outstanding outfield grabs five days later in Kansas City: "Thompson made two of the phenomenal catches for which he is noted."[46]

Sam's best offensive performance of the year was a five-for-five effort against Kansas City's Pete Conway on August 14, including a triple and an opposite field home run: "In the seventh ... Thompson, who had been slugging terrifically, then hit the sphere to left for a clean home run."[47] After Conway was sold to Detroit a short time later, Sam let Pete know that his prior hitting barrage against him was nothing personal by going four-for-four in support of the recently acquired pitcher against New York. Thanks to Sam's help, Conway registered his first Wolverine win in this game.

Such fine offensive performances continued to be equaled by Sam's prowess in the field. In a 10–2 loss to Philadelphia on August 24, "Thompson made a splendid catch off a long hit foul ball that went back to the seats near the right field foul line."[48] During the opening game of a crucial series with Chicago in late August, his strong throw and a tag by catcher Charley Ganzel cut down Mike Kelly, who was trying to score from second on a George Gore single in the fifth inning. Kelly was one of the league's best and most daring runners, and his failure to make it home ended a rally by Chicago, who lost the contest, 5–4. "When fifteen feet from the plate, Kelly sprung in the air and shot out feet first. Had he struck catcher Ganzel, the latter would have been useless for baseball purposes for the future. He avoided Kelly, however, and touched him neatly with the ball Thompson had thrown so unerringly."[49]

It was not uncommon for Sam's offensive and defensive heroics to occur in the same game. During a 14–5 blowout against Philadelphia on August 25, for example, he "came to bat and [center fielder] Andrews moved out. It was no go. Sam put 200 pounds of force into the whack he gave the ball and it plowed the air straight down centre field, sailing six feet over Andrews' head. It rolled clear to the fence.... Thompson crossed the plate before the ball was fielded to the diamond."[50] In the fourth inning, Sam collected one of his two game assists after Dan Brouthers had made an error at first, the ball dribbling into right field. "Bastian also tried to score, but was thrown out at the plate by Thompson."[51]

The stress of competing in a tight pennant race, and the frustration of losing the lead to Chicago after holding it for most of the season, began to wear on the Wolverines. Manager Watkins started fining players for miscues or otherwise poor play. Pitcher Getzien was the first victim of the new policy, receiving a $100 fine for a poor performance against Kansas City ($10 for each run allowed). As we shall see, Watkins' punitive measures only served to promote further disaffection and revolt against him among the players.

With every game on the line, the Wolverines also had to contend with what they considered unfair umpiring down the stretch. In a game against New York in early September, Detroit was trying to regain the league lead from Chicago. The Giants, meanwhile, were in third place and closing in behind them. In the sixth inning, Big Sam tripled, but was declared out by Umpire Phil Powers for not touching second base. Powers himself, however, had not seen the play, but was informed of it by New York's catcher, Buck Ewing, who had a well-known reputation for trying to influence umpires. "About the time Sam reached third, [umpire] Powers was waving his mask at him, having just received a communication from assistant umpire Ewing [*assistant* here is a sarcastic term, since Ewing was New York's catcher, not an umpire]. It was to the effect that Thompson had not touched second."[52]

In what soon would be known as Thompson's customary response to perceived unfair calls, Silent Sam made no comment about it, or on Powers' reliance on Buck Ewing's judgment to make it.

This was not the case, however, with the next batter, veteran Fred Dunlap, who commented to on-deck hitter, Ned Hanlon, "What do you think of that, Ed [Ned Hanlon's actual first name was Ed]?"[53] Umpire Powers promptly fined Dunlap $10 for this comment. When the second baseman tried to explain that he was talking to Hanlon and not to him, umpire Powers added another $10 to the fine. The game then resumed and the decision stood. The next day, the *Detroit Free Press* laid more of the blame on Ewing than on Powers. "It requires considerable nerve in a catcher to chin [argue with] an umpire for nine innings, but Ewing has the requisite supply."[54]

Two weeks later, the Detroit newspaper reported a similar incident involving Powers that worked to rival Chicago's favor in a game against Kansas City. "Umpire Powers seemed to have done good work for the Chicagos yesterday. In one instance in the morning game he called McQuery out because Hardie, the [Chicago] change catcher, called to his attention the alleged fact that Mac [McQuery] did not touch third base."[55]

The bad blood between the Wolverines and Umpire Powers came to a head in a do-or-die series with Chicago in late September. Detroit had dropped the first two games to the White Stockings, and was losing the third game by a score of 6–4. Umpire Powers, who allegedly had been seen drinking the previous night with members of the Chicago team, had made several calls that went against the Wolverines. In the seventh inning, with Detroit in the middle of a rally that included a home run by Brouthers and a single by Richardson, Powers called an end to play due to darkness, indicating that game would revert back to its sixth-inning score:

> It was about twenty minutes to 5 when Powers announced he would call the game back to the sixth inning [when Detroit was down, 6–3], giving no reason therefor [sic]. It had been cloudy all afternoon, but the clouds had begun to break, and at the time the game was called it was growing bright…. Powers, seeing the larceny of the game was accomplished, wanted it stopped right where it was … a wild scene followed the calling of the game. The enraged spectators chased Powers into the dressing room and then waited for him to come out. Friends of the caged umpire shouted that a row was taking place in the street, and when the crowd went to see, Powers was smuggled into a hack and driven away.[56]

The decision stood, but the following day, with Powers again officiating, Detroit closed out its home season, with a 6–2 win.

For the most part, Sam Thompson's bat was quiet during the last month of the season. He did hit another inside-the-park four-bagger against Washington on September 8 that was characterized as a "tremendous homer to centre,"[57] and he collected three hits in a Sept. 13 game at Kansas City. The home run against Washington, a triple against Chicago on Sept. 23, and two triples and a double in later contests, however, were his only extra base hits in his final 28 games.

Fatigue may have played a significant part in this let-down during Sam's first full major league year. His minor league seasons, including non-league exhibition games, never totaled more than 100 games. Thompson's game total in 1886, including exhibition contests which were played on all off-days except Sundays, may have approached 150 games. Bat fatigue, however, did not mean arm fatigue, as the New York Giants' speedy John Ward, who would steal 111 bases in 1887, discovered in an early September game, in which Sam threw out "that lightning runner Ward, at the plate, he running from second base on a hit."[58]

The Detroit Wolverines' .707 winning percentage in 1886 is the highest ever recorded for a second place finish in the National League. The difference between second place and Chicago's .726 winning first-place percentage, the third highest of all time, was due to the White Stockings offensive superiority. Both teams' pitching staffs had a similar ERA (Chicago 2.54; Detroit 2.85), but while Detroit lead the league in batting average and hits, and tied with Chicago in home runs, the White Stockings led in runs, doubles, triples, RBI, walks, stolen bases, and slugging and on-base percentage.

At the annual owners' meeting at the end of the year, Detroit's president, Frederick Stearns, received unexpected bad news. Aware that Detroit's chronic low game attendance was insufficient to cover the salaries of the big stars that he had signed, he counted on the percentage of gate receipts (25 percent) granted by the league to visiting teams to make ends meet. In cities like Boston, Chicago and Philadelphia, that could often draw five to ten thousand fans per game to see Detroit's Big Four play, the percentage rule translated into big paydays for the visiting Wolverines. For 1887, however, the magnates exacted their revenge on Stearns for his underhanded tactics in signing players by voting to rescind the league rule granting 25 percent of gate receipts to visiting teams, substituting instead a flat rate of just $125 per game. This decree spelled financial ruin for the Wolverines, who would capture the pennant in 1887 but fold as a franchise just a year later.

The 1887 season represents the high watermark in baseball's attempt to establish parity between pitchers and hitters. Rules changes now required the pitcher to stand 5.5 feet further away from home plate (55"6'), and for the only time in the history of the sport, walks counted as hits, and it took four strikes to strike out a batter. Baseball statisticians later corrected the 1887 batting averages by discounting the walks that originally contributed to them for this year.

The pitcher was compensated for these hitter-friendly changes by a rule that ended the hitter's right to request either a low or a high pitch, and by the doubling of the size of the strike zone, which now would extend from the top of the hitter's shoulders to the bottom of his knees. While the rules changes did result in a jump of 13 points in the overall league batting average, the average of the circuit's top five hitters surprisingly dropped from .367 in 1886 to .348 in 1887. By 1888, a further drop in the league average to .240, and in the top five hitters' average to .321, demonstrated that pitchers, most of whom were now throwing overhand, had quickly regained their dominance over hitters.

The 1887 season was also the high watermark for the Detroit franchise, as the Wolverines ended Chicago's dominance by winning the pennant, and then soundly defeating the St. Louis Browns in the World's Series. It likewise was the season that established Sam Thompson as a major star. He led the league in batting average (.372), slugging (.571), on-base percentage (.426), total bases (311), RBI (166), and triples (23), and he became the first player to reach the 200 mark in hits (203), doing so in a remarkable 127 games. Defensively he registered over 20 assists (24) for the third consecutive year.

The Wolverines planned no major changes in their 1887 roster, but as the season wore on, injuries forced them to make some adjustments. The often-injured Charley Bennett caught just 45 games, and the slack behind the plate was taken up by Charley Ganzel and new man, Charles "Fatty" Briody. Former 42-game winner Lady Baldwin developed a sore arm due to overwork, and was in and out of the rotation, but Charley Getzien won 30 games, and new pitchers Stump Wiedman and Larry Twitchel added a combined 24 wins, with Twitchell finishing with a promising 11–1 mark. Each of the four hurlers won at least ten games, marking the first time that four pitchers on the same team reached double figures in wins.[59]

All members of the Big Four hit over .300, and slugger Dan Brouthers led the league in runs and doubles. But it was Thompson's remarkable year, combined with the accomplishments of the Big Four, which gave the Wolverines the offensive muscle to win the pennant. The Detroits never lost the league lead, were only shut out twice, and led the Senior Circuit in hits, runs, doubles, triples, RBI, batting and slugging.

While the Big Four's exploits continued to garner most of the national press's attention, the league geared up for the 1887 season, and Washington, D.C.'s *National Republican* humorously reiterated Sam Thompson's importance to the Wolverine's future success. "Detroit makes formal announcement that her happiness and prosperity for the year 1887 are assured. Sam Thompson has signed to play for the Wolverines this season."[60]

As was Detroit's custom, the team prepared for the regular season by barnstorming from late March to late April, starting in New Orleans and then moving on to Savannah, Charleston, Birmingham, Memphis, Louisville and Nashville. Sam played well, including a home run, a double and a double-play assist in a game in New Orleans in late March, and a double and a triple in Savannah a few days later.

Big Sam would prove to be the Wolverines' iron man in 1887, playing in every pre-season contest, every exhibition game during the season, all regular league games and the ensuing World Series. In November, *Sporting Life*, quoting the *New York Clipper*, suggested that this performance set a new record. "Sam Thompson, of the Detroit team, is said to have played in 185 games in 1887. This number, if correctly stated, being the largest number of games ever credited to a player in any one season. The present record was 175 games each by O'Neill and Welch of the St. Louis Browns in 1886."[61]

Although such a schedule could be grueling, some stops along the way during spring training offered special benefits. After Detroit finished its southern tour, the team swung north, ending up in Minnesota and Wisconsin just before the start of the regular season. After a game against a Minneapolis nine in late April, the Wolverines were treated to a special event. "This evening by invitation of Thatcher, Primrose and West, the Detroits occupied boxes at the theater and witnessed the entertaining performance of that minstrel troupe. At its close, the Detroits, in company with the minstrel company, repaired to the parlors of the Tonka club, and were delightfully entertained with songs, recitations and a toothsome repast."[62]

A few days later, the team played a rain-shortened contest in Lacrosse, Wisconsin, where Thompson reunited with his former teammate, Gene Moriarty, and no doubt had occasion to be grateful for his good fortune when compared to the luck of the former Hoosier and Wolverine outfielder: "Among the Lacrosse players is Eugene Moriarty, the fine fielder who was injured by running against the back seats at Detroit, the latter part of 1885. It was his injury that developed Sam Thompson's value."[63]

Detroit opened the 1887 season at Indianapolis before a crowd of 5,000, many of whom had made the 20-mile trek from Danville to see their native son, Sam Thompson, play.

> Danville, where Sam Thompson lives, has about 700 population. It is safe to say that 698 Danvillians saw big Sam accept four chances and make a two-base hit in today's game. Two men and a dog were left in Danville to prevent anybody from running off with the town. There were also present half a dozen tall, strapping young men with light moustaches and a strong resemblance to our big right fielder. They were Sam's big brothers, and when they yelled in unison they drowned out the shriek of the remaining 4,994 excited enthusiasts.[64]

THOMPSON, R. F. Detroits
COPYRIGHTED BY GOODWIN & CO. 1887.
GOODWIN & CO. New York.

Iconic 1887 Sam Thompson tobacco card portrait (courtesy Library of Congress).

In the first inning, Emmet Seery, whom, as we have seen, had twice been previously victimized in the same game by Sam's outfield play, managed to escape the same fate a third time, thanks to an error by catcher Charley Bennett: "Denny hit a hard one to right, which the pride of Danville [Thompson] captured nicely, and then made a fine throw to the plate to cut off Seery, but the ball slipped out of Bennett's hand."[65]

In the last game of the season-opening four-game series against the Hoosiers, Sam hit his first home run of the season, a drive "down to the center field fence,"[66] off pitcher Egyptian Healy. Healy's unusual nickname was inspired by his home town, Cairo, Ohio's nickname, "Little Egypt." Five days later, back at Recreation Park in Detroit and again facing "the Egyptian," Sam connected for a "sky-scraping quartette hit [four-bagger]."[67]

In an 18–2 blowout the next day against the Hoosiers, Sam Thompson entered the record books as the only player to hit two bases-loaded triples in the same game. The feat was made even more unusual by the fact that the hits were made in consecutive at bats, and that on each occasion the same runners were on the same bases when the blows were struck. In the seventh inning with Fred Dunlap on third, Jack Rowe on second and Dan Brouthers on first,

> Danville Sam made a tremendous hit to right and the three giants [Dunlap, Rowe and Brouthers] raced over the plate in a bunch. Sam was left [at third] … the same thing happened in the ninth. Dunlap had a two-bagger and Rowe and Brouthers got first on balls…. With the same three men on base as in the seventh, Sam lifted the ball to right and it looked good for over the fence. It, however, got tangled in one of the canvas signs and when it dropped it was fielded and only one man was on base. That was Thompson, and he was at third. Richardson's single sent him home.[68]

Detroit won four of its next five home games against Pittsburgh and Chicago, thanks in large part to the hitting clinic put on by Thompson. He collected 15 hits, including three doubles and two triples, with the three-baggers having been hit in the same game. On both these three-base hits against Chicago on May 12, however, Sam was thrown out at the plate trying to stretch them into home runs. Such overzealousness on the base paths prompted *Sporting Life* to observe that "despite his size, Sam Thompson is one of the swiftest runners on the Detroit team. Nevertheless he is a poor base-runner."[69] Perhaps so, on this occasion, but his 232 lifetime stolen bases, including eight years with 20 or more, suggests otherwise. In fact, Sam was a consistently aggressive runner, both on the base paths and when running down fly balls in the outfield, and in the great majority of cases, this trait proved to his advantage.

In late May, the Detroits, now prematurely dubbed "the coming champions"[70] by the *Detroit Free Press*, arrived in the nation's capitol for their first series of the season with the Washington Nationals. The press's brief description of the entire team's accommodations there provides a startling contrast to those enjoyed by modern teams. They consisted of eight rooms and a parlor on the third floor at Willard's hotel, located "but a few steps from the White House."[71]

Detroit took two of three from Washington, but then lost two of three against both Boston and New York before returning home. The team may have stumbled on its road trip, but Sam Thompson did not. In the field, "the long-legged Thompson was invariably in the right spot."[72] At the plate, he "made thirty-eight hits in sixteen games of the trip just finished."[73]

Noting Sam's offensive performance, the *St. Louis Globe-Democrat*

THOMPSON, RIGHT FIELD, DETROIT.

D. Buchner & Co. chromolithograph tobacco card featuring Sam Thompson, 1887. Note that Thompson is depicted here as fielding bare handed. By 1889, Sam was using the Art Irwin fielding glove in right field (Library of Congress).

offered its own explanation for his aggressive hitting. "Thompson of Detroit can reach farther with the bat than any ballplayer in the profession. It takes a very wide outcurve to fool him. It is said that he doesn't want to get his base on balls and always desires to hit."[74]

Near the end of May, Manager Watkins benched third baseman Deacon White due to weak hitting, substituting Billy Shindle, who had been acquired from Utica of the International League. The temporary demotion humiliated and enraged the seventeen-year veteran White, and marked the beginning an ongoing feud with Watkins that would not end until the manager was fired the following year. It also marked the beginning of a contentious period between the rest of the team and its skipper that would threaten to undermine the drive for the pennant.

Shindle at least initially proved to be an able substitute

for White. In a June 10 game against Indianapolis, his defensive prowess helped add another assist to Sam Thompson's record. "[Jack] Glassock had reached first on balls when Shonberg made a hit to right. Capt. Jack [Glassock] made an effort to reach third on the hit. Thompson fielded the ball and made one of his celebrated throws to third. Billy [Shindle] scooped the ball from the ground and with a catlike movement clapped it onto Glassock as the latter slid into the base."[75]

By July 1, surging Boston had replaced Chicago in second place and was nipping at the Wolverines' heels. In the midst of a four-game series with Philadelphia, rumors surfaced that the Wolverines were in financial trouble and that the team was going to "get rid of some of its high salaried players,"[76] by selling them to Philadelphia. The list included Sam Thompson, Dan Brouthers, Hardy Richardson and Fred Dunlap. Clearly, the league's new flat fee of $125 per game for visiting teams, instead of the normal take of 25 percent of the gate receipts, was hurting Frederick Stearns' franchise.

It was not surprising that the Phillies coveted Sam Thompson, since he regularly pounded their pitchers. On July 1, he responded to the news of potentially being traded to them by collecting four hits against them including two singles, a double and a home run.

Troubles seemed to be dogging the Wolverines. A few days later in a game with Boston, Fred Dunlap and Thompson collided in short right field while trying to catch a pop fly. Dunlap suffered a fractured leg and was out for the rest of the season. By mid month reports were circulating of a "sale of the [Detroit] franchise to Eastern concerns."[77] Between July 12 and 26, the Wolverines won just two games against nine defeats, scoring 46 runs to their opponents' 89.

Tempers on the team frayed. Substitute catcher Briody and pitcher Wiedman were fined "heavily"[78] and suspended for drunkenness. Lady Baldwin, a teetotaler, defended the pair, declared the suspension unfair, and requested the same suspension in protest. Manager Watkins promptly granted his wish. The previous year's bad blood between pitcher Getzien and Manager Watkins then resurfaced: "Manager Watkins ... is said to have a grudge against Getzein [*sic*] and to be doing all in his power to harass him."[79]

Responding to a *Sporting News* observation that "the Detroits have no pitcher,"[80] President Stearns tried to dispel rumors that the club was

Engraving of Sam Thompson, 1887. Similar engravings of each member of the Wolverine championship team appeared together in a Detroit newspaper (courtesy Keith Thompson).

experiencing financial difficulties by announcing that "a procession of pitchers will soon begin to arrive in Detroit and we'll keep them coming until we get some good ones. We must have them, no matter how high they come."[81] The trio of new pitchers that he acquired, Ed Beatin, Henry Gruber and Turk Burke, pitched in only 11 games for the Wolverines, compiling a combined 5–5 record.

Sam Thompson kept doing his part in the outfield by preventing opponents from scoring runs, while at the plate helping to put runs on the scoreboard for Detroit. Against New York on July 9, he collected three outfield assists. In a July 20 game against Washington, with Jim Whitney on third, [shortstop Al] Myers hit a fly to right, "which Thompson pulled down, and by a beautiful throw, doubled up Whitney, who was legging it for home."[82] In the eighth inning of a game against rival Chicago, "Thompson hit a hummer to center. Ryan incautiously stuck out a hand as the ball whizzed by, and Thompson had crossed the plate long before Ryan got through rubbing his sore hand."[83] With Chicago's Marty Sullivan on first in the first inning of the next day's game against the White Stockings, "Williamson pounded a baser [base hit] to right and Sullivan started from first to make third. Thompson fielded the hit sharply and then lined the ball to White's hands to the discomfiture of Mr. Sullivan."[84]

Despite such efforts, Chicago, at 41–27, had moved past Boston to occupy second place by the end of July, and was again challenging the 43–26 first-place Wolverines. Thompson began August the same way he finished July—with good hitting and fielding. On August 1 he contributed a triple and an assist against Philadelphia. "The side was finally retired by Casey sending a fly to Thompson, who threw Clements out at the plate, the latter attempting to score on a sacrifice."[85] After hitting a home run and a triple a few days later against Boston, he came to bat twice in the ninth inning, singling both times and capping a rally that won the game, 12–11. In a crucial 5–3 win at Chicago 12 days later, Sam cut down speedy Jimmy Ryan trying to make it from first to third on Marty Sullivan's single: "Sullivan made a long hit to right but Thompson made a beautiful throw to third and caught Ryan in his effort to make two bases on the hit."[86]

The White Stockings took the second and third games of this series, however, and on August 18 their record was 50–34, just behind the first-place Wolverines, who were 52–32. Meanwhile, Detroit fans and both the home town and national press were lambasting Manager Watkins' actions.

> The Detroit people are complaining loudly of Watkins' incapacity to manage a good baseball club. His treatment of the pitchers is especially criticized. Getzein [sic], who is now the star twirler of the Detroit team, was laid off by Watkins simply because the two men were not on friendly terms. The public demanded that Getzein [sic] pitch more games and Watkins was compelled to yield. Getzein is now winning games right along.[87]

The *Detroit Free Press* chimed in with its own complaints, claiming that "the suicidal experiments attempted by Mr. Watkins and with such disastrous consequences on the previous trip, could not but be met with rigorous opposition."[88] The Detroit paper soon discovered that club President Stearns, showing remarkably little concern for the effect that his actions might have on the team, which was fighting for a pennant, had sent a letter to Chicago owner Al Spalding, offering him $10,000 for the services of the White Stockings' player/manager, Adrian "Cap" Anson. Spalding's succinct reply was that "no offer you make would be entertained."[89]

Despite the controversy, Detroit showed both poise and concentration by regaining its winning ways in the second half of August, successively sweeping Washington, Philadelphia and Boston, and pulling out to a substantial lead (58–35 versus 53–38) over stumbling Chicago. In the last win of this streak on August 30, Sam Thompson's glove and arm preserved the 7–6 victory. "The long-legged Thompson ... did some great fielding, and by scooping a low fly in the ninth and making a double play, he cut off the tieing run."[90]

The Wolverines managed to consolidate their lead thanks to one six-game and two four-game win streaks, and won their first—and only—pennant. Clutch pitching by Baldwin, Getzien and Conway, league-leading fielding, and the powerful bats of Thompson and Brouthers had accomplished the task. Over the last six weeks of the season, Sam Thompson's hitting and fielding remained as remarkably consistent as they had been all season.

During a home game against Chicago on September 5, Detroit fans arranged an on field ceremony to show their appreciation for all of Silent Sam's efforts.

Tall Sam Thompson was the first at bat in the second. He was just getting into position and putting on a three-base hit expression, when somebody handed umpire Powers a long, flower-enveloped article, which he proceeded to present to Samuel. It proved to be a gold-headed cane, presented to the great right fielder by some of his friends. "Wonder if it will rattle him?" was the apprehensive inquiry. It didn't, for he banged a single to center and raced to second on White's out at first. Twitchell then swiped one past short and Thompson galloped home with the first run.[91]

Highly stylized die-cut portrait of Sam Thompson, 1887. His name and position are inscribed on his uniform, lower-left. Die-cutting, or embossing, uses a steel plate pressed against the material to raise its surface (courtesy Transcendental Graphics/theruckerarchive.com).

Later in the game, Sam's three-run homer off John Clarkson preserved the win for Detroit: "Thompson ... drove the ball to center over Ryan's head for a home run, bringing in three earned runs."[92]

A few days later, Thompson's two stolen bases and two double-play assists helped seal a victory over Indianapolis. His first throw doubled up a runner at second. Then, his throw to third in the eighth caught the advancing Jack Glassock, and was described as "a magnificent effort."[93] Against Boston on September 12, "[Sam] Wise hit the ball with terrific force and on a line to Thompson. The big fellow ran backwards and caught it by jumping with one hand. So great was the momentum that Thompson turned a somersault, but he froze to the ball through this acrobatic performance like a blizzard to a Dakota hamlet."[94] The great catch was praised as "a shining addition to the long line of phenomenal plays made by the big man from Indiana."[95]

One of the most unusual events of Thompson's career occurred in a home game win against the Giants on September 23. Uncharacteristically, it consisted of an alleged violent encounter on the base paths with an opposing player, first baseman Roger Connor.

> A feature of the game was an incident that occurred in the eighth inning. It appears that Thompson and big Roger Connor had arranged for a Greco-Roman wrestling match, best two in three falls, the bouts to take place whenever Sam reached first. The big fellow went to first five times, each on a safe hit, but not till the eighth did he have time enough [since two of the hits were doubles] to take hold [of Connor]. On this occasion he made a sharp hit to D. Richardson [at second base] and beat the ball to first. The two gladiators grabbed each other without delay, and after a fearful struggle they came down in a heap ten feet from the base with a jar that shook the ten-cent stands. Thompson was on top and apparently won the fall. Referee [umpire] Daniels decided it was no fall, Connor having formed a bridge [with his arms and legs]. The contest will be resumed tomorrow.[96]

There certainly was bad blood between the Wolverines and the Giants in 1887. As we have seen in a controversial incident in which Big Sam was called out for not touching second base in a game earlier in the season, New York's up-and-coming team (they would win the pennant in both 1888 and 1889), was not above subterfuge, or even cheating, to achieve their goals.

Given the nature of the two gentle giants, Thompson and Connor, however, it is doubtful that this encounter was in reality any more than an accidental collision, which was written up as a 19th-century "clash of the Titans." Connor, like Thompson, rarely spoke on the field, played hard but fair, never questioned an umpire, and was never ejected from a major league game. Consequently, one of his many nicknames was the "Gentleman of the Diamond." The *Detroit Free Press*'s description of the collision as part of a vindictive grudge match between the pair, therefore, was more likely meant to be a humorous elaboration than an actual indictment of either player. Later in their careers, as we shall see, Connor and Thompson played together for a year in Philadelphia, and the two gentle giants roomed together during that season.

With the pennant finally secured, the Detroit press could not help but gloat over the Wolverine's victory over the league's traditional power-house teams. "It has of course been somewhat exasperating to New York, Philadelphia, Boston and other ancient landmarks of base ball to have a stripling like Detroit walk in and carry off the chief honors in the fore-most baseball organization in the country."[97]

As the team was closing out the season, negotiations were underway with the American Association champions, the St. Louis Browns, for a post-season series to determine "the champion of the world."[98] Although not recognized by Major League Baseball today, end-of-season series to determine a champion of baseball were played from 1884 to 1890, and were a natural consequence of the rivalry created by the existence of two leagues and their mutual acknowledgement as equals in the 1883 National Agreement.

Unlike their modern-day successors, however, these "World's Series" were primarily organized not by the leagues, but by the club owners of the respective champions, who received all the profits from the under-taking. As a result, the number of series games and their venues varied according to the whims and the financial imperatives of the teams' own-ers. The 1887 series was the longest, 15 games, continuing even after the Wolverines had clinched the title, and taking place not only in the home towns of the participants but in other cities across the country.

The teams competed for a modest $2,000 purse put up by the League and the Association. Each team also paid its players a fixed amount for their participation. Beginning in 1887, however, "the partic-ipants also competed for physical symbols of victory—a solid silver tro-phy known as the Dauvray Cup, and individual gold badges, with the player's name engraved on the reverse. The Cup and the badges were the gift of actress Helen Dauvray, an ardent Polo grounds fan who married New York star John Ward while the 1887 World's Series was taking place between Detroit and St. Louis."[99] The Dauvray Cup was the first American trophy competed for by professional athletes.

Even before Detroit clinched the pennant, conflict arose between the Wolverine players and the team's owners over the series' financial arrangements. Player contracts were due to expire on October 15, and the proposed 15-game schedule would require them to play six games after that date. President Stearns' original offer to the player was $25 per game, per man, for the extra dates. The players demanded a lump sum of $400 per player for the extra games, or $500 if they won the championship. Stearns initially countered with an offer of $300 per man and $400 for the championship, but was forced to back down and accept the players' demand.

The 1887 World Champion Detroit Wolverines. This rare version of this well-known photograph is personalized by a hand written message in the lower right corner from team owner and president, Frederick K. Sterns. The dedication reads: "Compliments of F.K. Stearns, Pres" (courtesy Keith Thompson).

The Wolverines' brief but successful pay and contract dispute is historically noteworthy. It was a clear indication of players' frustrations over the owners' tight-fisted and dictatorial policies, and it served notice that they soon might be ready for a more serious challenge to the League's monopoly. That challenge would become a reality in 1890.

A new National Agreement between the National League and the American Association ratified in 1885 had limited salaries to $2,000. This so angered some players that they formed a secret labor organization, the Brotherhood of Professional Ball Players. "Four years later the Brotherhood formed its own League, the Players' League, which had no salary limits."[100] Most Wolverine players, including Sam Thompson, Jack Rowe, Hardy Richardson, Dan Brouthers, Charley Bennett, Charley Ganzel and Charley Getzien, had joined the Brotherhood on May 11, 1886,[101] and by the end of that season they were joined by most players from all League clubs. Detroit's salary revolt that preceded the 1887 World's Series thus represents the first skirmish in baseball's labor/management conflict that would break out into full-scale war during the 1890 season.

Detroit's World's Series opponents, the St. Louis Browns, had won its league's pennant for three consecutive years. Their lineup featured outfielder Tip O'Neil, whose .435 1887 batting average is the second-highest in history, speedy third baseman Arlie Latham, who twice stole more than 100 bases in a season, but who was better known for his pranks and outlandish on-field behavior, and player/manager Charlie Comiskey, who revolutionized first base play by positioning himself well off the bag, and requiring the pitcher to cover the base on balls hit between second and first. The Browns' three-man pitching rotation of Silver King, Bob Caruthers and Dave Foutz had combined for 86 wins against 32 losses over the 1887 campaign. Detroit had to do without the services of slugger Dan Brouthers, who injured his leg stealing second base against Indianapolis in the last game of the season.

In a series that was played in nine different cities' ball parks (each park receiving a share of the gate), Detroit defeated the Browns ten games to five, clinching the series in the eleventh game on October 21 at Baltimore. The rivals split the first two games played at Sportsman's Park in St. Louis, with Sam Thompson collecting three singles over the eighteen-inning span. Detroit then won the next two games played at home, with Sam collecting four hits, including two doubles, and stealing a base. Games five and six, held in Brooklyn and at the Polo Grounds in Manhattan, were split by the Browns and the Wolverines, and Thompson collected just one hit in nine at bats.

Sam's hitting and fielding talents were again on display in games seven and eight, which took place respectively in Philadelphia and New York. He collected three hits, including a double, in the 3–1 win in Philadelphia, and in the eighth inning of the game his running catch of a low liner stopped a rally and preserved the victory. With two out, Tip O'Neil homered to center field, scoring the Browns' first run. Charlie Comiskey then doubled to right and Bob Carouthers singled to center, but Comiskey was held at third. "Foutz was next and he peppered an ugly one to center. It looked safe, but Big Sam was galloping towards it at lightning speed. Down went the capacious hands and the new ball cuddled in them. It was a close call."[102]

In Detroit's 9–3 victory at Boston the next day, "Thompson's slugging was terrific."[103] As the team's first batter in the second inning, "he set the crowd wild with a beautiful line drive to left on which he made the circuit of the bases."[104] After rapping a single in the fifth, Sam came up in the seventh "and smacked it over the center field fence and trotted around to the accompaniment of a general yell."[105]

After another win in Philadelphia, the *Detroit Free Press* declared that "with one more victory, Detroit will be the champion of the world."[106] That victory was delayed a day by rain, but on Saturday, October 22, the Wolverines won the Dauvray Cup by picking up a win in the second game of an unusual double header. A morning game played in Washington, during which Sam threw out Arlie Latham trying to score, resulted in an 11–4 loss. Then, "immediately on the close of the game at Washington the clubs rushed for the train and were whirled over to Baltimore, where without any delay the afternoon game was commenced."[107] Three thousand fans braved chilly weather there to watch Sam Thompson collect two more hits and the Detroits beat the Browns, 13–3. The *Free Press* proudly reported that "the members of the Detroit team are ornamented tonight with the Dauvray badges, and are a happy lot of players."[108]

In the anti-climactic last four games, played in Brooklyn, Detroit, Chicago and St. Louis, and split by the two teams, Sam collected five hits and an assist. Had the concept of a Most Valuable Player award existed

Detroit Wolverine Currency, 1887. Issued by a Detroit shoe store owner in honor of the World Champion Wolverines, this bill featured portraits of each Detroit player and entitled the bearer to a five per-cent discount on purchases of five dollars or more (courtesy Transcendental Graphics/theruckerarchive.com).

Commemorative portrait of the 1887 World Champion Wolverines featuring detailed cameos of each player (courtesy Keith Thompson).

at the time, he certainly would have carried off the honors. Playing in all fifteen games, he collected 21 hits, scored eight runs, drove in seven, hit .362 and slugged at a .621 rate, the latter marks being by far the highest of any player in the series.

Despite these accomplishments and his season league-leading marks in batting (.372), slugging (.571), hits (203) and RBI (166), a ceremony held in Detroit during the thirteenth game of the World's Series must have been frustrating for Sam. During the first inning of that game, Thompson's teammate, Dan Brouthers was awarded a "zylonite" (*xylonite*, an early plastic) bat, "presented by [White Stockings owner and sporting goods magnate] A.G. Spalding to the best batter of the Detroit Club."[109] Big Dan had indeed had another fine season, but it could not compare with Thompson's effort, and owing to a leg injury, he had played in part of just one game in the World's Series.

If Sam had any complaints or criticisms about his accomplishments being overlooked, he kept them to himself. Further frustrations would await him in 1888, his last season as a Wolverine, but just after Christmas, the Danville slugger returned to Detroit in good spirits from his Indiana home to sign his contract, and hinted that important changes were occurring in his personal life. "Big Sam Thompson, Detroit's pet right fielder, arrived in town [Detroit] yesterday minus his summer complexion, but in very good spirits, nevertheless. 'I'm here partially on business [signing his contract] and partially on pleasure,' he said. 'What are you laughing at? Can't a fellow pay his respects to a lady without exciting comment?'"[110] Within a year, the "lady" in question would be Sam's wife.

For Detroit in 1888, a combination of injuries, team dissention, poor attendance and long-standing financial woes led to one of the most sudden and startling changes of fortune for a major league franchise in the annals of baseball history. In the course of a season, the Wolverines went from the world champions to a defunct franchise.

In March, the team gathered in New Orleans to begin spring training. Deacon White and Ned Hanlon were contract holdouts. Both eventually signed, but rumors persisted that Hanlon would be traded, and White would only agree to play on the stipulation that Manager Watkins not critique his play.

Despite White's remarkable contract provision and the previous season's revelation that team owners were looking for a new manager,

Bill Watkins still was at the helm of the team, provided that, instead of watching the games from the stands and leaving the direction of the team to Captain Hanlon, as was his custom, he "resume his position on the player's bench."[111] Since "some of the players objected to his presence on the bench, he was loth [sic] to return,"[112] but did so. Under such circumstances, it was not surprising that he did not finish the year as manager.

In providing a pre-season assessment of the players and the team's chances to repeat as champions, the *Detroit Free Press* could point to only one certainty. "As to the right field, no comment is necessary. There is but one Sam Thompson in the world, and we have him. Had Detroit the choice of players in the world [if Detroit had the choice of any player in the world], Big Sam would be the unanimous choice."[113] Such confidence would prove to be premature, however, for before mid April, Sam suffered an injury that would radically affect his performance and production for the entire season.

Thompson's troubles started on his train journey to join the team for spring training in New Orleans. Heavy rains had flooded more than 40 miles of track south of Montgomery, Alabama, and another train had derailed nearby, further damaging the track. As a result, Sam was left stranded. "Every day for a week, it was rumored that a train would start south. The train would be made up, boarded by the gleeful passengers, start out, discover a new washout, and return with its disappointed load ... [Sam] secured a ... ball ... and kept in condition by banging it against a freight car."[114]

Thompson, it seems, was expecting to receive his first paycheck upon arrival in New Orleans, and had left home with little cash in his pockets. After a few days stranded in Montgomery, he sent a cryptic telegram to Manager Watkins:

Dead broke in Montgomery. Distance to Mobile 180 miles. Walking bad. Catch on? (signed) Thompson[115]

Mr. Watkins caught on, sending Big Sam $20.

Killing time in Montgomery, however, was not always unpleasant, as 28-year-old bachelor Sam Thompson revealed.

The railroad paid for my meals, and during the day I sat around the car, doing the gallant. Three ladies especially interested me. One was from

Cincinnati, another from Chicago, and a third from Detroit. They got to discussing baseball, and finally became all tangled up with respect to the virtues of the teams in their home cities. Here was my opportunity. I handed the Detroit lady my card and told her I should be glad to furnish any information in my power. "Why, are you Thompson of Detroit?" she asked, and I replied that I was. "Not big Sam?" "Yes." "Why my little boy said you were as big as Goliath." The long and short of it was that I got along famously.[116]

The unexpected layoff and subsequent lack of practice caused by the train delay soon proved unlucky for Big Sam. He finally arrived in New Orleans on April 1, and two days later against the St. Louis Browns, injured his arm so badly on a throw from the outfield that "he could not throw a ball 100 feet."[117]

A week later, while the team was headed to Louisville for a pre-season game, Thompson had another bad railroad experience, which the press found to be humorous. "About one o'clock there was a frightful crash, followed by a howl of pain.... There, in the middle of the aisle sprawling, was big Sam Thompson, he having tumbled off an upper berth and struck the floor with a crash resembling the shock of the collision of two speeding locomotives."[118] The train was stopped for four hours, and a Detroit newspaper offered a wry suggestion about the cause of the delay. "At first it was supposed that Sam Thompson's tumble had seriously injured the train and made a stop for repairs necessary."[119]

As the season progressed, the condition of Sam's sore arm did not improve, and veteran centerfielder Ned Hanlon, who also had a lame arm, gave a blunt assessment of the effect of both outfielders' injuries. "Neither Thompson or myself are able to throw as yet, and it is not a hard matter for a man to make two or three bases on a hard hit, where under other conditions he would be held at first."[120]

Sam's injury soon began to affect every aspect of his play. He registered just four assists in his shortened 56-game season (he had 24 in 63 games in 1885), and his fielding average fell 27 points. His hitting remained potent for a while, keeping him in the lineup. He hit three home runs in two days before a friendly crowd in Indianapolis, and slugged three more four-baggers in May and early June. By July 4, however, his average was nearly 100 points below the previous year's league-leading mark, and his extra-base hits had declined precipitously.

A swollen wrist, the result of an errant pitch, and a split finger suffered while unsuccessfully fielding a fly ball, further slowed him down.

The latter injury kept him on the bench for five days. "Everyone was wondering what was the matter, when Thompson lifted his left hand and shook some blood from it. Dr. H.O. Walker bandaged it up. 'Well, I might as well go on,' Thompson said. 'Well, I guess not,' retorted the doctor. 'You had better wait a week or so.'"[121]

Finally, in early July, Sam was laid off and sent home. The *Detroit Free Press* explained that

> few who have seen Sam Thompson play this last season have failed to notice the falling off in his work. The primary trouble was a lame arm, which interfered with his throwing, and a man at first invariably goes to third on a single. In addition, his fielding has been very poor, and to cap the climax, he has fallen off in batting. The past fine record of the great player has induced the management to continue him in the field in the hope of improvement, but as none came, they are compelled to lay him off for their own protection.[122]

After a month's rest, during which Detroit dropped from first to third place in the standings, Sam returned briefly to the team in early August. His arm was still lame, however, and although he collected seven hits in the five games in which he played, only one was for extra bases. His return coincided with the team's sixteen-game losing streak, and the owners, desperate to see some improvement on the club, now had no patience to spare. Once again he was laid off, this time without pay.

Sporting News provided a brief rationale for the club's decision to withhold Sam's salary: "It seems too bad that the Detroits should go to hair splitting over big Sam Thompson's salary. They have shut him off without pay on the pretext that his arm was weak before he signed at the beginning of the season."[123] On his departure, *Sporting Life* ominously reported that "it is considered doubtful if this great fielder and mighty batsman will ever be in condition to play ball again."[124]

Sam Thompson's difficulties in 1888 set the tone for the entire Detroit season. Frederick Stearns resigned as club president shortly after the successful 1887 World's Series, although he still retained membership on the Wolverine board. The League responded to this news by reinstating the percentage revenue system for visiting teams, but the move came too late to cure Detroit's financial ills, which now were caused primarily by a steep fall-off in the local fans' interest in the team.

Lady Baldwin, the 42-game winner in 1886, was laid off with a sore shoulder in June, and later was released. Hardy Richardson broke his ankle in early July and was out for the remainder of the season. Catcher Charley Bennett, long a favorite with Detroit fans, now complained that "the people in the grand stand behind him insult and abuse him ... and he wants to be released in consequence of it."[125]

With home game attendance in the hundreds instead of the thousands, the *Detroit Free Press*'s reaction to the team's dilemma proved to be prophetic. "It is ... a painful truth that very few people here [Detroit] realize the benefit conferred by the possession of a championship ball team, and there is not that general interest taken in the club which it deserves. If Detroit should wake up one fine morning and find herself without a ball team, the chances are there would be something of a wail."[126] *Sporting News*'s assessment was even more blunt: "The great craving of the Michigan public [the pennant] has been satisfied. Detroit has little to gain now."[127]

The Wolverines finished the season in fifth place, 16 games behind the champion New York Giants. A day after the season ended, Detroit sold its franchise to Cleveland in what the *Detroit Free Press* described as "the natural consequence of non-support of a grand base ball organization, and it serves the people of this city exactly right."[128] Cleveland, however, gained little from the deal, since the contracts for the Wolverines' highest salaried players were sold to Boston (Bennett, Brouthers and White), Pittsburgh (Hanlon and Rowe) and Philadelphia (Thompson).

For Sam Thompson, there was a personal silver lining to the troubles he experienced during 1888. Over the course of the sea-

Portrait of Ida Moratzke Thompson, taken in Indianapolis shortly after her marriage to Sam Thompson, late 1888 or early 1889. The couple married in Windsor, Canada in October 1888, and lived in Indianapolis until 1892 (courtesy Keith Thompson).

son, he had fallen in love with the young lady from Detroit whom he had mentioned to the press the previous December. She was Ida Moratzke (also spelled *Moraska*), a petite, dark-eyed, chestnut-haired young lady of Polish/German extraction, who was seven years his junior. The couple married on October 25, in Windsor, Ontario, just across the Detroit River from the City of Straits. It was a good match, lasting thirty-four years, until Sam's untimely death in 1922. The Thompsons had no children. After living in Indianapolis near Sam's family for several years, the young couple in 1892 settled in Detroit, where Ida's parents and siblings lived. She often accompanied her husband on his trips during his career.

Except in rare cases, such as that of John Ward's famous actress/wife, Helen Dauvray, donor of the Dauvray Cup, early baseball players' wives remained out of the their husbands' limelight. Little was reported about them, and consequently little is known about them today. This is true of Ida Moratzke Thompson, but in a letter Sam Thompson wrote to his parents on the eve of his nuptials the great slugger provided the briefest of suggestions that his new bride shared the same down-to-earth qualities that he did.

> I will be married tomorrow Thursday Eve. To the Lady I have been going with … it will be a very quiet affair as none but her folks will be there. I hope none of you feel slighted because you did not get a bid. We leave Friday for Indianapolis. Will get there at 6:45 and will come out home [to Danville] Saturday evening to spend Sunday. Now I don't want you to think of making any great preparations for it will not be expected and neither must you expect to see some Great-Society lady, for she is just as common as any of us."[129]

Reporting Sam's marriage, one Detroit newspaper found a way to use the news to put a lighter note on what otherwise had been a difficult season for the Danville slugger: "Sam Thompson was quietly married last night to a Miss Marotzke, of this city. The wedding took place in Windsor, and the couple left at once for Indianapolis. Sam had a lame arm all season. It is evident that his heart was also affected."[130]

A month later, a *Sporting Life* reporter from Indianapolis published an extensive interview with the newly-married Thompson in which he discussed the condition of his arm, his dispute with the Detroit owners over his back pay, and his reaction to the news of the sale of his contract to Philadelphia.

In what arguably is the most candid and extensive interview that Sam Thompson ever gave, he also put to rest forever the old stereotypes of his country-boy naivete and "Ah, Shucks" personality, revealing a mature, self-confident nature that befitted his status as one of baseball's recognized stars.

I saw Sam Thompson, the big right fielder, holding up a brick building on the sunny side of Washington Street [Indianapolis] and I went over and had a talk with the famous slugger. Sam is here with his new wife, a very pretty young woman, and will divide his time between Indianapolis and Danville, his old home, this winter. In answer to my question as to how he was feeling, the ex–Detroiter said, "I am feeling in fine shape. My arm seems to be perfectly well again, and I believe I shall have no more trouble with it. I have given it several thorough tests, and find that it holds up first rate. I shall nurse it this winter, however, and am satisfied that when spring comes, Samuel will be himself again. Will I go to Philadelphia? Well, now, I can't say just now. They want me, and the Detroit people are anxious to have me there, but I have not made up my mind fully yet. President Stearns wrote me that he thought I owed it to him to sign with Philadelphia, thereby aiding the Detroit Club people to realize as much as possible out of the transfer. He used the argument that he had treated me too well; that the Detroit Club paid my salary while I was unable to play last summer and all that sort of thing, but I do not look at it in that light. Detroit deserves no credit for paying me while I was unable to play last season. It was a case of force. They wanted to lay me off without pay, but when I kicked [complained] and asked for my release, they consulted a lawyer and found that they had to let me go or else pay my salary, and they concluded to do the latter with the hope of selling my release for a big price, which they have done, provided I consent to the transfer, which I am willing to do under certain conditions. I am in base ball for money, not sentiment. I would rather play in Philadelphia than Cleveland, in fact, would not go to the latter place at all. Detroit wants me to sign with Reach & Co. [Philadelphia] for the same salary that I got last year and I want more. A simple transfer means nothing to me. I want to realize something out of the deal and I think I am entitled to it. I am in no hurry to sign." Sam did not say so, but I think he would like a "divide" of the purchase money. He is looking well, and if his arm is all right next season, he will add great strength to any team that he joins.[131]

In just six years, Danville's "Sammy" Thompson had transformed from a gangly, inexperienced first baseman on his hometown amateur Browns to the most talented outfielder, and one of the most feared hitters in major league baseball. His greatest years and greatest challenges on the diamond, however, still lay ahead of him.

CHAPTER THREE

Philadelphia Sam: 1889–1892

"The Phillies have not in recent years secured a single player that has strengthened them so much as Thompson. The big Hoosier is a slugger from Sluggerville."—*Sporting Life*, April 17, 1889

Contrary to the myth that baseball was invented by a single individual, Abner Doubleday, the game actually evolved from a variety of children's ball and stick games that were subsequently adopted by adults as part of activities associated with social clubs to which they belonged. The oldest known ball-playing club of this type was the Olympic Town Ball Club of Philadelphia, organized in 1833. A retrospective article on the Olympic Club published in Philadelphia's *Sporting Life* newspaper in 1885 provides a description of its early town ball game. "The bases, if they may be so called, were five sticks, planted as to form a circle, the diameter of which was about thirty feet. The striker [hitter] was compelled to make a complete circuit in order to score. The runner was put out by hitting him with the ball, which was much lighter and softer than the ball of the present time."[1]

While it is a long stretch from this activity to baseball as we know it, the Olympic Club, and others like it along the East Coast, gradually incorporated rules developed and published in 1845 by Manhattan's Knickerbocker club into their games. These rules, for example, standardized the distance between bases at 45 paces (clarified as 90 feet in 1857), eliminated the practice of hitting runners with the ball to put them out, established three strikes for an out and three outs for a half-inning, and introduced the umpire as the game's arbiter. By the 1860s, the game these clubs were playing using these and other rules could be easily recognized as an early form of baseball.

The best known Philadelphia baseball club of the era was the Athletic (also written in the plural as the Athletics), which had various incarnations, first as an amateur or semi-pro team, then as a National Association team (1871–75), then briefly as a National League club (1876), and finally as an American Association team (1882–1891). In 1883, however, another city club, the Philadelphias, which had been organized as an independent in 1881, gained membership in the National League as the Philadelphia Quakers, after the dissolution of Worcester's Senior Circuit team, the Ruby Legs. Two years later, the club's nickname was changed to the Phillies.

Initially, the team's principal owner was British-born Al Reach, who was a legend in Philadelphia baseball and business circles, having played second base for various Athletics teams for two decades and partnered with local manufacturer, Ben Shibe, in a sporting goods business. Reach's primary Phillies partner was Philadelphia lawyer, John I. Rogers, who by the late 1880's had gained a majority control of the team. The investment goals of Reach and Rogers in the venture were polar opposites. "Reach was more interested in the game itself, and in its ability to promote the sale of sporting goods. Rogers, on the other hand, was looking for direct profit from his investment, and would let little or nothing stand in his way ... a fact that would come out more than once ... in part because Rogers tended to be arrogant and overbearing."[2] Years later, the normally quiet and compliant Sam Thompson dared to criticize Rogers publicly, and, as we shall see, he paid a penalty for his actions that had lasting consequences late in his career.

The demise of Worcester's short-lived National League franchise at the end of the 1882 season provided an entry slot for Philadelphia, but the transfer included no players. Consequently, the Phillies 1883 roster, a mix of rookies and marginal and over-the-hill veterans, posted a 17–81 first-year record, the worst year's total in franchise history. Al Reach's plan for turning around the horrible debut season began with the hiring of baseball legend Harry Wright as team manager.

A pious Episcopalian who didn't drink, smoke or curse, British-born Wright arrived in America as an infant, after his father was named the cricket pro for New York City's St. George Cricket Club. Wright apprenticed as a jeweler with the Tiffany Company as an adolescent, and although his first sport was cricket, in his spare time he learned to play baseball with the well-known Knickerbocker Club, whose rules for the game had helped to standardize regulations for the sport.

In 1865, Harry Wright followed in his father's footsteps and became the cricket pro at the Philadelphia Cricket Club. On Wednesdays, his off-day, he played baseball with the city's most famous ball team, the Olympics. A year later, he accepted a position as cricket pro for Cincinnati's Union Club, and in 1867 he helped organize the Cincinnati Base Ball Club.

In 1869, a group of Queen City investors hired Wright to organize the first recognized professional baseball team, the Cincinnati Red Stockings. Subsequently, as we have seen in a previous chapter, the team toured the country for two years, gaining national notoriety and popularizing the sport. From 1871 to 1875, Wright player/managed Boston's National Association team and won four consecutive pennants. In the ensuing eight years, he joined the National League, retired as a player, and skippered Boston to two pennants and Providence to one.

Among the many ideas pioneered by Wright that ultimately became commonplace in baseball are double headers, pitching rotations, batting practice, fielders backing each other up, and defensive shifts based on a hitter's prior record. His insistence on sobriety and decorum among his players helped diminish many negative stereotypes about ballplayers. Beginning his fifteenth year as a major league manager with the Phillies in 1883, Harry Wright was the most well-known and well-respected man in baseball.

Wright's leadership lifted the Phillies out of the cellar and into sixth place in 1884, and in the next three years, the team finished fourth, second and third under his tutelage. During his tenure with the Phillies, however, Wright's gentlemanly approach to the game was gradually losing favor to a more aggressive, no-holds-barred style of play that frequently turned violent on the field, leading to physical altercations between players, umpires and fans. Any and all such behaviors were anathema to Wright's style of play. By 1893, however, this radical change in the approach to the game, and the Phillies inability to capture a pennant, would lead to Wright's dismissal.

Sam Thompson's initial reluctance to sign with Philadelphia, which was expressed in his November 1888 interview with *Sporting Life* and discussed in the previous chapter, may have been just a ploy by the big right fielder to prompt the Phillies to sweeten the salary pot that he was initially offered, since just a month after the interview he came to terms with the team for the sum of $2,500, $750 more than his 1886 Detroit salary.[3]

After having being laid off by the Wolverines in August of 1888, Sam had resorted to an experimental electrical treatment to try to cure his arm.[4] Specifics of the treatment were not revealed, but a review of a similar procedure for a lame arm that was undergone by a contemporary, Giants catcher Buck Ewing, provides a glimpse of the lengths to which injured players went to try to heal their arms and revive their careers.

In 1892, Ewing underwent a series of massage and electricity treatments for his arm at Hot Springs, Arkansas. The massage was performed

The 1889 Philadelphia Phillies in their form-fitting uniforms, minus their famous manager, Harry Wright. Sam Thompson, seated, front row, center. Future Hall of Famer Ed Delehanty stands third from left, second row. Diminutive Art Irwin, inventor of the Art Irwin fielder's glove and future Phillies manager, standing, second row, far right. Left-handed catcher Jack Clements, third from left, top row, was the first player to catch 1,000 games (courtesy Transcendental Graphics/themarkruckerarchive.com).

by a mechanical contraption that shook Ewing's body. "It works with such force that Buck's entire body shakes, and one can see the muscles and veins bulge out as the machine does its work."[5] After fifteen minutes of this procedure, electricity was applied to the arm. "It is not the old shock, but a smooth current, applied with sponges. There is not a whimper from Buck as the sponges run over his arm, but just as soon as he raises his arm and the electricity touches the spot that was sore, Buck pulls away from the current as the pain passes through his arm."[6]

Harry Wright's first comments about his new right fielder's injury provided information which had not previously been included in reports about Sam's condition. The veteran manager had paid close attention to Thompson's arm problems the previous year on the occasions that the Phillies played Detroit, and after signing the great slugger to a Phillies contract in January 1889, he asserted that Thompson's problem was in the shoulder, and not in the arm or elbow. Wright then offered examples of several players, including former Wolverine Jack Rowe, who had learned to throw without using the shoulder after an injury, and thus prolonged their careers.[7] However, the improvised throwing style of using the arm, elbow and wrist rather than the shoulder would only be appropriate for the shorter throws required of an infielder.

As the Phillies gathered in Jacksonville, Florida, for the first half of their pre-season training in March 1889, it soon became clear what Wright had in mind for Thompson if his shoulder had not completely healed. After a few practice games with local teams, Philadelphia infielder Art Irwin reported that "all the boys were treated to a big surprise to-day. We all knew that Big Sam Thompson was a first class outfielder, but to-day he made the remark that first base was his home position. So we put him on the bag. Wait until you see him in Philadelphia. Nothing seems too high for him, and in the eighth inning with two out, Mulvey threw the ball about ten feet wide of the bag, but Sam pulled it in out of the sand as easy as though it was thrown in his pocket."[8]

Sid Farrar, Philadelphia's regular first baseman, was a spring training holdout who was seeking a salary increase, and Sam's initial good play at first base prompted *Sporting Life* to issue a warning to the Phillies veteran. "Thompson can evidently play first base in first-class style, so Farrar had better not hold out too long."[9]

As the pre-season continued, the Phillies returned home for another three weeks of training before the start of the regular season, and Sam began to reveal some weaknesses while playing his old position. In an April 7 loss to Philadelphia's other major league team, the Athletics, "Sam Thompson at first base failed to stop a throw from [pitcher] Buffinton which was intended to catch Stovey napping."[10] After Sam dropped a foul fly in the same game, "many voices in the crowd asked: 'Where's Farrar [the regular first baseman]?'"[11] Meanwhile, Manager Wright indicated that he "considered Farrar exceptionally strong on ground balls, but Thompson was superior to him on wide hit balls and thrown balls."[12]

Sid Farrar, clearly concerned about losing his starting spot at first base on the team, signed his contract in the first week of April, and after a poll of Phillies fans revealed that they were opposed to Sam playing first base in place of Farrar, Thompson returned to his customary right field position. It did not take long for the Phillies' pre-season opponents to test Sam's arm there, and to discover that it was now as strong as it had been before his injury. Playing at Brooklyn on April 12, in one of his first games back in his outfield position, he recorded two assists.[13]

Offensively, the Phillies new right fielder dominated the pre-season, leading the team with a .347 average during the club's Jacksonville stay, and putting on a three-week power display when the team returned home. His first home run in a Philadelphia uniform came in a 7–5 exhibition loss to Brooklyn on April 9. "Thompson just tapped the ball

For its 1889 tobacco card series, Goodwin Tobacco Card Company superimposed the Philadelphia logo in white lettering, thus barely visible here, on Sam Thompson's Detroit Wolverine shirt after he was traded to the Phillies (courtesy Keith Thompson).

in the sixth inning and it flew over the fence. It was one of those nice little hits that made the 'fans' feel sick two years ago when Thompson was with Detroit. Keep it up, Sam."[14] Thompson responded to the press's encouragement by collecting four hits a week later against Brooklyn, including a triple and a home run, and by scoring four times.

Philadelphia opened the 1889 season at Washington on April 24, with only two changes to its 1888 lineup: Sam Thompson in right field and Bill Hallman at shortstop. The Phillies' pitching starters were Charlie Buffinton, winner of 49 games since coming over from Boston in 1887, and Ben Sanders, who went 19–10 the previous year. Joe Mulvey, at third base, was in his eighth year with the club, and first baseman Sid Farrar was a seven-year Phillies veteran. Philadelphia-born Jack Clements, baseball's greatest left-handed catcher, and the first receiver to catch 1,000 games, was marking his sixth year with the team, as was San Francisco-born outfielder Jim Fogarty. Left fielder George Wood, originally Sam Thompson's outfield mate in Detroit, was entering his fourth and final year with Philadelphia.

Twenty-one-year old Ed Delehanty had debuted with the Phillies at second base in 1888. Although it was an inauspicious start (.228 batting average; 44 errors in 55 games), Manager Wright saw great promise in the Cleveland native, and had planned to start him at second again until he stepped on a rusty nail while running around the cinder bicycle track at the Phillies' park in April. The nail pierced the sole of the shoe and penetrated one inch into Delehanty's foot, keeping him out of action for a week. Then in May, with the regular season in full swing, Delehanty fractured his collarbone in a collision while sliding into second base. Returning to action in August, he reinjured the shoulder, this time sliding into third base. Although the young infielder played only 55 games in 1889, he blossomed into one of baseball's greatest hitters after later switching to the outfield, and compiled a .346 lifetime average, fourth all time. Delehanty earned a plaque at Cooperstown in 1945.

To fill the gap left by Delehanty at second base after his successive shoulder injuries, the Phillies acquired Al Myers from Washington in mid-season. Myers made his major league start with Philadelphia in 1885, but was sold to Kansas City the following year, where he led the team in batting and slugging. He moved on to Washington after the Kansas City franchise folded. A Danville, Illinois native, Myers had played against Sam Thompson while on the Northwestern League's Milwaukee team in 1884. Perhaps initially because of the coincidence that both men were natives of a town named Danville, although the towns were in different states (Illinois and Indiana), Myers and Thompson struck up a friendship, and would weather major controversies together after they both signed contracts to play for Philadelphia's Players' League team in 1890, and then jumped back to the National League Phillies. In later years, Thompson and Myers were co-owners of a Terre-Haute, Indiana, saloon.

Art Irwin was the one notable substitute on the Phillies' squad. The inventor of the Irwin fielder's mitt worn by most big league players of the era, including Sam Thompson, he had been Philadelphia's shortstop for three years, and also served as team captain, but after posting an anemic .219 batting average in 1888, manager Wright removed him from the lineup, replacing him with Bill Hallman, who as a substitute the previous year hit even worse than Irwin (.206)

Irwin's benching had as much to do with his strained relations with Harry Wright as with his weak hitting. As captain of the Phillies in previous years, he had numerous quarrels and confrontations with the Phillies manager over on field decision-making. In one well-documented incident in which the pair differed over the positioning of catcher Deacon McGuire behind the plate, Irwin, never one to mince words, shouted to Manager Wright, "You go back and sit down. I'm running these players."[15]

The underlying tension between Wright and Irwin was symptomatic of an evolving attitude in baseball with regard to the roles of team captain and manager. Although there were some exceptions, the early preference was for a player/manager, who could serve the dual function of team captain and club skipper. As would be proven by men like Frank Bancroft in Providence, Frank Selee in Boston, Jim Mutrie in New York, however, teams could also operate successfully with managers whose roles approximated those of today's team business managers, and who delegated field decisions to a team captain.

As baseball moved toward the modern era, the manager gradually assumed greater responsibilities for field decisions, while the captain's role became more symbolic. In the case of Wright and Irwin, Harry Wright initially prevailed, as the Phillies sold Art Irwin to Washington in June, 1889. Irwin, a Philadelphia press favorite, would eventually get his revenge when he was named Phillies manager in 1894, succeeding Harry Wright, whose contract was not renewed.

Big Sam Thompson went hitless in Philadelphia's opener at Washington on April 24, but after a few days' layoff due to rain, he connected for his first official Phillies home run, off Boston's future hall-of-famer, John Clarkson, on April 29. "Thompson got a ball where he wanted it, and over the wall into Broad Street it went."[16] The four-bagger proved to be his only extra-base hit in his first seven games. This fact, and some difficulty he experienced adjusting to the afternoon sun in right field at the Huntingdon Street Grounds, prompted a negative review of his early performance from the *Philadelphia Inquirer*. "The weak spot on the team is in right field. Thompson cannot get used to the glaring sun which he is compelled to face, and he does not cover enough ground. His batting has been very weak, and his base running is not up to Philadelphia standards. He muffed a fly ball in last Tuesday's game and gave the Bostons two runs, but his position on the team has never been in jeopardy."[17] Although he would soon silence the critics with regard to his hitting, base running and throwing abilities, Sam would continue to struggle for a time playing in what was considered the toughest sun field in the League.

Despite the Phillies' average won-lost record in the team's early years under Harry Wright, they were regularly outdrawing their city rivals, the American Association Athletics. In order to accommodate the larger crowds, Al Reach ordered a new park, known alternately as the Philadelphia Baseball Grounds or the Huntingdon Street Grounds, to be readied for the 1887 season. Its seating capacity nearly doubled that of Recreation Park, the team's former home, which "on its best days could really hold only about 6,500 people, which included 1,500 in the grandstand, 2,000 in the outfield bleachers, and the rest standing."[18]

Home plate at the Huntingdon Street Grounds faced east—a design incorporated to keep the sun out of hitters' eyes. Due to this orientation, by normal game time, 3:30 p.m. the sun was beginning its decline in the western sky, and was shining directly into the right fielder's eyes. Although Sam Thompson eventually adapted to the sun field by becoming one of the first players to use sunglasses, and by assuming a sideways stance while waiting for routine fly balls, throughout his career, sportswriters regularly noted the disadvantage he had when he took his position on his home grounds.

Offensively, the original design of the Phillies' park worked in Thompson's favor, as it did for all left-handed hitters. Like many parks of the era, it featured a non-symmetrical outfield, whose distances from home plate varied greatly. The left and center field fences were over 400 feet from home plate, but the distance down the right field line originally was just 310 feet. A 25-foot-high wall, stretching from the right field foul line to dead center field, formed an imposing barrier that prevented all but the most towering hits from landing on Broad Street, the north/south avenue that bordered the park's eastern side. A home run to right-center field would traverse the wall at about 365 feet. A four-bagger that cleared the center field fence traveled 408 feet.

As we have seen, a particular result of Sam Thompson's hitting style was a batted ball whose trajectory was both *high* and deep, and the Danville slugger soon developed a unique ability to "lift" balls over the right field wall in Philadelphia with regularity. An early 20th-century plat or cadastral map of the area around the Huntingdon Street Grounds lists Broad Street's width beyond the right and right-center field stadium wall as varying between 91 feet and 102 feet, not including the sidewalks on each side of the street.[19] Therefore, any home runs that cleared the right field wall at the foul line by any reasonable distance, traveled at least 370 feet to the middle of the street. The distance over the wall then increased proportionally from the right field line to right center, where a flag pole was positioned, and then to dead center, where another flag pole stood.

Season highlights for the Phillies included pitchers Buffinton and Sanders' combined 47 wins, centerfielder Jimmy Fogarty's league-leading 99 stolen bases and .961 fielding percentage, and the outstanding overall performance of newcomer Sam Thompson, who led the team in batting average (.293), slugging (.492), hits (158), doubles (36), RBI (111) and home runs (20). Defensively, he bounced back from his injury-plagued 1888 season with 19 assists and seven double plays.

Despite the efforts of pitchers Buffinton and Sanders, and of outfielders Fogarty and Thompson, the Phillies finished in fourth place in 1889, 20 games behind the New York Giants, who won their second consecutive pennant. Outside the friendly confines of the Huntingdon Street

Grounds, Philadelphia performed poorly, posting losing road records of 6–14 in June, 7–11 in August, and 2–6 in September.

Sam Thompson's fine first season with the fourth-place Phillies put to rest rumors that his career was over due to his arm injury and re-established him as one of the premier offensive and defensive performers in baseball. The 1889 campaign was a comeback year for him, both at the plate and in the field. His league-leading tally of 20 home runs marked only the second time that 20 or more four-baggers had been hit in a year (Chicago's Ned Williamson hit 27 in 1884). Over the next 30 years, only three other players would reach that plateau.

Big Sam's circuit blasts, either owing to their quantity, their distance, their frequency, or the game situations under which they were hit, solid-ified his reputation as one of the most dangerous long-ball hitters in the game. They often came in torrents. In August at Chicago, he hit home runs in successive games, the first landing in an unusual location: "in the fourth, Thompson made the circuit after banging the ball over the South fence and into a passing street car."[20] In mid–July, he hit five home runs in seven games, including a pair hit on July 20 in the second game of a double header against Pittsburgh. In early September, he hit three home runs in five games, including consecutive-game homers against Cleveland. One of these was of the tape-measure variety. "Thompson's hit was a terrific drive, the ball sailing over the centre field flag pole in close proximity to the stars and stripes, which hung suspended from where the league pennant is expected to float at some future date."[21] This flag pole was perched atop the center field fence, which stood 408 feet from home plate at the Huntingdon Street Grounds. A conservative esti-mate of this drive's distance, therefore, would be 425 feet, a long hit by today's standards, but a tremendous blast by dead-ball-era standards.

Another powerful blast hit earlier in the season off Pittsburgh's Andy Dunning may have been one of the longest home runs hit in the 19th century. "In the eighth inning Sam Thompson drove the ball out of the grounds near the flag pole, and it went sailing over Broad Street and the Reading Railroad tracks into the vacant lot beyond."[22] If the ball cleared these obstacles on the fly, it would have traveled at least 450 feet.

Besides being numerous and hit a long way, some of Thompson's 1889 homers were hit in dramatic fashion. Down by two in the ninth inning against Boston on August 28, for example, the Phillies came back to win, thanks to Sam's walk-off homer. With two outs, Al Myers and pitcher Ben Sanders connected for hits. Then, "Thompson made four grabs for his bat, and somebody in the press box predicted that the quartet of disappointments [grabbing for, and missing his bat four times as he prepared to hit] meant a four base hit. That somebody was right, for Thompson tried to break down the flag pole by driving the ball against it. Three runs were scored and the game was won."[23]

Another Philadelphia newspaper offered a more detailed and dramatic description of this game-winning inside-the-park home run. With two out in the ninth and Ben Sanders and Al Myers on base,

> a mighty shout rent the air as the figure of Big Sam Thompson loomed up at the plate, bat in hand. [Boston pitcher] Radbourn smile at Thompson, and then pitched a ball wide of the plate. "One ball," called the umpire. "He won't give him a ball [to hit]." "Thompson will go to first on ball [with a walk]." But "Rad" [pitcher Radbourn] did give Big Sam a ball, and now he wished that he hadn't
> The second ball pitched was a slow, straight one, which came in about waist high. As it neared the plate Big Sam drew back his bat, and then he swiped it. The ball went sailing straight up into the air and then described a curve toward the flagpole in right centre field. A big shout went up with the ball, and then there was a sudden lull.
> "It's going over into Broad street." "It's a home run," were some of the remarks that were heard. [Outfielder] Dickey Johnston ran down to the flagpole and looked up. [Base runners] Sanders and Myers logged it homewards, and Big Sam was sprinting toward second base when the ball came down. It didn't go over into Broad street, but struck the flagpole, then rolled swiftly up in centre field. Johnston chased it, picked it up on the run, and threw it to third base. The ball got by Nash, just as Thompson thundered around the third base corner, and in two seconds more the big fellow had crossed the home plate, and Philadelphia had won the game with two runs to spare.[24]

Under the standard rules of the day, the game should have been over when Al Myers, who represented the wining run, crossed the plate, but a recent ruling by National League President Nick Young had declared that "all runs scored and all bases made on a hit before the ball shall have been returned to the pitcher shall count."[25]

The circumstances surrounding Sam's grand slam in a 16–12 victory against Chicago on May 16 were even more dramatic. When he came to bat in the second inning, the Phillies had already scored two runs against starter Bill Hutchinson, and the bases were loaded. At this point, Chicago player/manager Cap Anson called Ad Gumbert in from left field to pitch to Thompson. Gumbert, a good hitting pitcher who hit over .300 twice in his career, often filled in for Anson in the outfield. "Gumbert only pitched one ball, and that ball big Sam Thompson lifted over the fence down near the flag pole, in right center, and while the crowd went wild with excitement, four runs came in. When Sam Thompson got to home plate, he modestly lifted his little white cap, while the men cheered him and the Belmont ladies [from the Belmont Cricket club] waved their dainty white handkerchiefs."[26] After his one disastrous pitch, Ad Gumbert returned to left field and Bill Hutchinson resumed his place in the pitcher's box for the White Stockings.

The most unusual of all of Sam Thompson's career home runs, however was one described by the *Philadelphia Press* as the four-bagger that "the umpire would not see,"[27] and consequently, one that, thanks to the trickery of Boston right fielder Mike Kelly, did not count in the record book. In the fifth inning of a close contest against Boston on July 29, Phillies hitters Bill Hallman and Al Myers both walked, bringing Sam Thompson to the plate. Sam then

> hit the ball over the high slats on the right-field fence for a home run. One man had scored, and Thompson had reached second when [outfielder] Kelly was seen to pick up a ball in right field and throw it in. No one appeared to know where the ball came from, but the umpire refused to allow the home run, saying the ball had not gone over the slats. It was plain to all, and was acknowledged by the spectators in right field that the ball had cleared the fence.[28]

The controversial call soon became the talk of the baseball world, and several days later, the *Pittsburgh Telegraph* noted that this was not the first time that Kelly had resorted to this trick. "Kelly used the extra ball trick at Boston Monday. The press reports all agree that Thompson's hit went over the fence, and that Kelly had an extra ball, which he threw against the fence, making it appear that the one Thompson hit struck there. The players and spectators saw it, but [umpire] Powers did not. Kelly played this trick here two seasons ago, according to Ground Superintendent Hebrank."[29] The umpire in question in this case, Phil Powers, was, we recall, the same arbiter who had ruled against Thompson and the Detroit team several times during Sam's years with the Wolverines.

Sam Thompson's defense was as important to the Phillies in 1889 as his offense. His ability to run down apparent hits frequently caught runners off guard. In a game against Washington on June 7, "Thompson made a good running catch when three Senators were on base, and by a beautiful throw to the plate, kept the runner on third, and [catcher] Clements, by a quick throw to [first baseman] Farrar, caught the runner off first to complete one of the prettiest double plays this season."[30] In a 6–5 win against Chicago on May 15, Sam committed Philadelphia's only error. "That was excusable because the sun got between Sam's eyes just as he was about to catch it."[31] He made up for the miscue by throwing out two runners on the bases for double plays. "Thompson's double play in the fourth, when he threw from the right field wall across to third, was very pretty."[32] An inning later, with Fred Pfeffer on second base, "Farrel ... hit to right, but the ball went high and Thompson caught it. Then Pfeffer started to third, and Thompson convinced the crowd that his arm was all right by throwing out the runner at third."[33] Two days later, Sam again registered another two assists in a game against Indianapolis.[34]

Such fine fielding and throwing continued as the season progressed. On July 4 against Indianapolis, the Hoosiers' George Myers singled, and then second baseman Charley Bassett followed "with a line hit to right field, which looked good for two bases. Myers was well on his way to third when Thompson, on the full run, pulled in the ball with his right hand and returned it to [first baseman] Farrar to make a magnificent double play."[35]

Against Washington on August 21, "Sam Thompson's brilliant running catch of Senator John Irwin's line drive in the seventh, when there were two men on bases and two out, saved a couple of runs."[36] During a mid–September contest against Indianapolis, "Thompson saved two runs in the sixth inning by a sensational fly catch. He took the ball literally off the wall and as high up as he could reach."[37]

Sam countered the previously-mentioned May 29 critique of his running ability by stealing 24 bases in 1889. After he scored four runs against Washington on August 19, the press opinion of the big slugger's running, if not his speed, was now positive. "Thompson uses excellent judgment in running the bases."[38]

The sacrifice became an official statistic in 1889, and in this era it truly was a *sacrifice*, since it counted as a time at-bat. Sam registered 19 by season's end, and had the current rules exempting a player from a time at bat for sacrificing been in place, his .293 season batting average would have been considerably higher.

Thompson's performance in a May 29 contest against Pittsburgh provides a good example of how valuable he could be to his team both defensively and offensively, even when he did not hit a home run. In that 15–4 victory, he collected two hits, both singles, scored two runs, stole two bases, walked twice, and had a sacrifice and an outfield assist. Now in his prime at age 29, he could beat you with his bat, his legs, his glove or his arm.

Thanks to his stellar offensive and defensive performances, by mid season, the Philadelphia press and public, many of whom had originally questioned his acquisition from Detroit, now expressed great satisfaction with work on the diamond. "Sam Thompson has been batting with all his old Detroit vigor and has proven a good investment"[39]; "Where now are the croakers who wanted Thompson retired early in the season?"[40]

As a result of Sam's popularity in Philadelphia, the local press began seeking the normally silent slugger's opinions on a variety of topics, and on occasion, the Danville slugger proved to be uncharacteristically talkative and employ an erudite vocabulary.

> When Sam Thompson, who is only 28 years old [actually, he was 29], was asked whether ball players age fast, he said, "Well, sometimes I think I am about 40 years old. They call me 'Old Sam' or one of the 'Big Four,' and speak of me playing as coeval with that of the introduction of the game in the country. Why, I have played only seven years. Newspapers, enthusiasts and cranks [fans] call us aged, but I don't care. I suppose I shall play until they term me 'superanuated' [sic]! I really think the laugh is on our side. But I will tell you who create these false impressions about our age—the cranks."[41]

Despite Thompson's remarkable comeback performance in his first year with Philadelphia and his growing popularity in the City of Brotherly Love, within a few months he would come under intense national scrutiny and criticism, not for his actions on the field, but for the position he eventually took in baseball's long-standing conflict between players and management, a conflict that would break out into full-scale war in 1890.

The players' discontent with their lot began in 1879, when the National League established the reserve clause. Their frustration grew in 1883, when it was extended to 11 players, a number that represented a team's full roster in the era. Two years later, with their control over the players' destinies complete, team owners moved to reduce costs by imposing a salary cap of $2,000, thus negating any increases players may have won during the bidding wars that followed the establishment of the American Association.

The Limit Agreement, as it was called, proved to be the breaking point for several New York Giants players, who were lead by infielder John Ward, who was completing a law degree at Columbia University. In protest, Ward and his teammates formed a union, the Brotherhood of Professional Base Ball Players. The following year, the Giants' Brotherhood players clandestinely enlisted men from other teams in their cause. The first chapter to join the Brotherhood after the New York squad was from Detroit. Sam Thompson joined on May 11, 1886, along with ten other Wolverine players.[42]

The last straw for the Brotherhood came in November, 1888, when the National League introduced a pay classification system for the following year that included consideration of each man's personal conduct on and off the field in determining his salary. In response, Brotherhood representatives met in New York on July 14, 1889, and voted to establish a new league, the Players' League, for 1890. Just months later, the league's architect, John Ward, announced that he had recruited backers for eight new teams, six of which were placed in cities with existing National League teams.

The Players' League outdrew its rivals, the National League and the American Association, in its only season, but startup costs for new fields, stands, equipment and lucrative player contracts proved to be prohibitive for its investors, and after a tumultuous first year in which the three leagues exchanged barbs and lawsuits, the Players' League folded.

A month after the 1889 season ended, Sam Thompson signed to play in 1890 with the Players' League Philadelphia franchise, the Quakers, but almost immediately seemed to regret his decision. The team's representative sent to Indiana to sign the Danville slugger reported that "he had some doubts, but Sam's only proviso was: 'I have got a family to support, and as long as you treat me right, you will find me with the [Players' League] boys.'"[43]

The National League, which was frantically trying to convince a number of wavering Players' League signees to return to the fold, then arranged for a series of meetings in Indianapolis in early December between the Hoosiers' owner, John T. Brush, and Thompson. It was a clever strategy, given Thompson's Indiana roots, and the fact that Brush, while not a native of Indiana, had a high profile in the state, not only as the owner of the Indianapolis baseball franchise, but also as the owner of a major department store in Indianapolis, the When Clothing Company, which had been in business there since 1875.

After the meetings with Brush, Thompson went back to the Players' League Quakers and asked for more money ($500), but was refused. Nevertheless, the pressure on him not to abandon the rebel league remained enormous. In its December 18 issue, *Sporting Life*, for example, warned that "if Sam Thompson plays the Brotherhood false ... he will deserve the contempt of every honest player and base ball patron."[44]

In a clear attempt to embarrass Thompson a few days later, the Quakers made public written correspondence between him and the club's owners, explaining that the team wanted to divulge to the public "the remarkable fact that Sam Thompson is in base ball for revenue only."[45] This ploy, aimed at making Sam look particularly venal, backfired, after an anonymous critic, identified only as a "well-known [baseball] enthusiast," remarked that "the Brotherhood capitalists say they only want to inform the public of the strange fact that Sam Thompson is in base ball for revenue only. Well, I would like to know what any base ball player is in the business for. Players, as a general rule, are not possessed of any more money than the law allows, and therefore it is hardly possible that they are in it for glory."[46]

Meanwhile, the Quakers' lawyer, J. W. Vanderslice, added to the pressure on Thompson by writing him that "this contract is binding upon you, and ... you will be held to the fulfillment of it.... Your fellow players who have stood by you in the past will stand by you in the future if you stand by them, as it is believed you will."[47]

Such pressure had the opposite effect on Thompson. A few days later, Sam signed a three-year deal with the Phillies. The press's announcement of the agreement was prefaced with the title "Two More Deserters," referring to Sam and his fellow Midwesterner and Phillies teammate, second baseman Al Myers.

The friends of the National League are jubilant over the fact that Sam Thompson and Al Myers, right fielder and second baseman respectively of the Philadelphia club, renounced their allegiance to the Brotherhood Monday morning, and each signed a three-year contract to play with the Philadelphia League club. The negotiations have been pending for some time, President Brush of the Indianapolis club, acting for the League. Both men express themselves as convinced that the players' combine will be a failure. Consideration [details about salary] [was] not stated, but the contract of each is for three years.[48]

In an interview with *Sporting Life* a week later, Thompson offered his rationale for the decision.

I've been thinking the matter over for some time and finally concluded that my best interests were with the League ... President Brush explained the situation very carefully, and I must say he has treated me a well as anyone could wish. I think he is one of the straightest men in the base ball business. I expect to be called a traitor and all that sort of thing, but I can't help it and have made up my mind to take matters as they come. As a matter of fact, I cannot see much show [future] for the Brotherhood now. It is going to pieces rapidly, and the player who does not come back into the League very soon will get the worst of it. I felt that I had waited long enough.... I would like to have remained with the boys, but became satisfied that they could never win under the present arrangement. The Brotherhood contract gives no assurance that the players will receive their salaries. I want to say here to [too] that I did not fully understand that document when I signed it. It was brought to me and I was urged to put my name to it before I had a chance to look it over. I asked to have it left with me so I could see what was in the thing, but this request was refused. However, I did not consider it binding, and do not now ... I think a great many more players will do as we [Thompson and Myers] have done.... For my part, I'm glad that I got things fixed.[49]

It is clear from Thompson's statement that in jumping back to the Phillies, he was well aware of the withering criticism he would receive from the Brotherhood and from many segments of the press. The confidence and admiration he expressed for John T. Brush, who convinced him to re-sign with the Phillies, is puzzling, since Brush was the architect of the Salary Limit Agreement, which led to the founding of the Players' League. Sam, however, may not have known that Brush developed the plan.

Thompson had the responsibility to read his Players' League contract carefully before signing it, but if, as he states, the team representatives first pressured him to sign it without proper review, and then refused to provide him with a copy, their actions were highly inappropriate and could not have been reassuring to him. By the same token,

Sam provides no rationale for asserting that he did not consider the contract binding, other than the implication that his reserved status with the Phillies precluded any other legal contract.

Critiques, explanations and justifications aside, the most probable reason for Sam's desertion from the Players' League Quakers was his belated discovery that the contract he signed with the team, like all contracts from the upstart league, gave no actual assurance that the players would be paid. As a co-operative enterprise, Players' League salaries were dependent on attendance rates at games. Additionally, after most of the players were in the fold, a new clause was added to the League constitution, stipulating that gate receipts would be used for salaries only after all other necessary expenses had been paid.[50] When this change was made known to prospective players who were wavering, a small but significant number of Brotherhood members, including Sam Thompson, made the decision to return to the National League.

Detail of an 1890 Philadelphia Phillies team photograph, featuring Sam Thompson. Thompson came under withering criticism in 1890 for defecting from the Players' League and returning to the National League Phillies (courtesy Transcendental Graphics/themarkruckerarchive.com).

While Sam's primary motivation for deserting the Players' League was the non-guaranteed nature of its contracts, his decision may also have been influenced by the fact that the urban "working-class union value system"[51] that the rebel league's actions embodied was not part of Thompson's ethic, which was rooted and nurtured in the family-owned farms and independent small businesses of the rural Midwest.

Besides Sam Thompson and Al Myers, other Players' League signatories who jumped back to the National League included future Hall of Fame pitchers John Clarkson and Mickey Welch, catchers Charley Bennett and Jack Clements, and Indianapolis shortstop, Jack Glassock. Critiques, condemnations and threatened law suits against the deserters figured prominently in the press at the start of the 1890 campaign, including one incident involving Sam Thompson and his wife, Ida, that revealed how bitter Brotherhood resentment was toward players who had deserted the ranks and re-joined the National League.

After several weeks of spring training in Jacksonville, Florida, in mid–March, the 1890 Phillies began an exhibition swing through the south that would conclude in Philadelphia just prior to the start of the season. While en route to Richmond, Virginia, the team encountered the Boston Players' League club at a stop in Wilmington, North Carolina.

> The Boston Brotherhood and Philadelphia League teams met yesterday in Wilmington, N.C., and the freezing reception given to Thompson, Myers, Clements, Shriver and Gleason by the 14 players of the Boston Club and Jim O'Rourke, of New York, will long be remembered by those who saw it. The Boston team arrived first, on the express from Savannah to Richmond. The Phillies were side-tracked on account of a wreck, coming from Charleston for Richmond. Word went around that the League club would come in on a special train, take dinner, and have their car hitched on to the regular express. The Players' League men lined up on the platform as the train pulled into the station.
>
> The Phillies came out in a bunch, with Sam Thompson in the lead, with his wife. The Boston men never made a move to speak to him, but stood like marble statues. Myers was next, and his wife was with him. Clements was lugging a big satchel. Gleason came along in the rear, trying to wear a smile, but the cold, iceberg stares he got from the Boston men turned the smile into a weird look. Manager Wright came along after the rest, and was cordially greeted by all the old players.
>
> After a ten minutes' lunch the Phillies marched back, the Brotherhood men turning their backs as the old players went by. This caused the crimson to rush to the cheeks of the ladies of the party.... Both teams rode on to Lynchburg, Va., where the Phillies branched off for Norfolk.[52]

Despite such unpleasant incidents, by mid-season, the press's focus had turned to the question of which league or leagues would survive. By 1896, Sam's last full major league season, both the rebel league and his role in it were forgotten by all but the most diehard Brotherhood supporters.

Having lost both of his starting pitchers, three infielders, and two outfielders to the Players' League, Phillies manager Harry Wright had to rely on rookies, cast-offs and unknowns to complete his roster for the 1890 season. His new pitchers were two 23-year-olds from New Jersey—rookie Tom Vickery from Milford, and Camden's "Kid" Gleason, who had compiled a weak 16–31 record for the Phillies behind former aces Charlie Buffinton and Ben Sanders in 1888 and 1889. Vickery and Gleason's battery mates were the team's old standbys, Jack Clements and Pop Shriver.

Al Myers at second base shared the infield with three newcomers: Ed Mayer at third, and Bob Allen at shortstop, both rookies, and Al McCauly at first, who last played in the major leagues in 1884. Back in 1883, as we recall from Chapter One, McCauly, using the pseudonym "Dickerson," was hired by the Danville Browns to pose as a Danville native and pitch against rival Plainfield.

Right-fielder Sam Thompson, at 6'2", dwarfed his two new outfield mates, who both stood just 5'6" tall: rookie Eddie Burke and second-year-man Billy Hamilton, who had been acquired from the American Association's Kansas City franchise after it folded.

Burke would enjoy an eight-year career in the majors, playing a decent outfield and compiling a respectable .280 batting average. Hamilton's hitting, run-scoring and base-stealing records in his thirteen-year major league career were of such high caliber that they would earn him a plaque at Cooperstown.

Born in New Jersey and raised in Clinton, Massachusetts, Billy Hamilton at age 13 was working full time in a cotton mill and playing ball in his spare hours. After hitting .351 and stealing 72 bases in 61 games for Worcester of the New England League in 1888, he spent the last weeks of that season with the fledgling Kansas City Cowboys of the American Association. The following year, Hamilton's 111 stolen bases and his .301 batting average with the Cowboys attracted the attention of Harry Wright, who was looking for an outfield replacement for Jimmy Fogarty, now a Players' League stalwart, who had led the National League in 1889 with 99 steals.

Hamilton did not disappoint. He hit .325 and paced the league with 102 steals in his first season as a Phillie. Over the course of his career, he stole 925 bases, third all time. He ranks third in on-base-percentage (.445) behind Babe Ruth and Ted Williams, and sixth (tied with Willams) in batting average (.344). In 1894, he tied George Gore's 1881 all-time record of seven steals in a game, accomplishing the feat in an eight-inning contest.

Hamilton holds the record for most runs scored in a season (196), most consecutive games scoring a run (24) and most consecutive games stealing a base (13). No man in the history of baseball has averaged more runs scored per game (1.06). After retiring from the big leagues in 1901, Hamilton spent another decade playing for and managing New England teams, winning three batting championships. In 1904, at age 38, he led the New England League in steals (74) and in batting average (.412).

During their years together on the Phillies, leadoff man Hamilton's run scoring abilities (first all-time in runs scored per game), combined perfectly with Sam Thompson's ability to drive in runs (first all time in RBI per game), and the pair became the most potent scoring combination in history. Elected posthumously to the Hall of Fame in 1961, Hamilton has the ironic honor of being one of the game's greatest but least-well-known players.

Harry Wright's patchwork roster surprised everyone by winning 22 of its first 35 games, and the team was riding high after winning a team record 16 straight in June. A series of setbacks then changed the course of the season. Harry Wright went temporarily blind due to the effects of a severe cold that settled in his eyes. Until he returned to the bench in mid–August, the managerial duties were shared by rookie Bob Allen and veteran Jack Clements. Allen, a banker's son who had worked in two of his father's financial establishments, handled the team's business affairs,[53] while Clements set the lineups, scheduled practices and determined on-field strategy. Clements, however, was soon sidelined with a hand injury, and second baseman Myers was laid off with a case of malaria.

Seeking to add some stability and maturity to the lineup late in the season, the Phillies sent Eddie Burke to Pittsburgh for veteran outfielder Billy Sunday. After just 31 games with the Phillies, Sunday retired from baseball to join the ministry, and in ensuing years, thanks to his fiery sermons replete with baseball imagery, became the most well-known revivalist preacher in America. As we shall see, a quarter-century later, one of Sunday's converts on the "sawdust trail" was his former teammate, Sam Thompson.

Pitchers Gleason and Vickery were overworked by midseason, and they ran out of stamina down the stretch as the Phillies ended up in third place, behind Brooklyn and Chicago. They closed out the season by dropping a doubleheader to the seventh-place Cleveland Spiders in an unusual way. Cleveland's 6'2", 210-pound rookie, Denton True Young, pitched and won both games of the twin bill. Due to Young's blazing speed, he had acquired a nickname, Cyclone, which was later shortened to Cy. When he retired 22 years later, Cy Young had amassed 511 wins, more than any other pitcher in the game's history.

Thompson and Hamilton were the bright spots in the Phillies lineup. Hamilton's 102 steals not only led the league, but marked his second consecutive season with over 100 thefts. In addition to finishing second in the batting race (.325), he also did so in on-base-percentage (.430).

Although Sam Thompson's home run total dropped to a career low of four in 1890, he raised his batting average to a healthy .313, scored 100-plus runs for the fourth time and drove in 100+ runs for the third time. He led the league in hits (172), and bettered his previous year's marks in triples (9), walks (42) and stolen bases (25). Defensively, he recorded 29 assists and posted his second-best defensive average (.939).

A slightly different version of Sam Thompson showed up to play in 1890. Sacrifices (24) and stolen bases (25) now often substituted for the long ball. There were just a few glimpses of 1889's home run leader during the season. In mid–July against Pittsburgh, his four hits included a home run, two triples and a single. At home against Chicago on August 30, he hit a "terrific home run over the flag pole."[54]

Two more four-baggers, hit in consecutive games against Brooklyn in June, never made it into the record books. The first left the park in the ninth inning against the Bridegrooms on a blisteringly hot afternoon, winning the game, but not counting as a home run. Two men were out, and the winning run, in the person of Billy Hamilton, was on third. Sam then knocked a pitch over the fence, but "only ran to first. He saw the game was won, and hurried to the dressing room. Hence he will only get credit for a single base. When asked why he had not run all the way round, he quietly replied, 'It's too hot.'"[55]

The next day, Sam hit the first ball pitched to him in the third inning out of the park, but an inning later, the game was stopped due to rain, prompting the *Philadelphia Press* to observe that "Thompson is in hard luck. Two home runs on two consecutive days, and he won't get credit in the official averages for either of them."[56]

Sam's home run production may have dropped, but the consistency of his fine fielding and throwing remained constant. In the same June game in which he settled for a single instead of a home run against Brooklyn, "Stallings hit a low liner along the foul line. That ball was traveling along an ugly 'don't cher [you] touch me' manner, and everybody thought it had the right-of-way—everybody but big Sam Thompson, and he came at it like a ram at a new farm hand. He caught it."[57]

Two Thompson outfield assists in a mid–June game against Boston temporarily kept the Phillies chances alive (they lost in the tenth inning). In the eighth, Sam caught Steve Brodie trying to stretch a single into a double, and in the tenth, with former Wolverine teammate Charley Bennett at second, Kid Nichols singled to right, and "Thompson fielded to the plate, where Clements caught Bennett."[58]

Against Cincinnati on July 7, Sam made a spectacular catch "with his right hand, the ball being caught far back over his head."[59] He made another great play in the fourth inning. "Marr was on third as a result of a three-base hit to left center. Knight sent a fly to deep right, and Sam caught it, Marr immediately starting home. He never got there, for the ball was lined in right to Clements, and 'Lefty' Marr was retired three feet from the plate. It was a great throw, and deserved all the applause it elicited."[60]

A similarly perfect throw in the third inning of a game against Chicago later that month erased another runner at home. "With one out Cooney and Carrol singled and Wilmot drove one against the wire over the right field fence for two bases. Thompson's throw was so fine that Cooney was caught before he reached the plate."[61]

Thompson's arm was still as strong near the season's end as it had been in the spring. Against Boston on September 4, he threw two men out trying to advance a base on hits. Six days later against Brooklyn, "Sam Thompson's fielding was the feature of the game. He made two brilliant running catches and two long, accurate throws, which resulted in double plays."[62]

The previously mentioned description of the Hoosier right fielder's brilliant catch against Cincinnati ("made with his right hand, the ball being caught far back over his head") merits further discussion. Sam is regularly described in baseball encyclopedias and in his Hall of Fame biography as both batting and fielding left-handed. If that is the case, catching a ball with his right hand would be a normal action for him, and would not merit special note in descriptions of the play. The fact that special mention *is* made of his *right-handed* grab suggests that such a catch was of an exceptional nature, that is, that he used his bare throwing hand to grab the ball. If so, then Sam actually threw right handed. As we shall see, this is not the only reference of its kind made over the course of his career.

As a condition of the agreement that dissolved the Players' League at the end of the 1890 season, a general amnesty was declared for all players who had jumped their National League contracts to play for the rebel league. Phillies owner, John Rogers, however, who had served as the National League's legal counsel during the 1890 season, adamantly refused to permit any former Phillie who had participated in the Players' League back on his team.

Phillies co-owner, Al Reach, managed to convince Rogers to make an exception in two cases. The first, "for basically public relations purposes,"[63] was made for popular outfielder Jimmy Fogarty. In his seven-year Phillies career prior to his Players' League defection, the 27-year-old Fogarty had played every position except catcher, but excelled in the outfield, twice leading the League in fielding, assists, putouts and outfield double plays. An average hitter, he was blessed with exceptional speed, and stole 102 bases in 1887.

Fogarty left his native California in February 1891, to return to Philadelphia, but "like countless other athletes, he prided himself upon his strong physique, and disregarded the advice of his friends, and persisted in going without an overcoat. The change from the genial climate of California to the harsh wintry weather that prevailed here [Philadelphia] was too much, even for his stalwart frame. And on Thursday last he was taken with hemorrhages [of the lungs] at his room in the Girard House."[64]

Fogarty was diagnosed with "galloping consumption" (tuberculosis), a malady that killed his father two years earlier, and would kill his brother shortly after his own demise, which occurred on May 20, 1891. Aware of Fogarty's condition, Al Reach convinced John Roger to sign the stricken outfielder for 1891, "probably after telling Rogers that the Californian would never play again."[65]

The other former Phillie invited back was Ed Delehanty, who, despite his unsteady performance since his debut in 1888, was still considered by Manager Wright to be "the best hitter on the team."[66] Wright's confidence in the Cleveland native would eventually bear fruit in the mid 1890's, when he transformed into one of the most potent sluggers the game has ever seen. Delehanty was the first major league player to hit .400 in three seasons, and his lifetime .346 average ranks fifth all-time. The great slugger's erratic behavior both on and off the field, as well as his alcohol addiction, would ultimately have fatal consequences. In the early hours of the morning on July 2, 1903, Delehanty, then 35, and en route to New York City from Detroit, was kicked off a train for drunkenness. While trying to walk across a single-track railroad bridge in the darkness, he fell twenty feet into the Niagara River and drowned, and his body was carried over Niagara Falls. His mangled remains were found a few days later.

John Rogers's stubborn refusal to re-admit the seven other former Phillies who had defected to the Players' League would not help the team's cause in 1891. First baseman Sid Farrar retired from baseball, and pitcher Dan Casey went home to upstate New York to play minor league ball. However, pitcher Ben Sanders, outfielder George Wood, shortstop Bill Hallman and third baseman Joe Mulvey found a home on the American Association Athletics. Former ace Charlie Buffinton spent the year pitching for Boston's Association nine.

Left fielder Wood, who hit .309 in 1891, was not missed by the Phillies, since his replacement, Billy Hamilton, hit .340. Hallman and Mulvey, however, hit .283 and .254 respectively for the Athletics, while their Phillies counterparts, Al Myers and Billy Shindle, hit just .230 and .210. The loss of Rogers' scorned pitchers, Sanders and Buffinton, who posted a combined 40–14 mark on their new teams, most affected the Phillies, since their substitutes, Kid Gleason and Duke Esper, won four more games than Sanders and Buffinton, but lost 23 more than the former Phillies duo.

As a cost-saving measure, the Phillies abandoned spring training in the south in 1891 in favor of the New Jersey beach resort of Cape May. As was the case the previous year, several players' wives, including Ida

Thompson, accompanied their husbands there during the pre-season, taking up residence in the Aldine Hotel.

Returning to Philadelphia in early April, the team played a series of exhibition games against local college and independent clubs until the start of the regular season on April 22. Manager Wright started Ed Delehanty at first base, but after he committed ten errors in 11 games, he moved him to Jimmy Fogarty's old center field position. Although "Del" would continue to substitute occasionally at second and first for injured teammates, he gradually made the outfield his home, where, along with Billy Hamilton and Sam Thompson, he soon would become a regular in what would be known as "the greatest outfield ever assembled."[67]

In order to spell front line hurlers Gleason and Esper, the Phillies experimented with nine other pitchers over the season, the majority of whom were unproven local rookies. For most of the year, John Thornton, whose major league experience consisted of pitching one game for Washington in 1889, did the bulk of the support work, finishing with an undistinguished 15–16 record. A testament to the team's desperation to find pitching help came with the signing of veteran sidearm hurler Tim Keefe, who had been released by the Giants. A future Hall of Famer, Keefe was in the last phase of a brilliant career, during which he pitched more than 5,000 innings, while compiling a 342–245 record. He had little left in his right arm to help the Phillies in 1891, compiling a 3–6 record.

In signing Keefe, Phillies owner John Rogers had to swallow his pride and sacrifice his dignity. Having refused to allow seven former Phillies to return to the club after they spent 1890 in the Players' League, Rogers was now paying Keefe, the highest ranking Players' League and Brotherhood member after John Ward, to pitch for his team. Rogers' penchant for trying to fix his team's ills by signing over-the-hill former stars or unproven rookies would continue through the 1890's, as would the team's fruitless quest for a pennant.

The hum-drum 1891 Phillies finished the season in fourth place, 18½ games behind the Boston Beaneaters. The performances of Billy Hamilton and Sam Thompson were the only bright spots in another disappointing season. Hamilton established himself definitively as a League star, leading the Senior Circuit in batting (.340), on-base percentage (.453), hits (179), walks (102), runs (141) and stolen bases (111; his third consecutive year with over 100 thefts).

Hampered all season by a series of hand injuries,[68] Sam Thompson recorded three-year lows in batting average (.294), slugging (.415), doubles (23), RBI (90), and his home run total of eight, while double that of the previous year, was still far below his record 20 four-baggers in 1889. However, in a season in which only five men hit above .300, Sam's .294 batting mark placed a highly respectable seventh in the league.

In contrast to a performance decline in several areas, Sam achieved three-year highs in walks (52), sacrifices (21) and assists (a league-leading 32) in 1891. His record in the season's first two games, while unlike the overpowering offensive performances of the past, reminded the front office and the hometown fans of the multiple ways that he could contribute on the field. On opening day versus Brooklyn, he collected one hit, a double, scored a run, drove in a run, and had two sacrifices and an outfield assist. The next day, again against the Bridegrooms, he hit two singles, drove in a run, stole a base, and made two fine catches. "Thompson caught Foutz on a high drive three feet from the right field wall, and then captured a line fly from Carouthers' bat, on the dead run, not over a foot from the ground, both being brilliant catches."[69]

Details from Sam's most significant multiple-hit games of the season give further evidence of a power decline, probably caused by the hand injuries. He registered four hits in a game three times, but on each occasion, all four hits were singles.

In the two previous seasons combined, Thompson had missed only three games. He missed five in 1891, with three of them due to an accidental self-poisoning rather than to a physical injury.

> Big Sam Thompson is just recovering from a poisoning. Feeling a little glum at Cleveland, he took two kinds of patent medicine, and he couldn't play that afternoon. Bell boys were his only friend, and they vowed they couldn't find a physician. Thompson lay in agony until the team's return, when some of the boys took a coup and went out in search of a doctor. They found one just in time. Thompson says he never wants another experience like that.[70]

When he did miss a game, the press gave specific examples of why his substitute, Bill Grey, was a poor replacement. "Had Thompson been playing in this inning, Zimmer's two bases would have been reduced to a single, and Denny's two bases would have been an easy fly catch."[71]

In late June, Sam gave another demonstration of the importance of his presence in the outfield, when his successive assists on successive days resulted in a double play and an out at the plate. After a game against Brooklyn, the press praised the "great one hand catch of Daly's line fly to the centre field wall by Thompson, who, by an accurate throw, caught Burns at first."[72]

The next day against the Giants, with speedster George Gore at first base, Roger Connor hit a grounder to short stop Bob Allen, who then threw the ball wildly into right field. "Gore kept moving, and was well on his way to the plate, when our friend Thompson, who inhabits right field and had been chasing the recreant sphere, secured it, and with one of his peculiarly accurate throws, caught Gore at the plate."[73]

Sam brought in three runs with one swing of the bat twice during the season. The first time he did so, it was in the traditional Thompson manner. With two on against New York on May 1, "Thompson lost the ball over into Broad Street and brought in three runs."[74] In mid–August, however, batting against Pittsburgh's Mark Baldwin with the bases loaded, Sam brought three men home in an unusual manner. "Thompson bunted the ball toward [pitcher] Baldwin, who made a hair-raising throw, the ball going to the extreme corner of right field."[75] Three runs scored on the play.

Like most long-ball hitters, Sam typically had little respect for the bunt, and it was the least-used element in his offensive repertoire. Whether he chose to use it on this occasion because it was a set play called for by Manager Wright, because he found pitcher Mark Baldwin difficult to hit (he struck out three times against him in the game), or whether he did so on his own initiative to surprise the defense, in this case, this rare Thompson stratagem proved successful.

Sam's 29 stolen bases and head's up base running provided another dimension to his play in 1891. A press account of a close 4–3 win against Chicago in late May, of example noted that "in the third, Thompson went to first on balls … stole second, went to third on a wild throw by [catcher] Kitteridge, and scored on Brown's single to center."[76]

Despite his solid 1891 performance, Sam's age (31), and his three-year Philadelphia record suggested to some that his best years were behind him. In every offensive and defensive category except home runs, however, he still had not reached his peak.

The American Association, mortally wounded financially by the Players' League revolt of 1890, had soldiered on for another year before finally capitulating at the close of the 1891 campaign. In its subsequent agreement with the now all-powerful National League, four Association franchises, St. Louis, Baltimore, Washington and Louisville, were assimilated into the League for 1892, and the remaining teams dissolved. The new League supremacy came at a stiff price. It now consisted of a cumbersome 12 teams, with each franchise forced to surrender ten percent of its gate receipts until the debt incurred by the buyout of the defunct Association teams was paid.

This debt, and the League owners' awareness that they now had no rivals, prompted them to strengthen their financial position at the expense of the players. Three months into the 1892 season, team rosters were reduced to 13 and salaries cut across the board. Owners agreed not to hire any player fired for refusing to accept the pay cut. In the third year of a $3,500 per year contract, Sam saw his salary reduced to $3,000. Within another year, he would see it drop another $1,200.

Infielders Bill Hallman and Joe Mulvey returned to the Phillies in 1892 after spending a year with the now-defunct American Association Athletics. New to the team were four-year Association and Players' League pitcher Gus Weyhing, who was 31–20 with the Athletics, and who would become the only player in history to win 30 games in three successive seasons, each time in a different league.[77]

A second newcomer, 6'3" former Giant, Roger Connor, now in the twilight of his career, already had slugged 129 of his 138 career total home runs in his 12 previous major league seasons. Born in Waterbury, Connecticut, Connor honed his baseball skills playing for his home town Monitors when not putting in arduous hours helping to support his family by working in a copper foundry. He debuted in the major leagues with the Troy Trojans, and then spent eight years in New York with the National League and Players' League Giants. Over the course of his career, first baseman Connor led the league four times in fielding, and at least once in hits, doubles, triples, home runs, RBI and batting average. It was not determined definitively until the early 1970s that Connor's career home run total (138) topped Sam Thompson's (126), making him the 19th century's home run king.

On the days that Tim Keefe pitched for the Phillies in 1892, one of baseball's rarest events took place. With Keefe in the pitcher's box, and Roger Connor at first base, Billy Hamilton, Ed Delehanty and Sam

Thompson in the outfield, and with Harry Wright directing the team on bench, six future Hall of Famers represented the Phillies at the ball-park.

The 1892 Phillies should have been serious pennant contenders. They led the league in hitting and tied for the lead in fielding. Three team members (Hamilton, Delehanty and Thompson) were among the top eight batting leaders, three (Connor, Thompson and Clements) figured among the top ten in slugging, and three (Thompson, Connor and Hamilton) were in the top ten in on-base percentage. Pitcher Gus Weyhing notched 32 wins, and Tim Keefe and Duke Esper each contributed 19 victories.

Despite such statistics and a 16-game win streak from May 28 to June 28, Philadelphia finished fourth in the new 12-team league, 16½ games behind Boston, a fact that has had baseball pundits and historians scratching their heads for more than a century.

Late in the season, *Sporting Life* blamed the team's poor finish on the unsettling effect of multiple injuries that plagued the club down the stretch. "Clements was knocked out for an entire month, and after that, Cross, Reilly, Hallman, Delehanty and Hamilton were successively injured, so there has been more or less shifting for nearly two months."[78]

Additionally, Manager Wright did himself no favors when he chose two highly unusual replacements, Phil Knell and "Brewery Jack" Taylor for backup pitcher Duke Esper, who was released at the end of July. Since 1890, Esper had compiled a 36–21 record for the Phillies, and prior to his release had won six in a row.

Pitching for Columbus of the American Association in 1891, Knell won 28 and lost 27, but along the way hit 54 batters, made 24 wild pitches, and issued 226 walks.[79] Signed by Washington in 1892, Knell walked 166 and hit 28 batters, compiling a 9–13 record until he was fired by Manager Art Irwin for insubordination. He went 5–5 after signing with Philadelphia late in the season.

The aptly nicknamed "Brewery Jack" Taylor was acquired from Albany of the Eastern League by the Phillies. Known throughout his career for his recurrent drunken altercations with teammates, Taylor was 1–0 in his brief stint with the 1892 Phillies.

Manager Harry Wright's need to rely on veteran castoffs like Tim Keefe, or contentious hurlers like Knell and Taylor, highlights one of the significant reasons for Philadelphia's poor showing in the 1880's and 1890's—the refusal of Phillies owners Rogers and Reach to provide the financial resources to acquire quality pitching.

Current-day baseball historians have placed the blame for the Phillies lackluster 1892 performance on team captain Jack Clements for lacking the "quick witted, on field take charge instincts" of other captains, such as John McGraw or Mike Kelly,[80] or on the fact that none of the great Phillies hitters, Thompson, Hamilton, Delehanty and Connor, brought a "hard-nosed, in-your-face style of play to the ball field."[81] Others blamed the teams disappointing season on the quality of their opponents, noting Boston's ability to "put a virtual All-Star conglomeration on the field."[82] Whatever the reason for the talented Phillies' continued struggles, Philadelphia fans, the press and the team's owners were rapidly losing confidence in Manager Wright's ability to lead the team.

The Phillies started spring training in 1892 in Gainesville, Florida, swung through the south playing exhibition games, and finished up the pre-season at home, playing college nines and the newly independent Philadelphia Athletics, late of the American Association. After the Florida warm-up, Sam Thompson showcased both his offense and defense on the road back home. Playing the Washington Nationals in Savannah, "Thompson made a fine throw to third which resulted in a double play."[83] Two days later, again against the Nationals, he banged out five hits, including two doubles, and scored three runs. The following day he caught a ball in deep right field and fired it to Joe Mulvey at third base, again resulting in a double play/assist. After returning to Philadelphia's Huntingdon Street Grounds in game against the University of Pennsylvania, "Big Sam Thompson surprised the crowd by stealing five bases."[84]

After making several fine catches and collecting seven assists in the first thirteen games of the regular season, *Sporting Life* concluded that Sam had now conquered the Huntingdon Street Ground's right field sun problem. "Sam Thompson has the optics of an eagle. He can look at the sun and catch home run hits without wincing."[85]

Commenting on a 12-inning victory over Louisville on May 29, in which Thompson had four hits, including a double, scored two runs, and collected a double-play assist, the *Philadelphia Inquirer* declared that "Thompson was the hero of the day. In the third inning, with Connor on second, he drove the ball high over the right field fence and trotted in with a home run. He also secured a two bagger and two singles.... Thompson added to his record by making several brilliant catches in right field."[86]

Sam was active in different ways during a three-game series against Chicago in early June. In the first game, a 12–3 win, he collected four hits, including a double. The next day, he scored three runs, and one of his two hits was a four bagger. "Thompson started the sixth by sending the first pitch over the right field fence for a home run."[87] In the game the following day against the White Stockings, a seven-hit, 4–0 victory by Tim Keefe, Sam unsuccessfully tried to catch Cap Anson sleeping at first base. "In the sixth, Thompson bunted down the first base line, which Anson took in charge [took charge of]."[88] A few days later, the better-known home run slugger re-emerged, when Sam hit four baggers in successive games against Cleveland and Pittsburgh.

In a late September blowout against Washington, Sam recorded four hits, but as was the case three times the previous year, all four were singles. In the game, Lave Cross had three hits, Ed Delehanty two, and speedster Billy Hamilton collected three bunt singles. The press waxed eloquent about this hitting spree. "Thompson, Cross and Del [Delehanty] had a large number of able bodied base hits concealed about them, and as often as the bunters and the waiters reached first, these knights of the wagon tongue [bat] proceeded to hammer the ball until the thunder of Philadelphia feet around the bases sounded like hail stones on a roof."[89]

In the four years that had transpired since Danville Sam Thompson joined the Phillies, he married, overcame a serious shoulder injury that threatened his career, weathered withering criticism from players and the press for abandoning the Players' League, hit 20 home runs in a season, and led the league in hits, doubles, home runs and assists. In doing so, he established himself as a premier clutch hitter, a superlative outfielder, and a crafty veteran who could beat you with the long ball, the bunt, a clutch single, a steal, a phenomenal catch, or a deadly accurate outfield throw to any base. Over these four years, Thompson hit an even .300, and averaged 169 hits, 109 runs, 102 RBI and 27 outfield assists per season.

Despite such accomplishments, Thompson's age (he would be 33 before the start of the 1893 season), the drop in his power numbers, and news that he would be partnering with Al Myers as co-owner of a Terra Haute, Indiana saloon over the winter, prompted some to think he may have played his last major league season. Listed among *Sporting Life*'s "baseball possibilities for 1893," for example, was the suggestion "that Sam Thompson may really retire from the diamond."[90]

There was no truth to such speculation. Al Myers, whose friendship with Thompson had been forged in the fires of the criticism the pair endured when they jumped their Players' League contracts and rejoined the Phillies, had retired from baseball after the 1891 season. Sam helped finance Myers' saloon, but never oversaw its daily operations, and had no plans to retire. Over the next four years, the aging veteran would lead the league twice in hits, doubles, RBI, slugging and fielding, and once in home runs, extra-base hits, assists and double plays. Now in his mid–30's, most of the Hoosier slugger's greatest accomplishments were still ahead of him.

CHAPTER FOUR

The Greatest Outfield Ever:
1893–1898

"Sam Thompson is the grand old man of baseball."—*Sporting News*, August 10, 1895

Poor attendance at National League games in 1892 was blamed on a weak economy and fan disenchantment with low-scoring, pitching-dominated games. Team owners could do nothing about the country's financial condition, which by Opening Day, 1893, had deteriorated into a full-blown depression on par with the Great Depression of the 1930s. Five hundred banks closed, a quarter of the nation's railroads went bankrupt, and hundreds of thousands lost their jobs.

Even before the economic downturn, baseball's owners, still obliged to surrender a percentage of their gate receipts to pay off league debts, had decided to cut player salaries drastically. Sam Thompson was no exception, and saw his career-high 1890 salary of $3,500 reduced to $1,800. Other than sitting out the season without pay, players had no option but to accept the cuts.

In an attempt to increase attendance under the trying economic conditions, the League opted to promote more offense by moving the pitching distance back five feet to the present 60'6". The pitcher's box was eliminated, and the pitcher was now required to keep one foot on a 12-inch by four-inch rubber slab, termed the pitcher's plate, while delivering the ball. The rule change achieved its desired effect, as 1893 league batting averages rose 35 points, and teams scored 1.47 more runs per game.

With the exception of the first base slot, the Phillies returned the same team to the field as in 1892. Veteran Roger Connor, whose hitting and league-leading fielding at first base had proved very valuable to

Philadelphia in 1891, returned to New York after the Giants hired John Ward as the team's manager. Connor had been a vocal Brotherhood and Players' League advocate and participant, and Ward, the rebel league's architect, rewarded his loyalty by providing him with the opportunity to play in New York again for a final season.

Connor was replaced at first base for the Phillies by Cincinnati native Jack Boyle, a journeyman utility player who had seen action with five different teams in a seven-year career. Standing 6'4", Boyle was one of the tallest men on the field in the 19th century.

All members of the four-man Phillies pitching staff, Gus Weyhing, Kid Carsey, Tim Keefe and Jack Taylor, had seen duty with the club the previous year, but in 1893,Weyhing and Carsey averaged twice the innings of Keefe and Taylor. The traditional two-man rotation that had been common throughout the 1880's was now evolving into a three- or four-man rotation, thanks to the extra stress placed on pitchers' arms due to the increased throwing distance to the plate.

Frigid Philadelphia served as the Phillies' spring training site for 1893 after the team's customary southern trip was cancelled for financial reasons. Sam Thompson began his preparations for the season in Detroit. "Thompson writes that he is practicing daily in a Detroit gymnasium and taking long runs. He is in splendid shape."[1] Sam's workout site was the Detroit Athletic Club, where he would play amateur ball and manage teams for a decade after his major league retirement.

As soon as he rejoined the Phillies, Sam gave notice that he was in fine form. He collected six hits, including two doubles, against a Richmond minor league squad in early April. Over the next nine exhibitions games, he banged out 13 hits, including two home runs, and scored 19 runs. His four-bagger against the University of Pennsylvania's team on April 19 was hit "over the centre field scoreboard"[2] at the Huntingdon Street Grounds, and traveled a minimum of 425 feet.

Sam's pre-season hitting prowess was a prelude to an outstanding offensive year. Playing in 131 games, he hit .370, stroked 11 home runs, scored 130 runs, drove in 126, and led the league in hits (222) and doubles (27).

Although reaching the 200-hit plateau in a season has long been regarded as the hallmark of a great hitter, the modern 154 or 162-game schedules have provided players with dozens more games per season in which to accomplish the feat in comparison to their 19th-century counterparts, whose seasons between 1883 and 1896 usually ranged from 100 to 135 games. Awareness of this disparity makes Sam Thompson's 222 hits in 131 games in 1893 an even more remarkable accomplishment. Only three players in baseball history (Tip O'Neill in 1887, Hugh Duffy in 1894, and Willie Keeler in 1897) have amassed more hits in fewer games in a season than Big Sam did in 1893.

The hot hitting of Philadelphia's outfield (Delehanty, .368; Hamilton, .380; Thompson, .370) kept the 1893 Phillies in the pennant race until August, when the sudden serious illness of a star player and a disastrous three-week-long season-ending road trip left the team in familiar territory—fourth place—14 games behind league-leader Boston. Speedy outfielder Billy Hamilton was leading the league in hitting five months into the season when he became sick after a series at Boston. Unable to recover from his illness, he missed the next two series with Washington and Baltimore. Then, on August 10, the *Philadelphia Inquirer* reported the grave news that "William Hamilton ... is lying seriously ill with typhoid fever at his residence ... Hamilton's condition was so critical on Tuesday that his wife was telegrammed for, and she arrived from her home in Clinton, Ma., yesterday."[3]

Philadelphia baseball fans were familiar with the seriousness of Hamilton's diagnosis, and they feared the worst. Six years earlier, Phillies pitcher Charlie Ferguson, who had won 96 games in four seasons with the club, contracted typhoid fever during spring training. On April 29, 1888, twelve days after he turned 25, Ferguson died of the disease.

Fortunately, Hamilton survived his illness, but he was lost to the team for the remainder of the season. Comfortably lodged in second place on August 4, the Phillies lost seven games and tied one in the immediate aftermath of Hamilton's departure from the lineup. By August 17, the team had dropped to fourth place. A poor final road trip, capped off by five losses in the team's last six games, eliminated any chance of moving up in the rankings. In its summary of the club's season, the *Philadelphia Inquirer* attributed the poor finish to bad luck, referring to Harry Wright's team as the "hoodooed Phillies."[4]

Turning 33 during spring training, Sam Thompson was older than any man on the team except Tim Keefe, 36, who was in his last season. Nevertheless, Sam swung the bat in 1893 with the vigor of a man ten years his junior. He had 60 multiple hit games, including 27 two-hit, 24 three-hit, seven four-hit and two five-hit efforts. To this total he added a remarkable 35 sacrifices, which, under the applicable 1893 rules, still counted as times at bat. Had the current practice of not counting sacrifices as official times-at-bat been in place, his season average would have been .392 instead of .370.

Sam was hot all season at the plate, but on certain occasions he was on fire. He had twenty hits in an eight-game stretch in early May, including six doubles and a triple. He contributed two sacrifices in each of three consecutive games in early June. He decimated Brooklyn pitching in a pair of games in late July, collecting eight hits in the two games, and in early August, his six hits in two games included three doubles and two triples.

Two of Sam's eleven home runs in 1893 were tape-measure shots whose descriptions in the Philadelphia press require further explanation, since they refer to some unique city topography. In a home game against Washington on July 20, Thompson took Senators pitcher Al Maul deep: "In the seventh, Thompson knocked the ball over the Reading Railroad Hump, and the cheers of the crowd lent wings to his No. 10 russets [shoes] as he made the circuit of the bases."[5] A month later against Louisville, he homered off Jock Menefee in the third inning: "It was Thompson's turn next, and he caught the ball on the nose, sending it clear over the 'hump' at Broad Street, scoring himself and Del [Ed Delehanty]."[6]

The "hump" referred to in both these descriptions was a man-made solution to a safety issue created by the intersection of two Reading Railroad tracks with Broad Street, along the eastern border of the Huntingdon Street Grounds. In order to eliminate this dangerous mix of road and rail, Broad Street was elevated and the railroad depressed, "so as to carry the street over the rail road."[7]

The change of grade began at the intersection of Broad and Cumberland Streets, one block south of the Huntingdon Street Grounds, rose to its highest point near the right-center field wall of the Grounds, and then descended as Broad Street approached Lehigh Avenue. At Huntingdon Street outside the southeast corner of the baseball grounds, Broad Street was elevated nearly 12 feet. Half way up the block, it was raised almost 15 feet. At Lehigh Avenue, the northeast corner of the ball park, it was raised almost 13 feet.

The newspaper descriptions of Sam Thompson's "hump" home runs do not pinpoint the precise location of the balls hit over the Broad Street hump, which spanned the entire block that bordered the ball park's eastern side. However, a ball hit over the hump—that is, over Broad Street—at the right field foul line would have traveled at least 410 feet. One hit over the right-center field fence and the Broad Street hump would have traveled at least 450 feet. In either case these were tremendous home run distances during the Dead Ball Era.

Many attempts were made to explain how the Phillies, who led the League in doubles, home runs, RBI, batting average and slugging, ended up in fourth place, 14 games behind league-leading Boston in 1893. Harry Wright attributed the poor finish to the absence of Billy Hamilton in the lineup: "The loss of Hamilton at the bat and in the field has been a very disastrous one for us."[8] Others placed the blame on Wright's overworking two of the four pitchers on the staff, Kid Carsey and Gus Weyhing, whose combined 663 innings were nearly twice the total hurled by Tim Keefe and Jack Taylor.[9]

For some, team dynamics, not actual player abilities, were the cause to the poor finish. The fact that the fourth-place Phillies took nine of 12 games from third-place Cleveland, but lost nine of 12 from tenth-place St. Louis, suggested that they were "a group of underachievers,"[10] thanks to their tendency to do well against teams above them in the rankings, but fare poorly against teams beneath them.

Another conclusion, one that may have exercised the greatest effect on the future of the team's manager, was that Harry Wright's methods were outmoded. In owner John I. Roger's words, "Harry has been too long in the game. He goes back to those Cincinnati Reds of the sixties. We're playing a different kind of baseball in the nineties."[11]

In the 1890s, baseball's new emphasis on the hit-and-run play, base stealing, and bunting for a hit or to advance runners, required a new attention to strategy, skillful team work and speed. Many other less commendable tactics, often described as "dirty ball playing," were, however, also part of the new approach to the game. They included throwing the catcher's mask or bats into the path of runners trying to score, grabbing runners' jerseys or otherwise interfering with their progress, spiking defenders or running into them in an effort to make them drop the ball, verbal and at times physical harassment of the umpire (known as "kicking" in the era), and taunting or fighting with opposing players. The owners' new tendency to wink at rowdy behavior encouraged a state of lawlessness at the ballpark that frequently led to riots by angry or drunken fans.

The new rowdy, "hoodlum" style of play, favored by teams like the Baltimore Orioles and the Cleveland Spiders, was the antithesis of the on-field Victorian propriety espoused by Harry Wright. The inability to adjust to the changes in the game or to win a pennant finally took their toll on the legendary manager, whose twenty-four-year career ended when he was released by the Phillies in November.

Wright's sterling reputation and contributions to baseball were well-known and admired by owners, players and fans across the country, all of whom referred to him affectionately as "Uncle Harry." His release provoked a public outcry, and boycotts were planned for future Philadelphia games. The National League let Phillies owner John Rogers off the hook by creating a new, paid position for Wright, that of Chief of Umpires, for 1894. It was largely an honorary post, since his responsibilities were limited to observing umpires and submitting reports to the National League office.[12]

The following year, Wright's health declined rapidly, and on October 3, 1895, he passed away in Atlantic City, New Jersey. E.J. Lanigan, a reporter for *The Sporting News* who was not present at Wright's death, claimed in his obituary that at the moment of his passing, the veteran manager awoke from a coma, raised two fingers, exclaimed, "Two men out!" and expired.[13]

A month before Wright's November 1893 dismissal by the Phillies' owners, Sam Thompson gave a long interview to *Sporting Life*'s C.K Mathison that sent shock waves through the baseball community, not only for its combative tone and critical nature, but also for the fact that "Silent Sam" Thompson, known by all as the most "inoffensive" ballplayer in the league, was the player who was issuing the complaint.

> Sam Thompson, the giant right fielder of the Phillies team, arrived in Detroit yesterday, and will spend the winter at his home, near the Michigan Athletic Association [the Detroit Athletic Club]. The big left-handed hitter looks well, and says he has gone through the season with nothing more serious than a case of Charley-horse. Thompson never played better ball than he has in '93. Of his prospects he says:
> "I shall not play again in Philadelphia, and I told Harry Wright it would

be a waste of time to write me about signing. The cheese-paring [cheapskate] methods of the management together with the fact that for five years I have had to face the sun in right field have been the causes leading to my resolution. The crowds that have turned out to see the game in Philadelphia have been astonishing. The management have made a barrel of money, but they grind the players into the dirt.

"Nothing would suit me better that to play ball for Detroit, and if the League knows its business, it will drop such dead rabbit towns as Louisville, St. Louis and Washington, and take in a few cities like Detroit. A League team in this city would draw [fans] to a certainty. It always was a good League town and players have always been treated decently. From talk I have heard from League people, I should say there is a decided leaning toward Detroit. With Charley Bennett and one or two other Detroit favorites, a League team would be a big success."

Thompson says the methods of John I. Rogers are particularly objectionable to the players, and Harry Wright's grinding the players down only subjects the men to unnecessary annoyance and does not help himself any.

As an instance, when the season started, the players were told to dress at the grounds. The men thereupon paid for their own bus, and Wright finally engaged [paid for] the bus. The team had to put up at the poorest hotels and travel on the cheapest [rail] roads. When Thompson told Wright he would not play again in Philadelphia, the veteran manager said, "Don't know if I'll be there myself."

Sam always says the reason the club slipped down at the finish was that a number of strong players were on the hospital list, and their places on the team were filled by amateurs. Thompson says he does not object to salaries coming down to reasonable figures, or to players being held to strict discipline, but he thinks the Philadelphia management is unnecessarily rubbing it on [in].[14]

Such critical commentary issued by a star player known throughout the league and the nation for his gentlemanly and inoffensive nature, makes clear that poor player morale was another significant factor in the Philadelphia franchise's continued mediocre performance. Sam's assertion that he would not play again for the team is a good indicator of his level of anger and frustration, but it was a useless threat, thanks to the stranglehold of the Reserve Clause.

Thompson's account of the club's initial refusal to pay the players' transportation from their hotel to the field while on the road reveals the lengths to which the Philadelphia ownership attempted to pinch pennies. His assumption that the team was doing well financially, which he based on his observation of the size of the home crowds, was well-founded. A week after his interview was published, *Sporting Life* reported that the Phillies led the league in attendance (290,000) and earned an estimated $40,000 in profit.[15] None of it was shared with the players.

The great slugger's identification of Harry Wright as the person assigned by the club to "grind down" the players may be understood in a dual light. On the one hand, Wright was the individual required to make decisions on team accommodations and travel on the road based on the amount of money owner John Rogers allocated for these necessities. Wright himself, however, also drew criticism from the team for his vigorous mandatory morning workouts before every home game, which consisted of "two or three hour simulated game practices."[16] Players felt that these constant sessions depleted their strength and energy reserves needed for the afternoon games followed.

The most significant aspect of Thompson's commentary is his identification of owner John I. Rogers as the person primarily responsible for the poor treatment of the players. Rarely in the era was a player so bold as to openly criticize the owner who, due to the Reserve Clause, held his future livelihood in his hands.

Sam came under some criticism in the press for his comments, but by the following season, as we shall see, reports indicated that the Phillies travel and accommodations on the road had improved greatly, thanks in great measure to his candor. For the remainder of the great slugger's years in Philadelphia, however, John Rogers regularly tried to trade him, but could not arrange a financially satisfactory exchange.

Rogers' real revenge came a few years later, when an aging and injured Thompson asked for his release. Sam planned to play for and manage a minor league team, but Rogers put a price of $5,000 on the release. It was an amount that no major or minor league team would pay for a player his age, and a price that if paid by Sam himself, would negate any income that he might make as a minor leaguer. Given the fact that Sam was fit enough to substitute successfully for the Detroit Tigers for eight games in 1906, ten years after his last full season, there is little doubt that had he managed to obtain his release from Philadelphia, he would have been able to extend his professional career either in the major or minor leagues, and benefit financially for many more years.

Thompson, known as Silent Sam early in his career, also began to speak out on other issues, including critiques of his play on the diamond.

Once, news of a dispute that he had with sportswriter O. P. Caylor found its way onto the sports pages. Caylor was known for his witty columns that often tended to drift into sarcasm, "cutting both friend and foe."[17] According to Francis Richter, editor of *Sporting Life*, the Ohio-born Caylor "lacked judgment, and therefore, was always eager to enter into controversy."[18] As a consequence, "he made more enemies than friends."[19] Big Sam briefly became one of those enemies, but his confrontation with the journalist had a humorous rather than a violent resolution.

> Big Sam Thompson of the Phillies is the most sensitive in the National league to newspaper criticism. An unfriendly sentence by a baseball writer will throw him into spasm and a paragraph will cause him to sulk for a month.
>
> In the old days, when O.P. Caylor was baseball editor of the Philadelphia Press [actually, Caylor wrote for the Philadelphia-based *Sporting Life*], he, for some reason, conceived a dislike for Thompson, and for weeks at a time he would miss no chance on [to] toast the big fielder for his playing. The most trivial errors were magnified until Thompson grew fairly desperate. He consulted with his friends and determined at last that the only thing left for him to do was to make it a personal matter, and either thrash his critic or be thrashed by him.
>
> Accordingly, he made his way to the Press office one evening after a particularly vicious attack had been made on him. He landed in the city editor's room and asked for Caylor.
>
> "Second door to the right as you got down the hall," briefly directed the city editor, and Thompson, after pulling himself together in anticipation of the impending conflict, knocked softly at the door in question.
>
> "Come in," was the response, in a weak, piping voice.
>
> "Sounds like a woman," growled the huge fielder in his deepest bass, but he pushed the door open and stepped in.
>
> At the desk directly in front of him sat a weazened [sic] man of nearly 50, who could not have weighed more than 110, and who peered out from behind strong eyeglasses.
>
> Thompson was staggered, but he quickly rallied.
>
> "Are you Mr. Caylor?" he asked, in his fiercest tones.
>
> "I am," was the response. "What can I do for you, sir?"
>
> The gigantic tall player eyed the little man from head to foot. Evidently satisfied with his inspection, he inflated his lungs, and, blowing a huge puff of air at the astonished Caylor, he turned on his heel and walked out, remarking as he went: "That settles you: you're dead."
>
> Caylor told the story on himself, and he and Thompson became fast friends.[20]

Events that transpired in baseball in 1894 gave clear indication that an era of change was at hand. The year began horrifically when veteran catcher Charley Bennett, a close friend and former teammate of Sam Thompson, suffered a terrible accident. In January, while heading to New Mexico for a hunting trip with pitcher John Clarkson, Bennett stopped briefly in a small town in southern Kansas to see an old friend. The pair talked briefly at the train station, and then Bennett prepared to re-board the train and continue his journey. Bennett's own account of what happened next appeared six months later in *Sporting Life*:

> It was raining and the platform was wet. I swung round to catch the railing. My foot slipped and I fell, the left foot going over the rail. I pushed my right foot against the rail to force my body back, but it slipped and went over also. The wheel went over my left foot and right leg at the knee. The train was stopped and I was put on the coach. John [Clarkson] decided to take me to Ottawa [Kansas, near the Kansas/Missouri border] where I could get medical attention.... They cut off both legs, one just above the ankle and the other one just above the knee.... While of course my baseball days are over, I think that I still may be able to hunt some. I was in good physical condition when hurt, and the stumps have healed so perfectly that I hope to be able to stand a good deal of pressure on them."[21]

After the accident, Bennett became adept at using crutches and artificial legs, and made a living as a china painter and a cigar store owner. In later years, as we shall see, Bennett and Sam Thompson were inseparable, attending almost every Detroit Tigers home game together. Each year, Bennett, standing briefly without crutches, caught the ceremonial first pitch on Opening Day at the Tigers' ballpark, while Sam Thompson, at Bennett's side, served as honorary umpire.

In October, 1894, John Ward, founder of the Brotherhood union and the Players' League, ended his 17-year career to devote full time to his successful law practice. He became an avid bicyclist and a scratch golfer, and frequently represented ballplayers in suits brought by them against team owners and the League.

A month after Ward's retirement, Mike "King" Kelly, baseball's first superstar and the first player to write and publish a biography, died of pneumonia in Boston. A splendidly gifted athlete, Kelly played most of his career in Chicago and Boston. Able to man every position on the field, he led the league twice in hitting and electrified crowds with his head-first base stealing, which was celebrated in a popular song of the era, "Slide, Kelly, Slide!" On one occasion, we recall, Kelly's antics on the field involved hiding an extra ball in his shirt and substituting it for a ball hit over the fence by Sam Thompson. Alcoholism compromised Kelly's talents and cut short his career. He died penniless at age 36, leaving behind a young wife.

The departure from the game of these and other members of baseball's old guard was followed in 1894 by the meteoric rise of a team that came to prominence by espousing rowdy ball. Managed by former Detroit Wolverine Ned Hanlon and led by a quartet of rough-and-ready Irish-American players—John McGraw, Joe Kelley, Hughie Jennings and Willie Keeler—the Baltimore Orioles combined skill, daring and aggression to claw their way to the pennant in 1894 after an eighth-place finish the previous year.

John Rogers' first order of business for the Phillies in 1894 was to hire a new manager. He chose a familiar figure, Art Irwin, the light-hitting infielder and inventor of the first fingered fielding glove, who spent three years as the team's shortstop in the late 1880's before being fired by Harry Wright for insubordination. The Canadian-born Irwin, who had skippered the American Association Boston Reds to the Association's last pennant in 1891, was a proponent of the new style of play that he and other players termed "scientific baseball," which featured place-hitting, bunting, base running and the sacrifice.

Rogers' decision to hire Irwin, a staunch Players' League participant and supporter in 1890 and a constant thorn in the side of Harry Wright during his prior service with the club, is clear evidence of how desperate the Phillies' owner was to secure a league pennant.

Studio Portrait of Ida Thompson, Philadelphia, 1890s (courtesy Keith Thompson).

Irwin's two-year tenure in Philadelphia was stormy. Constantly compared to his predecessor, the beloved Harry Wright, he instituted a complex system of signs and signals that confused his men, often made tactical moves that cost the team victories, and humiliated players, including stars like Billy Hamilton, by criticizing them in front of teammates or the press. Irwin's abrasive managerial persona masked an even more complex personality off the field. In July 1921, the then 63-year-old ex-manager withdrew $5,000 from a New York bank and boarded an overnight steamer for Boston. When the boat docked the next morning, Irwin was not on board, and his disappearance was declared to be a suicide. It was soon discovered that for decades he had been leading a double life, with a wife and family both in New York and in Boston. A year after his alleged death, however, a retired player who knew him well swore that he had recently seen him in Oklahoma.[22]

The Phillies opened the 1894 season with no changes to their previous year's lineup, but after playing in just 46 games, veteran catcher Jack Clements broke his ankle and was lost for the season. His substitutes behind the plate were 25-year-old rookie Mike Grady, from nearby Kennett Square, Pennsylvania, and a 35-year-old journeyman, Dick Buckley.

In mid June, Phillies starting shortstop Bob Allen was hit in the face by a pitch thrown by Cincinnati's Elton "Icebox" Chamberlin. Allen's cheekbone was shattered, effectively ending his career. His replacement, Joe Sullivan, hit .352 for the remainder of the year, but posted a miserable .887 fielding average.

The retirement of Tim Keefe left the bulk of the pitching duties to Jack Taylor, Kid Carsey and Gus Weyhing. In a clear indication of the team's major weakness—the franchise's unwillingness to spend money to support the staff—11 different hurlers were shuffled in and out of the rotation as a replacement for Keefe. A half-dozen were rookies, and three of their number, John Johnson, Al Lukens and Al Burris were "one and done" pitchers who never played again in the major leagues after their debut game with the Phillies.

In addition to arousing the ire of the Philadelphia management, Sam Thompson's disparaging remarks about the team's parsimonious ways and his own dissatisfaction with playing for the Phillies suggested to other teams that a trade for the veteran slugger now might be possible. In January, rumors that Thompson would be traded to Baltimore for pitcher

Sadie McMahon were denied by new manager Irwin. "It is true, I will sign a good pitcher if I can get one, but I'm not going to give away my best player in exchange…. Sam can play the difficult right field in the Philadelphia Ball Park better than any man we could get, and I don't propose to let him go."[23]

Two months later, however, St. Louis owner Chris von der Ahe offered pitcher Kid Gleason "and a cash bonus of a large size,"[24] for Thompson. Even though Phillies owner Al Reach "couldn't see his way clear to a deal which involved the transfer of Thompson to St. Louis,"[25] *Sporting Life* reported that manager Irwin, who in January insisted he would not trade Thompson, had "worked hard to effect a trade [of Thompson] with the St. Louis club for pitcher Gleason."[26]

Trade speculation ended temporarily after Sam signed with Philadelphia just before the start of the season, and the local press, after a sarcastic jab at the big right fielder for his now-famous complaints, conceded that his value to the team would make it difficult to let him go. "Thompson … has said that he will never again wear a Philadelphia uniform because the team does not travel in parlor cars and stop at ten-dollar-a-day hotels. Big Sam, however, is so popular here, and … is such a good fielder and batter, that the club will not let him go without a struggle."[27]

Studio Portrait of Sam Thompson, Philadelphia, 1890s (courtesy Keith Thompson).

While the Phillies fourth-place finish in 1894 did little to hold fan interest, more than enough drama and excitement were generated by news of an injury and subsequent operation endured by a star player, a fan riot at the ball park, a fire that completely destroyed the Huntingdon Street Grounds, and the advent of the greatest offensive season ever put together by three members of a major league outfield. The Phillies pinched pennies during the pre-season for the second straight year, opting to use the University of Pennsylvania's facilities in West Philadelphia for spring training instead of wintering in Florida or touring the south.

Sam Thompson seemed to thrive in Philadelphia's cold weather while he was sharpening his batting eye against college and Eastern League pitching. In the twelve games prior to the start of the regular season he collected 21 hits, including home runs in three consecutive games, scored 22 runs, and stole seven bases, including a pair of thefts in consecutive games.

Thompson's transition to hitting against major league pitching after the season opened had no effect on his hot streak. In fact, he hit the big league pitchers even better than the college and minor league hurlers, collecting 31 hits, including six doubles, four triples and a home run in his first 16 league games. He also stole three bases and collected an outfield assist and a sacrifice.

Over the winter, the sacrifice rule had been amended, limiting it to bunts, and for the first time not counting sacrifices as times-at-bat. Over the course of the season, power-hitting Sam would show his ability to bunt for a sacrifice seven times. His long fly-ball outs, which accounted for his 35 sacrifices the previous season, still allowed runners to advance a base, but they no longer counted in the statistical record as sacrifices.

Big Sam's first home run of the season, hit off Boston's Jack Stivetts, was a tape-measure clout over the Huntingdon Street Ground's center field fence, located 408 feet from home plate. "The climax was reached in the second inning, when big Sam drove the ball directly over the new high board fence in centre field. It was a terrific hit, and the crowd didn't stop yelling until Sam sat down on the player's bench."[28]

In mid–May, however, Thompson's hot-hitting streak ended abruptly when he was sidelined after injuring his hand in the outfield. "Thompson has a gathered [jammed] finger, the result of catching a hot liner."[29] The little finger of his left hand suffered the injury.

In the seven previous years in which he had the opportunity to play a full season, Sam had missed just 16 of 942 games. Thanks to this first major injury in his career, he would miss six weeks and 30 games of the 1894 season.

It soon became apparent that the injury was more serious than originally thought. The finger swelled alarmingly, so much so that Sam's doctors recommended amputation.

> Sam Thompson submitted to an operation at the Samaritan Hospital last Sunday which will prevent him from playing at least six weeks, so the hospital surgeons say. Thompson was put under the effects of ether [on] Sunday noon, and the operation was performed by Dr. John A. Roger, one of the surgeons at the hospital, who is also the physician of the Philadelphia Club.
>
> About two weeks ago the little finger on Thompson's left hand began swelling up, and it has daily grown worse until he could no longer endure the pain, which finally induced him to submit to yesterday's operation. The finger had been injured so often by coming in contact with hard-hit balls that several small bones in it became afflicted with some chronic disease which the physicians called "dead bone," and the only way to relieve him was to either take out these bones or amputate the finger. Thompson preferred to have these small bones taken out, but the surgeon advised that he submit to the amputation of the finger, which he refused to do.
>
> At the hospital, it was thought that since these dead bones had been removed, Thompson's finger might get well again in about a month's or six weeks' time, but, if it did not, then it would have to be amputated, which would prevent him from playing for still another month.[30]

The details of Sam's injury and surgery again raise the question of whether he threw left-handed or right-handed, an issue that was discussed previously in Chapter One. As we recall, Sam used the Irwin glove when playing the outfield. The glove provided minimal protection for the hand and fingers, and players wearing it were still subject to injury from hard hit balls. It is possible that Thompson's gloveless hand may have received multiple injuries from hard hit balls, but the greater probability is that the gloved hand, which always made contact with every ball that he attempted to catch, would suffer more injuries than the gloveless hand. If Sam's gloved hand were the injured [left] hand, this would indicate that Sam threw right handed.

In mid–July, the Huntingdon Street Grounds were rocked by violence during a game. In the first inning of a home contest against Boston, Billy Hamilton started things off for the Phillies in one on his favorite ways—he walked and then stole second base. Boston's first baseman, Tommy "Foghorn" Tucker, known around the league for his foul mouth and aggressive demeanor, vociferously protested the safe call of Hamilton at second base, peppering his complaint with a string of profanities. A few minutes later, Hamilton scored the Phillies' first run, setting Tucker off again. Local fans responded by booing the Boston first baseman, who retorted with more profanity. Each inning thereafter as he took the field, his exchanges with the fans grew more insulting and aggressive.

In the eighth inning, with Boston behind and a rainstorm threatening, the Beaneaters began to use delaying tactics in order to drag the game out until the rain began, at which point they hoped that the umpire would declare the contest to be canceled. Boston refused to field Phillies hits, ultimately forcing Sam Thompson to retire the side by running across the diamond from first base to third base without coming near second, in order to force the umpire to call him out. Boston then refused to bat, and the team's captain and best hitter, Hugh Duffy, grabbed the game ball and ran around in the outfield with it, hoping to further delay the action. At this point, the umpire declared the game a forfeit, giving the Phillies a 9–0 victory.

The decision in favor of Philadelphia was not enough to placate the irate home town fans, who swarmed onto the field in search of Tom Tucker and any other Boston player they could run down. Tucker was felled by several blows to the face, one of which broke his jaw. Police and the Philadelphia team managed to move the Boston players to safety under the grandstand, but on their return to their hotel, their horse-drawn omnibus was stoned by an angry mob. Thus, less than a year after the departure of Harry Wright, the gentleman of the diamond, "rowdy ball" had made its debut in Philadelphia.

The fiery display of emotions at the ball park in July was followed by an actual fire there the following month, one that destroyed the Huntingdon Street Grounds. On August 6, while the Phillies were conducting their morning practice, a fire of unknown origin broke out in the grandstand. All efforts to put it out failed, and after burning for several hours, "the only remains left to show that the Philadelphia park had stood at 15th Street and Huntingdon Avenue were a patch of badly scorched turf, the fence in dead center field, and part of the brick wall running along Huntingdon Street."[31]

After the fire, the Phillies embarked on a three-game road trip, and then played six "home games" at their spring-training site, the University of Pennsylvania's Varsity Grounds, located at 37th and Spruce Streets in West Philadelphia. Meanwhile, club owners Reach and Rogers ordered round-the-clock construction of a temporary grandstand and bleachers at Broad and Huntingdon Streets. The team resumed play there on August 18.

Despite the series of misfortunes that plagued the Phillies in 1894—injuries to key players, the July riot, the August fire and the Phillies fourth-place finish, Philadelphia fans were witness to a remarkable performance from three members of their team that has never been duplicated in baseball's long history: all of the Phillies' regular outfielders, Ed Delahanty, Billy Hamilton and Sam Thompson, hit over .400 for the 1894 season.

After years of up-and-down offensive performances, 26-year-old Ed "Del" Delehanty finally began to fulfill Harry Wright's 1892 prediction that he would be a great hitter. That year, he first hit over .300 (.306) for the first time, and from then until his untimely death in 1903, he never dropped below that mark. After hitting .404 in 1894 and again in 1895, he soared to .410 in 1899. Delehanty's .345 lifetime batting average ranks fifth all-time, and is second only to Rogers Hornsby among right-handed hitters.

Besides hitting .403 in 1894, Phillies center fielder Billy Hamilton was busy on the base paths. He set all-time records for runs scored in a season (196) and most consecutive games scoring a run (24), and in an eight-inning contest against Washington on August 31, he tied George Gore's 1881 all-time record of seven stolen bases in a game.

Sam Thompson hit .415 in 1894. He played 83 of his 99 season-total games after he had the tip of the little finger on his left hand cut off, and in 54 of those contests he had at least two hits. Although he feasted on Brooklyn's pitching, collecting four hits in a game three times (April 27; May 8; July 23), he proved himself to be an equal-opportunity ball-basher by also collecting four hits in a game against Boston (August 8), Pittsburgh (August 25) and Cincinnati (September 4). His eight hits in a double header against Washington on August 11 included a five-hit effort in the first game. A week later against St. Louis, he hit for the cycle, and then added two more hits, for a total of six. "The particular feature of the game was the Phillies batting. Sam Thompson led. He was seven times at the bat, and made six hits for twelve bases, his longest being a home run."[32]

Late in August, Thompson's triple against Pittsburgh in the fourth inning "hit the centre field fence on the fly."[33] He followed this effort in the ninth inning with "a home run drive over to the 'hump.'"[34] His two home runs against Cincinnati on September 6 included a grand slam: "Sam made a home run in the third inning when one man was on base, and in the sixth he came to bat with the bases full. 'Put her over the fence again, Sam,' came a shout from the bleachers. Sam is nothing if not accommodating, so when [the pitcher] Mr. Whitrock laid one right on his bat, Sam put it over the hump and four striped legged Phillies trotted leisurely home."[35] The latter blast cleared the scoreboard in right center before clearing the Broad Street hump, a distance of at least 450 feet. Thompson also victimized Cincinnati pitching when the Reds were at home. In a double-header on September 20, he hit a four-bagger in the first game, once again off Bill Whitrock, and another in the second game, off of Tom Parrott.

Although he missed 33 games in 1894 due to his finger surgery, Sam still led the league in RBI (147) and slugging (.696). Defensively, he led the league in fielding with a .972 mark, and while his 12 outfield assists were a career low, his throwing accuracy remained consistent, earning high praise from the press: "Thompson's throwing this season has been something remarkable. From deep right he throws to home plate almost on a line."[36]

By mid season, the Danville slugger was grateful to have overcome his injury, but was also pleased that his criticism of the Philadelphia franchise's penny-pinching ways had led to positive changes for the players. He responded to a sportswriter's request for a statement while staying at the Monongahela House Hotel in Pittsburgh during a road trip in July with a mixture of humor and satisfaction. "'All I know,' said Sam Thompson dryly, 'is that we are stopping at a good hotel. I could stand this all the time.' Just then, Del [Ed Delehanty] blurted out, 'We stop at good houses everywhere this year.' That kick [complaint] of Thompson's last winter had some effect after all."[37]

Two months later, the Phillies returned to the "good hotel" in Pittsburgh when the team was in town for another series with the Pirates. At the time, the city was also playing host to the Grand Army of the Republic (G.A.R.) Encampment, an annual reunion of Union Civil War veterans. Each year the old soldiers met in a different city, where they reminisced about their war experiences and remembered their fallen comrades. "Ball players are lost in the shuffle in Pittsburg[h] this week. The G.A.R. Encampment holds sway, and even the [league-leading] Orioles wouldn't create much of a commotion if they were here."[38]

One G.A.R. member attending the reunion also had a chance to reunite with his son, who was playing for the Phillies against the Pirates. "Sam Thompson's dad, wearing the [Union] blue, was here during the series."[39]

Having reached the .400 mark in hitting, led the league in fielding, and had his major complaints about team travel and lodging resolved, a satisfied Thompson headed home at season's end, after having done something else he had never done before in his major league career. "Sam Thompson has returned to Detroit. He has signed with Philadelphia for next season, the first time in his life before the close of the [previous] season."[40]

The fire that destroyed the Huntingdon Street Grounds was one of four that occurred at league parks in 1894. The worst of these, which took place in Boston, was dubbed the Great Roxbury Fire, after the neighborhood near the Boston Beaneaters' South End Grounds that it partially destroyed. The fire started under the right field bleachers during a May 15 game, and spread to the left field seats by way of the outfield fence, forcing the fans onto the diamond for safety. The flames then jumped to the roofs of nearby houses to the south, and within an hour had destroyed 200 buildings and left 1,900 homeless.

The baseball fires of 1894 vividly highlighted the inherent dangers posed by the all-wooden ballparks. In response, Philadelphia owners Reach and Rogers replaced the original Huntingdon Street Grounds at the close of the season with a new park whose transitional design reflected such safety concerns. Its seats and seat platforms were still made of wood, but the remainder was built of brick and steel. Thanks to the strength of the new construction materials, the new grandstand upper deck was able to be cantilevered over the lower seats, allowing fans an unrestricted view of the field. The addition of bleacher seats in right and left field, however, significantly reduced the distance to the respective fences—from 400 to 341 feet in left field, and from 310 to a mere 280 feet in right.

Sixteen years after the construction of the new Huntingdon Street

Grounds, Forbes Field, the first ball park made entirely of steel and concrete, was erected in Pittsburgh. It featured wide ramps instead of stairways for moving fans quickly to their seats, and an elevator to the third-level luxury boxes. The major league's last all-wood ballpark, Chicago's South End Grounds, was built by former first baseman Charles Comiskey for his new American League team, the White Stockings, in 1900.

Although it would take a decade for team batting averages and ERAs to return to their levels prior to the increase of the pitching distance to 60'6", the 1894 season represented the high water mark in terms of the effects of the new distance on hitting and pitching. By 1904, the league batting average (.249) was roughly the equivalent of the 1892 average (.245), and the league ERA that year (2.72) was even lower than its 1892 counterpart (3.28).

Despite the precipitous ERA rise that occurred in the first years after the 60'6" rule was established, the three best pitchers of the 1890s, Boston's Kid Nichols, Cleveland's Cy Young, and New York's Amos Rusie, adjusted much more rapidly to the new rule than most pitchers. Nichols, whose 297 wins in the 1890's is the most for any pitcher, recorded a 2.84 ERA in 1892, but ballooned to 4.75 in 1894, the second year of the 60'6" rule. By 1896, however, his ERA had dropped to 2.83. Cy Young's remarkable 1892 ERA of 1.93 rose to 3.94 in 1894. By 1898 it was 2.54 Due to contract disputes, Amos Rusie pitched for only eight seasons during the decade, but averaged 29 wins per year. Nicknamed the "Hoosier Thunderbolt," he was widely considered the hardest-throwing pitcher in the game, and his ERA was unaffected by the 60'6" rule. In fact, it was higher (2.84) the year before the rule was implemented than it was in 1894 (2.78).

For pennant-starved Philadelphia fans, the 1895 season was like a recurring bad dream. Although the Phillies managed to move up a notch to third place in the final standings, they finished 9½ games behind the Orioles, who won their second consecutive league championship. The Phillies' fine hitting (.330, first in the league) could not overcome their weak pitching (5.47 ERA, tenth in the league). The three members of the fabulous Philly outfield, which was in its last season together in 1895, either led or finished in the top three in every offensive category. Sam hit .392 (third) and was first in slugging (.654), home runs (18) and RBI (165). Hamilton hit .389 and led the league in runs (166) and stolen bases (97). Ed Delehanty pounded the ball for his second consecutive .400+

season (.404), led the league in on-base percentage (.500) and finished second behind Sam in slugging (.617) and total bases (296).

For the second straight year, Manager Irwin placed the pitching burden on two starters, Kid Carsey and Jack Taylor. Between them, they won 50 and lost 30, but their ERAs (4.92 and 4.49) hovered near five runs per game. Although Irwin experimented with eight other pitchers, including several rookies who never played again after 1895, journeyman Willie McGill and rookie Al Orth shared the bulk of the pitching load after Carsey and Taylor, although their combined innings pitched were 100 fewer than either of the latter two starters. McGill, who had pitched for five teams in the previous six years, brought a 56–61 record and a 4.66 ERA to Philadelphia, where he went 10–8 with a 5.55 ERA.

The 22-year-old Orth, a Missouri native who grew up in Danville, Indiana, and watched Big Sam play for the Browns there as a teenager, was the bright spot among the new pitchers, going 8–1 with a 3.89 ERA and hitting a cool .356. A lifetime .297 hitter, Orth remained with the Phillies for six years, occasionally substituting in the outfield. In 1902 he jumped to the new American League, pitching for Washington and the Yankees through 1909. Nicknamed erroneously as "the Curveless Wonder," Orth's arsenal actually included a number of different breaking balls, some of which resembled the modern-day slider.[41]

A singular but unheralded event took place in Baltimore just prior to the start of spring training in 1895—one that eventually would exercise an enormous influence on major league baseball down to the current day. On February 6, a child was born to a German-American couple there, at 216 Emory Street, in a neighborhood called Pigtown. The infant's name was George Herman Ruth, Jr.

Although Sam Thompson trained all winter at the Detroit Athletic Club near his home, he arrived late for spring training at Hampton, Virginia, thanks to the lingering effects of "an attack of grip [flu]."[42] His performance in the final six games before the Phillies broke camp and headed north, however, indicated that he had regained his health. Playing intra-squad games or against local Virginia clubs, he hammered out 18 hits, including three triples and a home run, and scored 14 runs. Seven games into the regular season, he hit the first of his league-leading 18 home runs for the season, a walk-off, three-run blast against New York. The details were creatively recounted in the press.

The ninth was Thompson's inning. Delehanty and Hallman were flirting around second and third bases when Sam came to the bat and spat on the plate for luck. Then something cracked. It was an awful crack. Some fellow who wasn't looking that way thought one of the cantilevers in the new pavilion had "busted," but it was only the concussion of wagon tongue [bat] and good tough horse hide [ball]. Away sped the ball hugging the heaven far out over the right field fence, and still it did not drop. It had heard that there was an Inquirer [a Philadelphia newspaper] [hot-air] balloon floating around and went chasing it. Three pairs of number ten feet pattered around the bases and the smile on [Phillies owner] Colonel Rogers' face was all wool and a yard wide. Sam had to doff his cap a dozen times and the little bald spot on the top of his pate glistened charmingly in the rays of the May day sun.[43]

Thompson's home runs in 1895 are notable not only for their quantity, but for their distance and the circumstances under which they were hit. Although considered a dead pull hitter for his entire career, one-third of his 18 home runs this year were hit to dead center, several to right center, and one to left. He hit home runs in consecutive games three times—twice in May and once in September, and in August he hit two four-baggers in a game against New York. Like his walk-off against New York, mentioned above, his dramatic September 19 three-run homer in the eighth inning gave the Phillies the lead and eventually the win against Washington. With two out and none on base, "it looked mighty blue for Philadelphia, and more than half of the crowd stood up ready to move out and go home to supper."[44] However, Ed Delehanty reached first on a bunt and then Lave Cross singled to right. Lefty Jake Boyd, the Nationals' second left-handed pitcher of the day, then faced Sam Thompson.

Boyd drew back his southpaw and delivered the ball. On it came with a slight curve just above the knee and right over the plate. Thompson's bat described a backward, then a forward stroke. There was a crush, and sailing high in the air went the ball. The higher the ball went, the farther out it went, straight for center field. Tom Brown went back until the fence stopped his further progress, and the ball dropped safely into the Reading Railroad tracks. "It's over," yelled the crowd, and cheer after cheer rent the air as three black-legged Phillies sprinted across the plate and we were one run ahead.[45]

In late June and early July, Sam had three memorable extra-base hit streaks. Between June 11 and June 21, he established an all-time record (subsequently tied by Jimmy Johnston in 1923 and George Brett in 1976) by collecting three or more hits in six consecutive games. His ten hit total in three games against Baltimore in late June included three doubles, a triple and two home runs. These efforts were just a prelude to what would follow. In ten games between June 22 and July 3, he stroked 29 hits, including 11 doubles, four triples and a home run.

Although the hitting of the veteran right fielder was legendary in the league, his fine fielding and throwing were equally recognized in 1895.

> "Thompson robbed Brown and McGuire of two base hits by pulling the ball off the wall."[46]
> "Lange hit to center for two bags, but was thrown out at the plate by Thompson while trying to score on Everett's single to right."[47]
> "The fielding and throwing of Sam Thompson were the particular features of the game."[48]
> "Sam Thompson made two splendid throws to the plate, putting out one man and holding another at third."[49]

The historical significance of Sam's outfield performance in a game against Brooklyn on August 1 has unfortunately been overlooked, thanks to inconsistencies in descriptions and game accounts of the contest. Over the course of the 1895 season, Sam recorded 31 outfield assists, and on four occasions registered two assists in a game. In this game against the Bridegrooms, if Philadelphia and Brooklyn news accounts are correct, he doubled that total. In its review of the game, the *Brooklyn Eagle* noted that "Thompson carried off the fielding honors, nipping four runners at the plate."[50] The *Philadelphia Inquirer* game summary also stated that Sam "threw no less than four men out at the plate."[51]

The *Eagle* provided details of two of Sam's assists. In the third inning, "Treadway tried to score from second on Anderson's single, but was caught at the plate by Thompson's fine throw."[52] With the bases loaded in the fourth inning, George Treadway doubled to right, but Sam threw out third baseman Billy Shindle at the plate.[53] The *Inquirer* clarified that the Shindle putout went from Sam in right field to Bill Hallman at second, and then on to catcher Mike Grady.[54]

Unaccountably, however, box scores of this game in the *New York Times*, *Sporting Life* and *The Sporting News* credit Sam with only 3 assists, and provide no details about them. However, even if these accountings, and not those from the Philadelphia and Brooklyn newspapers, are the accurate ones, Thompson is still in exclusive company, since only three other players, Dummy Hoy, Jim Jones and Jack McCarthy, have recorded three outfielder-to-catcher assists in one game.[55]

In many ways, 1895 may be considered Sam's best overall season. Not only were his offensive and defensive numbers some of the highest of his career, but his work ethic and steady, year-after-year performance were finally getting the recognition they deserved. Boston manager Frank Selee went on the record as considering Thompson "the best right fielder in the profession."[56] *Sporting Life* agreed with Selee, going into further detail: "Sam Thompson does not make much noise, but at the end of the season Sam is always well up among the leaders in batting, and he can get around the bases as quick as any of them. He is a great thrower and can beat any man in the business playing right field for the Phillies."[57] In a year-long contest among the famously fickle Philadelphia fans to determine the team's most popular player of 1895, Sam Thompson was awarded a silver loving cup for finishing in first place, beating out teammate Lave Cross by over 1,200 votes.

Despite such accolades, there were subtle hints in 1895 that age was beginning to creep up on the great slugger. He was still a rugged and determined player, even able to shake off a beaning and finish a game: "Big Sam Thompson was hit on the head with a pitched ball in the game at Louisville, the sphere going into the grandstand on the bound from his cranium. It never phased him."[58] However, Sam missed 14 games in 1895, due to a "Charley-horse," or other minor arm, hand or leg injuries. This total is equal to that of all the games he missed from 1886 through 1893. In mid November, *Sporting Life* reported that "Sam Thompson is hunting shell-barks [presumably, birds that inhabit or live near the shell-bark hickory tree] in the woods around Detroit, Michigan."[59] As he relaxed after another long season, the Danville slugger must have given some thought to his age and his physical condition, and wondered how many years he had left in baseball.

The disappointment of Philadelphia owners Reach and Rogers over their team's third-place 1895 finish—ironically its best since 1887—was intensified by the Phillies' miserable play in the final eight games of the season. After having won 35 of 49 games from August through mid September, the club still had an outside chance to catch second-place Cleveland and then compete for the Dauvray Cup against Baltimore. That hope was shattered when the Phillies dropped successive series to Baltimore and Brooklyn, losing five, tying two, and winning just one game. Club play was so bad that rumors circulated in the press that the Philadelphia players had "thrown the final games to Baltimore,"[60] forcing an irate John Rogers to offer $1,000 dollars for proof of such action. None ever surfaced, but it was clear that Manager Irwin, whom *Sporting Life* declared, "was never popular here [Philadelphia] as a player or a manager,"[61] was in grave danger of losing his job.

Rather than wait to be fired, Irwin resigned in mid October and moved on to New York, where he would fare even worse, leading the Giants to a seventh-place finish the following year. Phillies owner Rogers named his long-time administrative assistant, Bill Shettsline, as the team's business manager, and then began a search for someone who could serve both as an on-field manager and play full-time as team captain.

His choice was Boston's captain and third baseman, Billy Nash, a lifetime .275 hitter who in a decade of covering the hot corner had led the league four times in fielding and twice in assists. Nash became expendable in Boston with the arrival of rookie Jimmy Collins in 1895, whose defensive prowess eventually earned him a Hall of Fame plaque in Cooperstown. Collins revolutionized third base play, "edging in when notorious bunters were at bat and staying back for strong pull hitters … charging in on slowly hit balls and bunts, scooping them up barehanded and firing in one motion to first or second."[62]

Trading for Billy Nash would require the Phillies give up one of their best players. Reach and Rogers decided on Billy Hamilton, who hit .389 in the just-concluded season, led the league in runs (166) and stolen bases (97), and finished fourth in hits (201) and second in on-base percentage (.490). However, Hamilton for years had complained about his poor compensation, and despite his quiet demeanor, had unjustly acquired the reputation of a troublemaker. The Phillies would regret the decision to trade him for years to come.

Nash hit .247 for the Phillies in 1896 and led the team to an eighth-place finish. On May 15, he was beaned by Louisville pitcher Tom Smith, subsequently suffered continuing bouts of vertigo, and was never the same on the field. He spent only one more complete season in the majors, hitting .243. In contrast, Hamilton hit .359, stole over 200 bases and scored over 400 runs in his first three seasons with Boston, and helped lead the team to two pennants. Over the course of those three seasons, the Phillies finished eighth, tenth and sixth. The Hamilton-Nash exchange today is regarded as one of the most lopsided trades in baseball history. Nearly 120 years later, Billy Hamilton still holds all-time Philadelphia records for batting average (.361), on-base-percentage (.468) and stolen bases (508).

The trade of Hamilton for Nash broke up the best outfield ever assembled. Between 1892 and 1895, the trio of Thompson, Hamilton and Delehanty "averaged 191 hits, 106 RBIs, 133 runs, 32 doubles, 15 triples and nine home runs, and 44 stolen bases per season."[63] Thompson averaged 25 assists per year during this time period, Delehanty 24, and Hamilton 16. Hamilton's speed allowed him to get to balls that eluded most outfielders.[64] Delehanty's greatest defensive asset was "...his aggressive outfield play. Newspaper accounts marvellled at how [at the Huntingdon Street Grounds] he ran up the terrace into the roped-off crowds of spectators to catch fly balls."[65]

In his definitive essay on the great Thompson/Delehanty/Hamilton combination, Delehanty's biographer, historian Jerrold Casway asserts that "there have been outfields that had extraordinary statistics, but nowhere does an outfield trio have such consistently high offensive production and defensive efficiency.... If readers put aside their 19th century prejudices and the fame of outfields graced by immortal players like Cobb, Ruth, DiMaggio and Mays, they may appreciate how Delehanty, Hamilton, and Thompson rank as the greatest outfield ever."[66]

Things went from bad to worse for Philadelphia in 1896. Poor pitching, the loss of base stealer and run scorer Billy Hamilton, a steep decline in Sam Thompson's power statistics, and a lack of on-field leadership, lead to a drop from third to eighth place in the league standings.

The Phillies replaced Hamilton in center field with 23-year-old Duff Cooley, who was purchased from St. Louis. The Leavenworth, Kansas, native, who hit lefty and threw righty, hit .339 for the Browns in 1895, but had a reputation as a hard drinker. In St. Louis, Cooley "hooked up with the Brown's German duo of [pitcher] Ted Breitenstein and [catcher] Heinie Peitz to form 'The Five Cent Gang,' so dubbed after they found a bar in Washington that sold beer at 5 cents a bottle. The gang spent around $50 in the place each night in town."[67]

Philadelphia acquired left-hander Bill Hulen from Minneapolis of the Western League to replace Joe Sullivan at shortstop. Sullivan was already exhibiting the early symptoms of consumption [tuberculosis], the disease that would take his life in 1897. Hulen's 73 games at the position marked the last time "that a left hander would play more than half of his team's games at an infield position"[68] other than first base. Hulen hit .265 for the Phillies, and his miserable .874 fielding average (51 errors in 73 games) was largely responsible for the team's tenth-place fielding ranking among league shortstops.

In 1896, John Roger continued his habit of acquiring aging veterans at a low price in hopes of a short-term-high-return by purchasing 38-year-old first baseman Dan Brouthers from Louisville for $500. Arguably the most dominant hitter of the 1880s, Brouthers, a member of the "Big Four" and Sam Thompson's teammate in Detroit, led the league five times in batting and on-base percentage, seven times in slugging (including a consecutive stretch of six years) and eight times in OPS (on-base percentage plus slugging).

One of the mysteries of the 1896 season is why Philadelphia released Brouthers after just 57 games. It has been argued that he "fielded poorly and stranded too many base runners,"[69] and also that "the infirmities of old age kept Big Dan off first base a lot."[70] He did miss a week of play in late June for unspecified reasons, but he was hitting his lifetime average, .344, and fielding .983 (.005 below the top league average for first basemen in 1896) when he was laid off.

It appears that Brouthers, who during his career was extremely sensitive to any criticism of his play, became involved in personal squabbles with his teammates over this issue. A few weeks after his release, he blamed the Phillies players' criticism of each other's play for their lack of success.[71] After the season ended, the normally reticent Sam Thompson defended his teammates and blamed Brouthers himself for such criticism: "Sam Thompson says that 'knocking' [criticism] is what caused Dan Brouthers' to be released by Philadelphia. Almost every member of the team was down on 'Old Wappinger' [a Brouther's nickname]."[72]

A month after Brouthers' departure, his place was taken at first base by Napoleon Lajoie, a rookie from the New England League's Fall River team. The stocky Woonsocket, Rhode Island, native hit .326 with 12 doubles, seven triples and four home runs in 39 games with the Phillies. He made just two errors at first base, recording a .995 fielding average. Lajoie spent another two decades in the major leagues, retiring with a .338 lifetime average. Like Dan Brouthers, the man he replaced, Lajoie was elected to the Hall of Fame after his retirement from the game.

The Phillies' poor pitching was one of the biggest reasons for their woes in 1896, thanks to their overreliance on Jack Taylor's right arm (359 innings, 20 wins, 21 losses, 4.79 ERA) and their penny-pinching penchant for experimenting with rookies or aging veterans as backups. A parade of 14 pitchers toed the rubber for the team in 1896, including 36-year-old Bill Whitrock, 38-year-old Ad Gumbert, and 35-year-old Bert Inks, all in their last year in baseball, and five rookies, two of whom, Harry Keener and Charlie Jordan, were in their first and last seasons. The result was a disastrous combined 5.20 ERA, tenth in the league.

In addition to personnel issues, the Phillies suffered from inconsistent field leadership in 1896. Although owner John Rogers insisted that Billy Nash would have full control of the team,[73] Rogers had for years been notorious for his interference, and his hand-picked Business Manager, Billy Shettsline, owed his allegiance to the club's owner and not Captain Nash. Disinclined to be a disciplinarian, Nash lost control of the team. In Sam Thompson's words, "As soon as the players realized that the manager was helpless and that he was not the boss, they commenced to make life a burden for him. There are some men on the team who would drive a saint to drink. Nash took orders every day from Colonel Rogers. He was a nonentity."[74]

Nash played infrequently after was beaned in July, and in August put Jack Boyle in charge of the team and left town to comb the Northeast for talent. Under such circumstances it is not surprising that the press complained that there was too much divided authority on the Phillies.

Sam Thompson, who turned 36 during spring training, was the ninth oldest player in baseball,[75] and one of just a few dozen men still on the diamond who were playing in the 1880s. "There were 117 players in the big League [National League] in 1889, and of that entire number, just thirty three are still holding the honors that they then achieved [that is, still in the major league] ... twenty nine are now in the minor leagues."[76]

There were dramatic contrasts between Sam's offensive and defensive play in his twelfth big league season. His batting average, although still a respectable .298, represented a 94 point drop from his 1895 effort (.392). His extra-base hitting also fell off precipitously. Playing in the same number of games (119) in both the 1895 and 1896 seasons, he recorded 57 fewer hits (211 vs. 154) in 1896. His doubles dropped from 45 to 28, his triples fell from 21 to 7, his home runs from 18 to 12, and his stolen bases dropped from 27 to 12. Despite such an offensive tailspin, he still managed to score over 100 runs (103) for the tenth time, and to drive in an even 100 runs, reaching the century mark in that category for the eighth time.

Reviewing the season in late October, Sam admitted that his hitting was off, but offered no explanation other than bad luck, or the possibility that he was having vision problems: "I don't know whether my eyes ... went back on me or not, but my average is lower than it ever was ... I made as good swing at the ball as usual, and the boys tell me that I picked out the good ones, but the fact remains that when I hit the ball hard it went straight at some fielder. Every player has his off year. This was mine."[77]

During 1896 spring training in the South, it seemed as if the same hard-hitting Sam Thompson of old was back for another season. He collected three hits against Lynchburg on April 4. Back home in Philadelphia a week later, he banged out four doubles against a Syracuse Eastern League club.

After the regular season opened there were occasional glimmers of the old slugger, including a pair of three-hit games against New York and three and four-hit outings against St. Louis. After a five-hit outburst at Boston on June 29 (a double and four singles) and two long home runs in August, one into "the hanging garden [cantilevered bleachers] in left-center"[78] and another "home run drive to the club-house [beyond the 408' center field fence],"[79] Sam's extra-base hit and multiple-hit games decreased dramatically. Nevertheless, the great slugger was still able to bunt successfully when required to do so. In the seventh inning of a mid June game against Washington, "Del [Delehanty] sent a grounder past Joyce ... and Thompson bunted and played the role of Isaac in the intended sacrifice, both being safe."[80]

In the field, in contrast, Sam had his finest season. He lead all league outfielders in fielding (.974; a personal high), assists (28) and double plays (11, tying his personal record).

Of his two assists against Brooklyn on April 28, one helped complete a double play: "It was simply suicide for Tom Daly to try to score on Griffin's fly to Thompson. Sam nailed him a block [by a mile]. Thompson was very much in it fielding today."[81] A few days later against the Giants, "Tiernan made a single to right, but in trying to stretch it into a double, he was thrown out at second—Thompson to Hallman."[82] Three games later against St. Louis, "Myers sent one away over into right, which appeared to be a home run, but Sam Thompson made a great running catch with one hand."[83]

Buck Ewing, the Hall of Fame catcher who spent most of his career with the Giants, was a crafty-if-not-speedy base runner. The only catcher to lead his team in stolen bases (58 in 1889) he once stole five bags in a game. Playing for and managing the Cincinnati Reds in 1896, the veteran Ewing tried unsuccessfully to challenge Sam Thompson's throwing arm in the fourth inning of a game against the Phillies in early June. Ewing was on first base when Reds shortstop Germany Smith flied to right field. Ewing attempted to go to second on the fly out, "but ... was cut out [thrown out] by Sam Thompson's air-line throw to Hallman."[84]

In an 8–2 June loss to league-leading Baltimore, during which the Phillies committed five errors, Thompson, second baseman Hallman and catcher Grady combined for a double play. Noting the recent decline in Sam's offense, the *Philadelphia Inquirer* still praised him in this instance for his work in the field. "In the midst of all this abominable fielding, the work of Sam Thompson at [in] right shone out resplendent. Sam doesn't figure very numerously in the individual score, but the way he covered his quarter section of ground, partially compensated the cranks [fans] for the misrepresentations of the other members of the team."[85]

Unfortunately for Big Sam, he would have more problems to deal with at the end of the season than the decline in his batting. Unwittingly, he became embroiled in a controversy over statements attributed to him that blamed the Phillies' poor season on meddling by the club's owners.

In late October, Francis Richter, editor of *Sporting Life*, published an interview, "Sam Thompson Speaks at Length of the Phillies Fall," in which Thompson was quoted as having blamed the team's poor showing on meddling by the team's owners. Richter, claiming the interview first appeared in a Detroit newspaper, quoted Sam as affirming that there is no questioning the fact that we played wretched ball. Bad management was the cause. Billy Nash is a capital third baseman, but as a captain he was not strict enough with the team. He was altogether too easy. It was not entirely his fault either. He was handicapped and I suppose he simply tried to carry out to the best of his ability his orders. The players soon realized that he did not have full control and that made life a burden for him. Had Nash been given full swing there is no doubt the team would not have finished so low down in the percentage table. Really, there was no such thing as team work.[86]

A few months later, at the insistence of John Rogers, Richter issued a retraction of his article, blaming his source, Charley Steiger, editor of the *Detroit News-Tribune*, for the problem. In the interim between the October 1896 interview and Richter's January 1897 retraction, Philadelphia had hired a new manager, George Stallings, to run the club, and he was referenced several times in the retraction. Stallings, then the manager of the Western League's Detroit team, had played minor league ball, but had seen action in just seven major league games.

The Richter retraction consisted primarily of an explanation from his source, Charley Steiger, who stated that

Mr. Thompson was credited with saying some harsh things about undue interference with the duties of the manager. Even the Quaker sheets [newspapers] predicted that unless [new manager] Stallings was given absolute power his path as a manager would not be strewn with roses. As a matter of fact the statement that drove Mr. Rogers into hysterics was not directly made by Thompson, but it came from a source—a mutual friend—that seemed most authentic. The veteran fielder [Thompson] tells me that he did not knowingly make any such statements. He admits that he made 40 or more lame excuses to personal friends for the miserable showing made by the Phillies under the management of Billy Nash, but he never attributed any failure on the team's part to either Colonel Rogers or the scholarly Mr. Reach.

More discipline and plenty of it would have helped the club had it been rightly enforced. The laxity, however, it seems, was general, all members of the team falling into a state of innocuous desuetude and playing far below their recognized ability. There certainly was something rotten in Denmark. Where that rottenness is, if it still exists, will in time be revealed by Manager Stallings. As far as the club owners were concerned, they were most liberal in salaries and honorable in the treatment of the players, several of whom have for years received the League limit.

Mr. Thompson says that he never has been better treated than in Philadelphia, where he hopes to play until all his tenure in the right field position shall expire. His only failing is that he wants the Philadelphia Club to win the pennant. If Colonel Rogers only possessed a few more players of the Thompson stripe, his team would long ago have ranked with the best. If [new manager]Stallings is given absolute control, as the papers have it, Colonel Rogers can look forward to the time when the Phillies will finish one, two, three.[87]

Steiger's retraction did little to place Sam Thompson in a good light, especially, as we have seen, after the veteran slugger's prior statement that Billy Nash was hamstrung by John Roger's meddling intervention. Coming off a sub-par season, the aging veteran was now placed in a uncomfortable position with the team's owners.

There is an unfortunate similarity between Sam Thompson's brief 1897 and 1898 seasons. In each case, he started the year strong and in apparent good health, only to have to abandon the diamond due to injury or illness shortly after the season started.

The illness of Sam's wife, Ida, in Detroit, caused Sam to arrive late to the Phillies' 1897 spring training camp in Augusta, Georgia. He hit well in inter-squad games and against local Georgia teams, including a home run against Augusta on April 3, and he dutifully set about learning how to ride a bicycle, a new method of training introduced by new manager Stallings. "The most popular exercise at training camp was bicycle riding.... Unfortunately, bicycling had its drawbacks. Delehanty had trouble stopping his bike, and in one instance, after taking a tumble, was run over by an equally inept Napoleon Lajoie."[88] George Stallings, the bicycle promoter, was far from being an expert bicycler himself. While biking to the ballpark back in Philadelphia a month later, he had an unfortunate encounter with a trolley car. "Manager Stallings, while biking to the ground [the Huntingdon Street Grounds] last Thursday morning, collided with a street car, and had a narrow escape from serious injury. He was thrown into the fender of the car, and escaped with a few bruises, but his wheel [bike] was completely wrecked."[89]

Early reports on Sam's spring play were positive. "Thompson, in his old stand in right field, has been toeing the scratch in a manner that was scarcely to be expected at this time of year. He has pulled down a number of hard balls and has thrown in from right field in his usual fashion. Any man who beats Thompson out this year will know he has been playing ball."[90] Bad weather followed the Phillies north after breaking camp in Augusta, and Sam's arm was affected by the rain and cold weather after recording an outfield assist against Richmond. "Thompson's arm is a bit sore, and he would not trust it today and failed to throw to the plate when a runner might have been caught."[91] Returning to Philadelphia on April 9, the team played another half-dozen games before the season opener, with Thompson exhibiting his old reliable playing form. In three games before mid-month, he collected eight hits, stole two bases and laid down a perfect sacrifice bunt.

In the league opener against Boston, Sam had two outfield assists, and would have recorded a third had Billy Nash not dropped the ball. "Tenney made a safe hit to right and Stahl tried to go to third on it. Thompson got the ball clean and made a beautiful throw, right into [third baseman] Nash's hands, and had Stahl out by ten feet, but Nash dropped the ball."[92]

However, after hitting a triple and scoring three runs in the next two games, Sam was pulled from the lineup due to an unspecified injury, and soon laid off without pay. *Sporting Life*'s comments on his departure provided a summary in the past tense that seemed to suggest that his career might be over. "His deportment on the field and off always was gentlemanly, and as a player he ranked with the best of his school."[93]

In addition to experiencing severe leg cramps, Sam was suffering from pains in his lower back that were attributed to kidney trouble. In mid–May, after his back discomfort failed to resolve itself, he returned to Michigan to undergo a month of treatments at Mt. Clemens, a Michigan mineral bath spa. His season was over, and his career was in jeopardy.

In August, Bob Allen, a friend and former teammate, reported that "Sam Thompson is all right again physically, but will not play with the Phillies [again] until he gets ready, because the club laid him off without pay last spring."[94] By October, that positive report was challenged. "According to Detroit advices [sources], Sam Thompson says he will not be able to play ball anymore, and therefore hopes to secure his release from the Philadelphia Club in order to accept the management of the [Western League] Detroit club, which has been offered him."[95]

In December, Sam himself tried to dispel such rumors, asserting that he was well, blaming his illness on the cold and wet weather he encountered during spring training in Augusta, and suggesting that he was willing to be traded under certain conditions.

Sam Thompson recalls the fact that he has written Manager Stallings that he will be back on deck next spring and try to play right field in his old style. In an interview with a Cleveland paper he is quoted as follows:

"I do not know where I will play next year. I would prefer to play in Philadelphia but may go elsewhere. Manager Watkins of the Pittsburg[h] Club [Sam's former manager in Detroit] has called on me twice within a few weeks, and has asked me if I would like to play with his team. I hear that Watkins is trying to arrange a deal by which Donovan will be given to Philadelphia for myself. Of course, nothing may come of it. I feel positive that I can report in condition for playing next spring, but will not guarantee to do so unless I have my own way of training. Last year I went to the training grounds in Augusta, Ga., with a lot of youngsters who never knew an ache or pain and [I] tried to keep up with their fast clip. That's where I made a mistake. Next season if I play ball I will dodge this tough preliminary work. I want warm weather to thaw me out, and I feel confident that I will be able to play as good ball as I ever did."[96]

In early February 1898, Manager Stalling's assertion that "a deal of Sam Thompson for [Cincinnati right fielder] Dusty Miller would suit him"[97] revealed that Sam's status with the Phillies was anything but certain. The normally reticent slugger, now increasingly and uncharacteristically more vocal, did not help his case with the Phillies by ending a statement he issued while visiting his parents in Danville with a critique of his club.

I am going to [be] playing again this season. I mean to begin gymnasium work as soon as I get to Detroit, and if I see I am all right, will play; but if not, and I see I will not be able to do the club and myself justice, I will not report for spring practice. In my eleven years [actually, 14 years] in the League I have never been fined or released. I do not want to be turned down, preferring to quit while my credit is good. What are the Phillies' chances this season? Six clubs, Cincinnati, Baltimore, Boston, New York, Cleveland and Brooklyn are bound to beat them, and they will have to fight hard to lead the second division, and I very much doubt if they can do that.[98]

Even though Sam's prediction about the Phillies' future standing in the league turned out to be more accurate than not (they finished in sixth place), his uncomplimentary assessment drew sharp criticism. "Not very diplomatic, was it, on the part of a man who is looking for a place on the team? Thompson is not regarded as so very strong anymore, and by making the team also look weak, he has simply materially affected his chance of becoming a member of it."[99] Waiting in the wings should Thompson fail, was 23-year-old rookie speedster Elmer Flick, who, after being given a starting role, hit .313 in a 13-year career, lead the league in triples three times and stolen bases twice, and was elected to the Hall of Fame eleven years before Sam Thompson, the man he replaced in right field.

Despite the pre-season controversy, Sam, accompanied by wife Ida, joined the team in Cape May, New Jersey for spring training, where it was reported that he was "back in his old form,"[100] and "in splendid shape."[101] In his first six regular season games, that assessment seemed accurate, as he collected eight hits, including two doubles and a triple, and threw out four base runners from his right field position. A report that Thompson was "as popular as ever and likely to hold his place as right fielder on the team,"[102] also included a note indicating that Sam was also making other plans in the event that his comeback was unsuccessful: "Rumors are in circulation that Charlie Bennett and Sam Thompson will purchase the [Eastern League] Toronto franchise and bring the Canadian city into the Western League next year."[103]

Meanwhile, Sam's fine field work was drawing rave reviews. His two assists in a game against New York on April 22 prompted a local paper to observe simply that "It's hard to beat the old man in right."[104] Giants captain Bill Joyce was even more effusive in his humorous statement of praise for Sam's hitting during the Phillies-Giants series. "Old Sam Thompson, whom one of the Western writers booked for an engagement at the Home For The Aged, is the shiftiest dead one I ever saw outside the morgue. Sam's lamps [eyes] located our pitchers for enough hits in our series with the Phillies to give the Big Hoosier a batting average of about .500."[105]

A half dozen games into the season, the *Philadelphia Inquirer*, employing a horse racing analogy, was ready to admit how important a healthy Sam Thompson still was to the team. "Thompson's absence last year had considerable effect upon the club's position in the race, for there is as much difference between Thompson's fielding and that of the two players who tramped around in the right garden last year as there is between a stake horse [one of high quality] and a selling plater [a low-quality horse]."[106]

A week later, *Sporting Life* recognized that much of Sam's value to the team went unnoticed. "With Big Sam Thompson at right, the outfield is 10 percent stronger than it was last season. The quality of his field work is not always indicated in the score, for the reason that there is no way of recording the extra bases he saves with his superb throwing."[107]

Sam continued his fine hitting and fielding through the first six games in May, collecting 11 hits, including two doubles, two triples, and an outfield assist, but after going 0–5 in a game at Washington on May 11, he was removed from the lineup due to illness. "Thompson had to lay off on account of some stomach trouble. In his absence, however [Elmer] Flick will do well enough."[108] A few days later, rumors about the condition of the big slugger became more alarming. "It is said that Sam Thompson has undergone a surgical operation, and that he may not re-enter the game. It is hoped that this rumor will prove unfounded, for the retirement of Big Sam would be a positive loss to the game."[109]

While there is no evidence that Sam underwent an operation, his back problems, which were believed by some to have been caused by kidney issues, did not improve. The Phillies' team physician, Dr. Boger, discounted the idea of kidney disease, but did not offer hopeful news. He described the ailment as "a chronic sprain of the muscles of the back," stating that Thompson "would never be able to play ball again."[110]

Two weeks later, Thompson left the club and returned home to Detroit without informing most his teammates or the club's owners. His sudden departure was criticized in the press, which now considered him retired.

> Sam Thompson has repeated his trick of last season, taking French leave [leaving without informing anyone] of the club and of Philadelphia. An effort has been made to shroud the thing in mystery, and to make it appear that there was some difference with the club behind it all. Nothing could be further from the truth. The club was anxious to retain Sam, and actually coddled him, not permitting him to play at all on cold or damp days, with the hope that he would be in prime condition when the hot weather arrived. Sam furthermore received his salary in full whenever due despite his disability. The fact is that Sam despaired of complete recovery from the trouble in his back, told Secretary Shettsline so and finally concluded to return to his Detroit home without more ado. That he did so without saying goodbye to President Reach or Colonel Rogers is only in keeping with his peculiar disposition. A year ago he did precisely the same thing, and moreover, never answered any of the club officials' letters until very late in the season, when he condescended to make announcement of his intention to return to the game this year. Thompson's financial independence probably encouraged him in these little eccentricities.[111]

After this critique, the article's author, *Sporting Life* editor Francis Richter, softened his tone, became nostalgic, and wished the old slugger well in his retirement.

> There is little doubt ... that Thompson's retirement will be permanent, and that, therefore, the National game will lose another one of its old landmarks. Thompson was not only a great player in his day, but always a square, honest and straightforward man, and a gentleman on and off the field. His many friends will wish him all manner of luck and happiness in his retirement, and success in any other businesses he may engage in.[112]

The Phillies' team physician's diagnosis of Sam Thompson's health problems may or may not have been accurate. His prognosis, however, that Sam would never play again, was off-base. The veteran slugger would play amateur ball for another decade, and at age 46, eight years after his departure from Philadelphia, he would return to the big league diamond for an eight-game curtain call.

CHAPTER FIVE

Late Innings: 1899–1922

"Taking all his good qualities into consideration, I never knew the equal of this man Thompson as a great fielding, hard-hitting right fielder."—Tim Murnane, ex-big league first baseman and outfielder and *Boston Globe* sportswriter in the *Sporting Life*, October 15, 1904

During the twilight years of Sam Thompson's career, events were unfolding in baseball that would alter the organizational structure of the National Pastime for the next six decades. To Thompson's satisfaction, these changes would eventually bring major league ball back to his adopted hometown of Detroit. They would also provide him with the opportunity at age 46 to don a major league uniform again and play right field for the American League Detroit Tigers.

By the mid 1890's, the National League's baseball monopoly was experiencing significant difficulties on multiple fronts. Almost from its outset, the twelve-team, single-division format that had been in place since the demise of the American Association in 1891 was lopsided and unworkable. "In a given year at least seven or eight teams were out of the pennant race almost from the beginning.... Fans of teams that were 20 or 30 games out of the running naturally lost interest and stopped buying tickets."[1] Some clubs on the lowest rung of the league ladder in the 1890's were among the worst teams of all time. "In 1898, last-place St. Louis finished 39–110, and in 1899, Cleveland went 20–134 to finish an amazing 84 games out [of first place]."[2]

The National League had actually handcuffed itself in this regard in its 1892 consolidation agreement with the American Association by stipulating that there could be no circuit changes for the ten-year life of the pact. The single-league monopoly also meant the absence of a post-season World's Series, which had captured the nation's attention from 1884 to 1891.

Team owners exacerbated the inequality in the league in the 1890's through a system of "interlocking ownerships," a euphemism for a type of syndicate baseball by which individuals could own significant stock in two or more league teams. Arthur Soden, director of a large building supply company, owned one-third of the Boston team and was a minority owner of the Giants. Brewery magnate Harry Vonderhorst owned 40 percent of both the Brooklyn and Baltimore clubs.[3]

In perhaps the most blatant example of this practice, Ned Hanlon, former Sam Thompson teammate on the Detroit Wolverines, was both President of the Baltimore franchise and field manager and part owner of the Brooklyn team. "Openly announcing his intention to concentrate the playing strength of both clubs in Brooklyn, Hanlon took along enough of his Baltimore stars, including Hughie Jennings, Willie Keeler and Joe Kelley, to win two successive pennants in Brooklyn."[4] Under such circumstances, fair competition between league teams was not possible.

The National League's woes were not just structural in nature. The persistence of rowdy play, obscene language, gambling at the park among fans or between managers, players and owners, and umpire- and player-baiting that sometimes led to physical harm, all lent an unsavory element to the game, driving away middle-class fans. "There was scarcely an issue of the Sporting News that did not tell of kicking [complaining] and wrangling with umpires, fights among players, indecent language, and incidents of rowdyism in general."[5]

The imperious and often unethical personal behavior of some National League club owners toward fans, players and sportswriters did nothing to improve the circuit's image. Among such owners, Giants' owner Andrew Freedman topped the list. Freedman eliminated complimentary passes for reporters, banned sportswriter Sam Crane from the Polo Grounds for his published critiques, once punched a *New York Times* reporter in the jaw, and on occasion refused to let visiting teams practice before games as required by league rules.[6] At the end of the 1895 season, Freedman deducted $200 from 24-game winner Amos Rusie's final paycheck for unspecified "indifferent work." Rusie, then the game's most dominant pitcher, sat out the next season in protest, and without him the Giants finished seventh in the league, 24 games behind first-place Baltimore.

Phillies' owner John I. Rogers was not far behind Freedman on the most-hated owners' list. He once responded to a player's complaint by snapping, "If you're looking for a soft job, you should work in a sponge factory."[7] A lawyer by profession, Rogers was not above the use of underhanded tactics on the ball field. During a September 1900 home game, it was discovered that he had ordered a wire run from the Phillies' clubhouse in center field to a metal plate under the third base coach's box. In the clubhouse, reserve catcher Morgan Murphy would read opposing catchers' signals using a telescope, and "relay them, via electrical impulse, to the coach's box, where the third base coach could pick them up via his metal spikes."[8] The coach would then relay the information to the Phillies' batter. When the National League discovered this practice and requested that it cease, Rogers stated that "he thought this ploy was perfectly fair and legitimate."[9]

In the midst of this deteriorating state of affairs in major league baseball, one man, Byron Bancroft "Ban" Johnson, was working to change the landscape. Born in Ohio in 1864, Johnson played college ball at Marietta College, working behind the plate as a catcher, but disdaining to use either glove or mask in the process.[10] Disregarding his father's advice to study law, Johnson signed on for a salary of $25 per week as a sportswriter for the *Cincinnati Commercial-Gazette*, and in 1887 became the paper's sports editor. In the early 1890s, he developed a close friendship with Charlie Comiskey, then manager of the Cincinnati Reds, and former first baseman/manager of the St. Louis Browns. In the 1880s, Comiskey led the Browns to four American Association pennants. Both Johnson and Comiskey decried the sad state of the National League, and they in particular detested the rowdyism that dominated play on the diamond.

In 1894, Johnson took on the task of reviving the defunct Western League, which had dissolved two years earlier. Serving as the new organization's president, he established franchises in Detroit, Toledo, Minneapolis, Indianapolis, Kansas City, Grand Rapids and Sioux City. Bancroft's friend Comiskey took charge of the league's Sioux City franchise, transferring it to St. Paul the following year.

As league president, Johnson ruled with a strong hand, drafting schedules, transferring franchises, arranging team travel, prohibiting liquor sales at the ballparks, signing players, imposing a $200 per month salary cap, and fining or suspending players for any hint of vulgar speech or aggressive behavior. His reforms proved extremely successful. "Soon, Johnson's Western League had a reputation as the best-run minor league in the country. Johnson insisted that his umpires crack down on rowdy behavior. As a result, Western League games were now considered family entertainment, because sensitive fans would not witness violent behavior or hear bad language [at the games]."[11]

When the National League pared back its number of teams from 12 to eight in 1899, Johnson saw an opportunity to expand his circuit. He established new franchises in Chicago and Cleveland, signed many competent players from the four teams dropped by the National League, and officially changed the Western League's name to the American League. Then, in 1901, when a revival of the old American Association as a major league rival to the National League was being considered, Johnson, in a pre-emptive move, declared his American League to be on equal footing with the National League, and moved franchises into Philadelphia, Boston, Baltimore and Washington.

The National League scoffed at its new rival's bravado, but Johnson, taking advantage of the fact that the Senior Circuit has imposed a $2,400 salary limit, raided its ranks and offered lucrative contracts to players to jump to the new circuit. Eighty-seven National Leaguers did so, including such well-known stars as Cy Young, Jimmy Collins and Nap Lajoie. In 1902, American League attendance surpassed that of the National League. In 1903, the old league sued for peace, and the result was the bipartite National/American major league structure that remains in place today.

Given the state of affairs in the National League that led to the founding of Ban Johnson's American League, Sam Thompson's surprisingly vocal and public criticisms of owners and the league in the latter stages of his career, many of which were outlined in Chapter Four, can be viewed in a new light. Far from being the idle rants of a pampered star, as they were occasionally portrayed in the press, Thompson's critiques of weak teams that had no business in the league, the subsequent need for new venues, and his candid assessment of owners' meddling and poor treatment of players, were in reality some of the earliest public expressions of concerns that a few years later would lead to the founding of the American League.

After the dissolution of the Detroit Wolverines franchise in 1888,

Sam Thompson's adopted home town sponsored teams in the International League for a few years until it disbanded, but then was left without a club until Ban Johnson reorganized the Western League in 1894. Johnson included Detroit among his franchises and brought high-quality baseball back to the City of Straits. After seventh- and fifth-place finishes in 1894 and 1895, respectively, the Detroit club's owners hired George Stallings as manager. Stallings, as we recall, would move up to the majors for the 1897 and 1898 seasons as manager of the Philadelphia Phillies during Sam Thompson's last two abbreviated big league years.

Although Stallings moved the club up to third place in his first year in Detroit, 1896 is more often remembered today as the first season in which the "Tigers" nickname was applied to the team. In an interview with sportswriter Fred Lieb years later, Stallings claimed credit for it. "Among other things, I thought maybe a change of uniforms would change their [the Detroit players'] luck. I put striped stockings on them, black and a sort of yellowish brown. I didn't think of their resemblance to a tiger's stripes at the time, but the fans and some of the early writers noticed it, and soon started calling the club the Tigers, and they have been Tigers ever since."[12]

After George Stallings left to manage the Phillies in 1897, the newly-nicknamed Tigers landed in fifth and sixth place in Western League standings over the next two years, and in 1898 briefly counted future Hall of Famer Rube Waddell among the team's ranks. A talented left-handed pitcher, Waddell "possessed the intellectual and emotional maturity of a child,"[13] and was "known to miss a scheduled start because he was off fishing or playing marbles with street urchins,"[14] Waddell compiled a 4–4 record with the Tigers before abandoning the club to pitch in Canada after being fined for drunkenness. Rube would later lead the National League in strikeouts six times while compiling a lifetime ERA of 2.16. He was elected to the Baseball Hall of Fame in 1946.

George Stallings returned as the Tigers' manager in 1899, and shepherded the club through its transition from a Western League club to an American League team in 1901. A new baseball park was constructed for the fledgling American League Tigers at Michigan and Trumball Avenues. It initially was named Bennett Field in honor of the old Wolverines catcher who had lost his legs in a railroad accident, and later (1911) renamed Navin Field in honor of the club's owner, Frank Navin.

Besides Detroit, the new American League featured teams in Boston, New York, Philadelphia, Cleveland, St. Louis, Chicago and Washington. While some of these clubs' nicknames would change over the years, the circuit's cities would not change for decades.

Near the end of 1898, the *Washington Post* noted that "Sam Thompson has asked [Philadelphia owners] Reach and Rogers for his release. Sam is figuring on purchasing an interest in a minor league team next spring, though he is still on the Phillies' reserve list. Sam's reservation by the Quaker [Phillies] management recalls the case of poor Joe Sullivan, whose name appeared on the Mound City [St. Louis] reserved players' list two months after his death."[15]

Sporting Life clarified that Sam's minor league of choice in such a venture would be Ban Johnson's Western League, and that if successful, he planned to return to his original position on the diamond at first base. "He said that if he could secure his release at a reasonable figure he could get an engagement the coming season to play first base and manage a Western League team. Sam thinks he could play first base all right, because he would have no long throws to make."[16] Although a release from the Phillies was not forthcoming, and Sam's dream of owning a minor league franchise never materialized, the old slugger still managed to stay in the game in one fashion or another for another decade.

The early spring, 1899 report from Philadelphia was that Sam "was in shape to play again."[17] and had been tendered a contract, but was not satisfied with the terms. Apparently, he responded with a counter offer to the Phillies that was refused. "Sam Thompson is still in Detroit with his ear to the ground, waiting for the call that never calls [comes]."[18]

The Detroit to which Thompson returned after his decade in Philadelphia was a far cry from the town it was when the Danville slugger arrived there as a rookie in 1885. Thanks to its strategic location on the Great Lakes Waterway, the city had experienced slow but steady growth since the mid–19th century, particularly in the areas of shipping, ship building, pharmaceuticals and small manufacturing. Such progress in Detroit would soon be outpaced by the sudden and explosive development of the automobile industry.

In 1898, the year Sam Thompson last played for the Phillies, Henry Ford drove his first gasoline-powered prototype automobile through the streets of Detroit. In 1903 he founded the Ford Motor Company and built the first Model A. A decade later, he had designed the Model T and developed the basic techniques of the production line. The latter's effect was dramatic. Approximately 18,000 Model T's were hand-produced in 1909. Over 170,000 rolled off the automated production line four years later.

Ford had many competitors, including Ransom Olds, son of an Ohio blacksmith, who founded the Olds Motor Vehicle Company in 1897, David Dunbar Buick, whose Buick Auto-Vim and Power Company began two years later, and General Motors Corporation, founded by former carriage salesman William Durant in 1908. Thanks to the success of the auto industry, Detroit grew from a town of about 125,000 when Sam Thompson started his career with the Wolverines, to a city of nearly one million in 1920.

When it became clear after the 1898 season that Thompson's professional career was over, he returned to the diamond as an amateur, playing for an athletic club in Detroit where he customarily worked out during the winter. "Good old Sam Thompson is cavorting around the outfield for the DAC [Detroit Athletic Club] team, and proves [to be] a good drawing card, as he is very popular in the Michigan town."[19] Popular, yes, and also still potent at the plate: "The other day the old war horse [Thompson] in a game at Harbor Beach, Mich., made seven hits in as many times at bat, including 2 homers and 3 triples."[20]

Founded in 1887, the Detroit Athletic Club was one of many similar organizations established across the country in response to an increased interest in health and fitness in the last half of the 19th century that believed that fitness was "best achieved by athletic contests rather than gymnastic performance."[21] The DAC's original facilities were located on a large tract of land between Woodward and Cass Streets in a fashionable Detroit neighborhood. It included a clubhouse with a gymnasium, a library and a billiard room, a football/baseball complex encircled by a quarter-mile cinder track, and a dozen grass tennis courts. DAC's second president (1890–94) was a familiar figure to Sam Thompson and many Detroit baseball fans. He was Frederick K. Stearns, former owner of the Detroit Wolverines, who, we recall, kidnapped Thompson and other Indianapolis players for ten days after buying their franchise, in order to prevent them from being approached by any other major league team owners.

DAC baseball teams won two national amateur championships in the 1890s, and the club's football team was the first in Detroit to play a consistent schedule. For years during the college gridiron season, "the University of Michigan hosted its big football games against Minnesota and Cornell on the DAC field to accommodate Detroit area fans."[22] In February 1901 a lease was signed to use the club's baseball diamond as the home field for Detroit's new American League team, but the deal fell through at the last minute for unspecified reasons.

After its lease expired at the Woodward Avenue site in 1912, the club moved to its current location in downtown Detroit. It fielded its last baseball team in 1909.

Because of Sam Thompson's previously published opinions on the need for new major league franchises that could draw more fans, late in the fall of 1899 his name became mistakenly associated with a movement to re-establish the old American Association, the organization that had successfully challenged the National League in the 1880s. Reportedly, he and his close friend, Charley Bennett planned to purchase a franchise in the venture. "Sam Thompson and Charley Bennett ... wanted to be in on the deal [for an American Association franchise], but the other people, who own grounds within ten minutes' ride from the center of the city, got their money in first."[23]

A month after this report surfaced, it was denied by Thompson.

The veteran player, Sam Thompson, held under reservation by the Philadelphia Club, denies emphatically that he will have any financial interest in the new [proposed American Association] Detroit Club, although his name has been prominently mentioned in connection with the scheme. Upon returning from a hunting trip Saturday last, Thompson was interviewed, and spoke as follows: "Say for me that I do not know a blessed thing about it. I think that the proposed association, if reorganized on the proper lines, would be a good thing, and renew interest in the game. As far as I am concerned I have not been approached on the subject. It will take a heap of money to place the organization on a paying basis. If there is sufficient capital behind the scheme, I think there will be no trouble in securing players. There are a great many dissatisfied men in the Major League organization, and I think they would jump at a chance to go into another League, provided they were certain of their salaries."[24]

Although the new league that ultimately would rise to challenge the National League's monopoly would be Ban Johnson's American League, and not a revised version of the old American Association, it is significant that when such plans were being formulated, the press specifically sought out Sam Thompson's opinion on the subject, since in the past he had been at the forefront in pointing out the old league's problems. His final caveat, that players were ready to join another league *provided they were certain of their salaries*, is almost certainly a reference to and a defense of his own conduct during the 1890 Players' League revolt, when he jumped back to the National League after he discovered that his Players' League salary was not guaranteed. Public perception was that Sam was now sufficiently well-off financially to forego his baseball salary. "Sam Thompson now is living a life of ease in Detroit. He is one of the wise players who saved his money and now can afford to rest."[25] At the time he was laid off in 1898, Thompson's real estate investments were said to yield him a yearly income of $1,800.[26] This was no fortune, but combined with savings, it allowed Sam and Ida to live a comfortable, though by no means extravagant life after his major league career ended.

The first half-dozen years of the 20th century were busy ones for Sam Thompson. He played amateur ball, coached college teams, was sidelined for more than a year due to the recurrence of injuries that plagued his last major league seasons, said a sad farewell to his parents, finally secured his Philadelphia release, and for a brief period once again joined the major league ranks.

The national press caught up with the Danville slugger in January 1900. "Sam Thompson, good natured and deliberate as ever, is taking exercise this winter on the ice, where he is very much at home when mounted on a pair of skates. He says he would not advise his friends to put any money into a new league club, but hopes to see it come to life.... Thompson is still under reserve by the Philadelphia Club, but would doubtless play with a new league club if the chance presented itself."[27]

By March 1900, however, Sam was sidelined with some of the same ailments that had led to his departure from Philadelphia in 1898. "Sam Thompson, the veteran outfielder, now living in Detroit, had his injured leg examined recently by physicians in that city. They told him that, while much better, he could not hope to play this season. He is still having trouble with his back."[28] In late August, he returned to Danville for the sad duty of attending the funeral of his father. Jesse Thompson's brief obituary noted that the Civil War veteran "was respected by all who knew him."[29]

The following January, Big Sam was back on the diamond, playing winter ball for a "scratch" team against some of the Tigers' regulars,[30] and performing so well that the press reported that "It is quite likely that the veteran Sam Thompson may be given a trial by [Tigers'] manager Stallings."[31] Although he did not make the squad, due at least in part to the fact that the new American League had a 14-player team limit, Sam was happy to discover that Phillies owner John Rogers finally had relinquished his stranglehold on the veteran's ability to play professional ball. Rogers had not suddenly become generous, however. His action was due to a new National League rule that limited a team's number of reserved players to 16. It had finally become too expensive for Rogers to indulge in his revenge against Thompson for speaking out against him years earlier. For all practical purposes, however, Sam's newfound freedom came too late to be of use to him.

In April, 1902, Sam's mother Rebecca passed away, 20 months after the death of her husband. A "most unusual and pathetic scene" at her interment occurred "when ... [her] six sons, all over six feet in height, strong, stalwart men, acting as pall bearers, bore the casket containing the remains of their mother and lowered it in the last resting place."[32]

Studio Portrait of an elegant and mature Sam Thompson, early 1900s (courtesy Don Thompson).

Brighter days lay ahead for the veteran Danville slugger. When the Tigers opened their 1903 home season, Detroit favorite, Charley Bennett, "and Sam Thompson, formerly the greatest batter in the country, sat on the player bench at the Detroit opening."[33] The two former Wolverine teammates rarely missed a home game, and soon a tradition developed at Bennett Park that would last until Thompson's death in 1922. Each year, as part of the Tigers' Opening Day ceremonies, Bennett, perched on his artificial legs, caught the season's first ceremonial pitch, which usually was thrown out by the Detroit mayor. Standing behind Bennett and holding the former catcher's walking-cane, Sam Thompson served as Honorary Umpire.

In July 1903, Thompson played briefly for a team in Monroe, Michigan, 25 miles south of Detroit. During the next two seasons, he coached the Albion College baseball team and player/managed the Detroit Athletic Club team, where he was occasionally assisted by Charley Bennett and Bennett's former Wolverine battery mate, Charles "Lady" Baldwin. The latter, at age 44, was still pitching for his hometown Hastings, Michigan, team. A brief newspaper portrait of Sam during this time period suggests that he was a contented man: "Still hale and hearty, he [Thompson] has developed new specialties. They are playing ball with the D.A.C. boys and catching bass at Elizabeth lake [*sic*]. He is as fine a performer with the rod and reel as with the bat."[34]

Several of Thompson's DAC team protégées went on to big league careers. Pitcher Fred Blanding spent five years with the American League

Detroit Athletic Club amateur baseball team studio photograph, circa 1907. Sam Thompson, with arms crossed, sits in the middle row. Charley Bennett, former Detroit Wolverine catcher, sits next to Sam, second from right. Charles "Lady" Baldwin, former Wolverine pitcher, sits next to Sam, third from left (courtesy Detroit Athletic Club).

Cleveland Naps, compiling a 46–46 record. His big league debut in September, 1910 was the most memorable game of his career. In that game he tossed a six-hit shutout against future Hall of Famer Walter Johnson of the Washington Senators.

Outfielder Harry Leibold played 13 seasons for four American League teams, hitting .266. Playing right field for the White Sox in 1919, he was one of three starters not implicated in the famous Black Sox World Series scandal of that year.

Catcher Frank Bowerman played for DAC before Sam Thompson completed his own major league career. A 15-year big league veteran, Bowerman is best remembered as "the first regular catcher for Christy Mathewson, who would go on to become one of the first five players inducted into the Major League Hall of Fame in 1936."[35] Born in Romeo, Michigan, 40 miles northwest of Detroit, Bowerman owned a 100-acre farm there, and often hunted on his property area with his frequent guest, Sam Thompson.

The Detroit Tigers, whose home games Charley Bennett and Sam Thompson rarely missed, experienced mixed results in their first few years in the American League, finishing in fifth place once, and in third or seventh place twice. A bright spot in their early lineups was outfielder Sam "Wahoo" Crawford, who had jumped his Cincinnati Reds contract after the 1902 season to join the Tigers. In 19 seasons, Crawford, whose unusual nickname was derived from the name of his hometown, Wahoo, Nebraska, would hit .309 and establish the all-time record for triples (309). Wahoo Sam was elected to the Hall of Fame in 1957.

Crawford soon was surpassed as the Tigers' best player by a teenaged firebrand from Narrows, Georgia named Ty Cobb, who joined the Detroit club in late August 1905, after having been acquired from a Class C minor league nine, the Augusta Tourists. Playing in 41 games for the Tigers, Cobb hit just .240 in 1905. It was the first and last time in a 24-year career that his average would dip below .300. In January 1906, Cobb signed a Detroit contract for his first full major league season as a backup outfielder behind starters Marty McIntyre, Davy Jones and Sam Crawford.

Early on in the 1906 season, however, Tigers manager Bill Armour's plans for his outfield began to crumble. After Sam Crawford and Davy Jones went out with leg injuries, Ty Cobb became a starter in centerfield. Then suddenly, during a mid-summer series at Boston, Cobb disap-

Game day at the Detroit Athletic Club field, Woodward and Cass Streets, Detroit, circa 1903. Numerous Thompson protégés from the DAC subsequently played professional baseball. Sam Thompson stands in the back row, sixth from the left. The club's logo featured its initials DAC inscribed in a triangle (courtesy Detroit Athletic Club).

peared. A few days later, Detroit made public the news that the 19-year-old Georgian "had been sent to a sanatorium,"[36] suffering from a nervous breakdown.

The full story behind Cobb's breakdown only became known years later. In late August 1905, a few days before he was to report to the Tigers for the first time, Cobb's father William was shot dead trying to enter his own house from a second story porch in the dead of night. The shooter, Ty Cobb's mother, Amanda, thinking her husband was an intruder, pulled both triggers on a double-barrel shotgun, blowing off her husband's head. Amanda Cobb was charged with voluntary manslaughter and released on bond, with her trial date set for March 1906.

Arriving in Detroit four days after his father's burial, young Cobb was soon subjected to the worst kind of rookie hazing by the veteran Detroit team. His teammates sent him anonymous threatening notes, refused to let him take batting practice, cut the fingers out of his fielding glove, sawed his bats in half and nailed his spikes to the floor.

The following March, Cobb interrupted his spring training to attend his mother's trial, and then returned to the team after she was acquitted. Shortly before opening day, his throat was so sore that he could not swallow. Taken to a doctor who later was discovered to be a quack, the young outfielder submitted to a brutal tonsillectomy without the benefit of anesthesia. The next day he was forced by Manager Armour to play seven innings of an exhibition game. He somehow managed to connect for a double before walking off the field. Then, after the season began, Cobb underwent an operation on his hip, which had become infected due to abrasions caused by his base-sliding while attempting steals.

In July, the stress caused by his family matters, his injuries, and the psychological abuse to which he was subjected by his teammates led to Cobb's breakdown. For almost seven weeks, he underwent treatment at a sanatorium outside Detroit. Toward the end of his stay, he sharpened his baseball skills by playing a half-dozen games for the Detroit Athletic Club's team, perhaps at the suggestion or invitation of the club's player/manager, Sam Thompson.[37] Cobb did not return to the Tigers until September, and even then his playing status remained day-to-day. Detroit, then in seventh place and with its outfield in tatters, desperately needed some temporary help until Cobb, Crawford and Jones could recover from their assorted physical or mental ailments. Forty-six-year-old Sam Thompson, who had last played full-time in the major leagues a decade earlier, surprised everyone, perhaps even himself, by volunteering his services to the team.

At least initially, there may have been an ulterior motive in the club's decision to select Thompson as an outfield substitute instead of giving a minor leaguer a chance at the job. Detroit's attendance was low and Manager Armour's job was in jeopardy. Thompson was a legend in his adopted hometown, and the prospect of seeing him in uniform again would fill the stands and might temporarily take the discontented Tigers fans' minds off the overall state of their team.

The idea of bringing back retired stars for brief curtain calls was promoted by Giants' manager John McGraw, who in 1904 invited both former Giant catcher Jim O'Rourke and former Detroit Wolverine first baseman Dan Brouthers to play a game in the Polo Grounds after New York had clinched the National League pennant. Thompson had been asked to make such a one-game curtain call in Detroit on numerous occasions, but had always refused. "This year, however, his health has been better than any time since he quit base ball, and his batting for the Detroit Athletic Club has been something terrific. Then too, while his speed in the field and on the bases is nothing like that of former days, he is still able to wing the ball in from deep right to the plate, straight on the line."[38]

On August 31, the Tigers began a home stand against the St. Louis team, and

> Sam Thompson, one of the greatest batters of a bygone era and revered in Detroit as a member of the town's greatest ball team and the only one that ever won a major league pennant, once more donned his spangles [uniform] as a professional player and took his old place in the Detroit right field. The management had announced the fact, and the stands and bleachers were full of special Thompson delegations; for the veteran player, since he retired, as well as during his active career, has always been one of the most popular members of his profession.[39]

Hitting fourth in the lineup, Sam had to face spit-ball-throwing right-hander Harry Howell in his first at bat. "The first time he appeared at the plate he was presented with a huge floral horseshoe and a bouquet as big as a washtub. These gifts hoodooed him, of course, and he struck out."[40] The second time he sent a fly to center. When he came up the third time, the bases were loaded and he faced left-handed reliever, Beany Jacobson. "He won the game hitting down the right line and sending in two runs. He thought the hit good for two bases, but Hemphill threw him out. His fourth attempt was a long fly that Hemphill caught."[41]

The press across the country celebrated his remarkable return with words of high praise. The *Washington Post*'s headline, "Sam Thompson, Back in Game, Makes Good," was followed by the observation that the old veteran "still has his batting eye ... forty-six years old, he retains [the] vigor of youth."[42] *The Sporting News*' story was prefaced by the statement, "Beyond His Prime, But Sam Thompson Can Still Smite the Ball,"[43] and the *Hartford* Courant affirmed, "Sam Thompson Shows the Youngsters How to Play."[44] Sporting *Life* added that "his batting on Friday was mainly responsible for Detroit's victory."[45]

In an interview after the game, Sam offered his thoughts on being back in the major leagues, on a new type of pitch that was now common in the game, and on the perennial comparisons between old-time and modern players:

It seemed the most natural thing in the world to be walking out on the field with the other leaguers. I struck out the first time. Howell was pitching for St. Louis, and that spit ball he was using was all Greek to me. In my day there was no such ball, and though I heard considerable discussion of it, I was completely fooled when I first attempted to connect with it. After playing just one game a man doesn't like to form a judgment as to whether baseball is faster now than it was ten years ago. I don't think the players to-day are any better that the stars of my time, but it is certain that there are more good players now than there were then. That is natural, for there are more first class men in all lines. This is noted particularly in the pitching. When I was playing with the Phillies first-class pitchers were not nearly so numerous, which accounts in great measure for the fact that the batting in those days was much heavier.[46]

Over the next ten days, Sam played in seven more Detroit games, including away contests in Saint Louis and Chicago. He collected six more hits and fielded his position flawlessly until leg cramps and joint pain forced him off the field. "Sam has lost none of his cunning, but his joints are a trifle stiffened with old age, and after a hard run he limps considerably."[47]

Thompson's game highlights in these contests included "pulling down five difficult flies in the outfield that helped his team to victory"[48] on September 1, two hits in the first game of a double header with St. Louis on September 3, and a dramatic three-base hit the next day against the Browns. "The old gray-haired Badger played a star game. He made a sensational catch which looked like a hit and had two more difficult flies which he gobbled in. Then he made the hit of the day when he tripled to right with a man on base and when the outfield threw to third, Thompson kept on to the plate, beating the ball by nose."[49] By referring to the Danville slugger as a "Badger," this Washington, D.C., *Evening Star* reporter evidently forgot that Thompson hailed from the Hoosier state, and not from Wisconsin, where the badger is the official state animal.

Years later, Charley Bennett added a humorous final note about one of the plays that Sam made for the Tigers that emphasized the fact that Danville slugger's slow and deliberate demeanor, which had been a hallmark of his play since his Wolverine days, had not changed. In one game as Detroit took the field, Bennet recalled that "he [Thompson] took his good ol' sweet time … so that he was standing on the foul line, still adjusting his sun glasses, when the pitcher pitched and the batter hit a line drive right down the line. Sam looked up just in time to catch it, far out of position."[50]

An expanded version of this story provides more details of the incident and emphasizes the veteran's quick reflexes.

> It took old Sam about five minutes to get over to his position, find his sunglasses over near the foul line [between innings, players left their gloves and sunglasses on the field in this era] and wipe them off and get set. Along late in the game, a fellow named Max Hoffman, who had been in a bad slump, led off for the opposition. Mullen, the Tigers' pitcher, didn't notice that old Sam was still out there along the foul line wiping off his glasses, his back turned toward the infield, when he pitched the first ball. Max got hold of it right and it shot down the right foul line on a line, a sure triple. Everybody looked that way and there was old Sam, just fitting on his glasses, his back still to the plate. "Sam-Sam-Sam!" the Detroit players yelled, and Sam whirled around, saw the ball coming, and took it just as pretty as anyone ever did. Everybody roared, that is, everybody except Max. When he got back to the bench, he said, "Well, if felt good, anyhow!"[51]

Thompson's remarkable return to the diamond a decade after his last major league season, and after having only played amateur ball intermittently in the interim, is a singular accomplishment in the annals of the sport. As noted by the *Washington Post* during his brief stint with the Tigers, "He is playing now merely as an experiment, but declares he has no intention of keeping it up. But no matter what he does, he has established a unique record and proved that the age limit for a baseball player is considerably higher than is generally supposed."[52]

Big Sam's curtain call soon prompted many requests from newspapers for his input on the National Pastime. The first of these was a brief eulogy for Buck Ewing, the great Giants catcher, who had died at age 46 of Bright's Disease (kidney failure) on October 20, 1906. A versatile athlete who played every position on the field, Ewing was a lifetime .300 hitter, and the first catcher able to nab men attempting to steal by using snap throw from the crouch position. An outstanding base runner, he is the only catcher ever to lead his team in stolen bases (53 in 1888), and once, taking a break from his duties behind the plate, he played third base and stole six bases in a game.[53]

"They're slipping away,"[54] remarked Thompson, referring to the growing number of players from his era that had passed on. Echoing the sentiment of others like John McGraw, Ned Hanlon, Clark Griffith,

Tim Keefe and John Ward regarding Ewing, Sam affirmed that "there never was a greater catcher or all-around player."[55]

A month later, in December 1906, Sam penned a long essay entitled "Baseball Reminiscences" that featured anecdotes about two pitchers, Tim Keefe and Brewery Jack Taylor. Both men for a time had been Sam's teammates in Philadelphia. Each story employs liberal use of humor, and each showcases Thompson's considerable skills as a storyteller— two traits not usually associated with the laconic Danville slugger.

In discussing Keefe, Sam reminded his readers that in the early days of the game, a hit batsman did not get a free pass to first base, and he credited Keefe's tendency to hit batters with the establishment of that rule.

> There was no penalty for hitting a batsman in the early history of the game. The way the pitchers used to feed the ball in close to the batsman before the penalty was added was a caution. I remember the first time I faced Tim Keefe. He was pitching for New York and he had speed to burn. I had not much experience in the big organization, but he had made something of a reputation among the bush leaguers. Tim speeded one over that sang as it came. Whish-zip expresses his speed. I thought he threw at my head; anyway, I save[d] my life by falling to the plate. With exactly the same motion he threw another ball, but it was a slow bender, and I caught it on the end of my bat for two bases. There were men on second and third and they loped home.... Keefe may not have intended hitting as many men as he did, but he kept us black and blue just the same.[56]

Sam then recalled an exchange between pitcher Keefe and Jim White, his former Detroit Wolverines teammate, after the former had plunked White with the ball. "'By ginger, old man, you almost got out of the way of that one [said Keefe]. Why do you insist on standing squarely over the plate? I'll have to keep 'em away from the plate when you are at bat if you don't quit it.' White would rub the bruised spot and exclaim, 'If I had your conscience, Tim, I'd go out and strong arm [rob] the rich. That would be an easier way to get money than by committing homicide.'"[57]

Thompson's second anecdote detailed the friendship between pitcher Jack Taylor and umpire Tim Hurst. The pair were drinking partners who were in the habit "on occasions too numerous to mention to wander away from their hotel after night had drawn her dusky curtains and spend several hours taking the town to pieces 'to see what made it tick.'"⁵⁸ Taylor was scheduled to pitch once after a night out with Hurst, and was in no condition to do so. Accordingly, he asked his friend, who would be umpiring the game, for help.

"Tim, I don't feel like pitching today. I just can't do it. It is all I can do to drag one foot after the other, but the manager insists on my going in." "Oi'll tell you what Oi'll do," said Hurst in his creamy brogue. "After yo've pitched three or four balls, kick like the divil on my decisions and Oi'll chase you out of the game." Taylor did as Hurst had suggested, and lobbed a few balls over that were strikes, but which Hurst called balls, and then he came down to the plate to protest. He came on the run, waving his arm, and shouting that Hurst was a "robber" and a "brigand" and a few other choice specimens of outcast society. "To the bench with you," said Hurst, waving his hand. "What's that?" yelled Taylor. "Out of the game ye go, my bye," repeated Hurst. Taylor went through a dumb show of anger for the manager's benefit and as he slowly walked away he said in an undertone to Hurst, "It's me to the hotel and to bed. I'm nearly dead on my feet."⁵⁹

In January 1908, as players and fans awaited the arrival of spring, Sam was profiled by George Pulford of the *Logansport* [Indiana] *Daily Reporter* in a story filed from Detroit. Although the veteran slugger would soon celebrate his 48th birthday, Pulford noted that

the years have been kind to Thompson, now one of Detroit's best known citizens. His tall figure is as straight and his gray eyes as gray as when he picked out the best in the repertoire of [John] Clarkson and [Amos] Rusie and poled them over the right field fence at Philadelphia. He is grizzled, but the fan of the 80's would not fail to recognize him. Blessed with a sufficiency of this world's goods and growing wealthier every year as the result of shrewd investments, Sam Thompson spends his summers playing ball with the Detroit Athletic club and his winters at his home or club, or in the hunting field near Danville, Ind.⁶⁰

Described as "one of the old-timers who believe base ball faster than it was in the 80's,"⁶¹ Sam elaborated on his 1906 comments on the spit ball and the overall improvements in the game in his interview.

It is natural that the game should be faster. There are many more good players than formerly. Base ball is a bigger game than it used to be. College ball furnishes heady players, and where a team formerly had one or two stars, they now have five or six.... Pitching is better than of old for the same reason. There are more pitchers and they are kept in the best condition. Why, Detroit in 1887 won the championship virtually with two pitchers—Getzein and Lady Baldwin. The greatest development in pitching is the spit ball. Whenever I face one of the fellows who uses it, I am at sea. A man is batting at nothing. You can follow a curve, but the spitter breaks at an angle after the batter starts his swing. I have read that some old timers used to throw the spit ball. There isn't a word of truth to that. [Charlie] Buffinton's name has been mentioned particularly as a spit ball pitcher. Buff [Buffinton] never threw the spitter at me or at anyone else on the Detroit club. He did have a wonderful drop, but it was a curve, not a spit ball.[62]

Three months after this interview, *Sporting Life*'s Detroit reporter announced that Big Sam had suffered a serious recurrence of the symptoms that caused him to retire from the Phillies in 1898.

It is a painful duty for me to inform "Sporting Life's" readers of the serious illness that has sapped the strength of Sam Thompson, the grand old man of local baseball, during the winter. Along in February, Thompson was stricken with a serious hemorrhage which defied treatment for weeks and ran the veteran down in weight until he is but a faint shadow of his former stalwart self. He is convalescent now and is managing to be up and around, though his strength has gone to a pathetic degree. He has already told his Detroit Athletic club friends that that they must fill his place in right field with someone else from now on, and doesn't think he will ever play ball again. Sam thinks that the trouble is the result of an old baseball injury that has manifested itself in various ways since his retirement from the diamond. It is needless to say that every baseball fan in Detroit acquainted with the situation is pulling hard for the veteran's complete recovery.[63]

By the following spring (March 1909), Sam was well enough to resume his sports writing career, publishing a story about legendary Chicago pitcher John Clarkson, who had passed away a month earlier at age 47.

I'll never forget the first time I ever faced Clarkson.... It was his first year in the National League and he was just as cocky as any other member of the Chicago team on which he played, and I don't suppose that there was ever a team that had the umpires as thoroughly cowed as they did. The first ball John pitched to me was a bit wide and the umpire called it so. Clarkson came galloping in and wanted to know what ailed that ball. The umpire told him. He grouched and went back. The second ball was an exact duplicate of the first. When the umpire proclaimed it a ball again, [Chicago's player/manager, Adrian] Anson bellowed from first base and Clarkson started to run in once more. Clarkson stopped and looked at me. "I don't see any medals on you for batting," he said in that cool, calculating way of his. "Well, maybe you will before this season is over," I came back. He strolled back into the box. The next one was a curve ball about knee high and square over. I hit it up against the right field fence so far there was really no use for the fielders to case it [run it down]. I sprinted at my best speed to third and had plenty of time to go home. As I trotted in I put my hand alongside my mouth and yelled to Clarkson: "Guess I've got one of those medals for batting coming to me right now, eh?" He never said a word—just kicked on the little hole he used for his right foot when he pitched. Well, all this sounds pretty fine from my standpoint, perhaps, but you may believe me, boys, I lived to see the day when I bitterly regretted getting into an argument with John Clarkson. I faced him after that in scores of games and I can truthfully say that never in all that time did I get another ball that came where I expected it or in the way in which I guessed was coming. That sounds impossible, but it's just exactly true. I'd make up my mind just what was coming, and so help me, I never guessed right. He'd take chances on curving them when a curve would never have been thought of by the average pitcher and then, when you'd get set for a curve, over it would come, straight as a string. I got a few hits off him, for the law of chance will always get in its work, but those I got were mostly luck. I never out-guessed him. Time and time again I've heard good, wise ball players argue that question of Clarkson's ability to read their thoughts. And he never set me down in a pinch when he knew I'd have given a year off my life for a hit, without saying something about those batting medals that he didn't see adorning my shirt yet.[64]

Although known throughout his career as a long ball hitter, Thompson nonetheless had a great appreciation for the "small ball" strategies of legendary New York manager John McGraw. In an essay he penned that employs surprisingly erudite vocabulary, Sam praised McGraw's approach to the "inside game."

McGraw has the science of the game at his fingers' ends. His team played like a well-oiled and perfect piece of machinery. The beauty of inside work is generally lost on the average fan, who is keyed up to cheer the spectacular play—hair-raising stops, balls pulled out of the air after long runs, etc. But it is the perfect playing together of the men, each a component and important part of the machine, a grasping of the opportunities and the execution with faultless precision that helps more than any one feature outside of hits to win games. I venture to say that errors of omission lose as many or more games than errors of commission.

McGraw is a great leader. Why, in 1895, we—Philadelphia—did not win a game from Baltimore, where McGraw was at the helm, during the entire season. I think that was pretty nearly a record. Of course, in baseball, the first desideratum is hits. Hit the ball. That is the primary lesson in the art of winning games, but in augmenting the efforts of the batsman[,] "inside work" is most important. It is growth [innovation] that the years have added. It was but natural that with the great array of talent contributed every year by the many minor leagues of the country, that the best players should be seized upon by shrewd managers and utilized for the benefit of their teams. That is what McGraw has done. He is fertile and inventive, and also he is emulative. He can grasp an idea, work it over, hammer it around, regild [regild] it and turn it out with the hallmark of originality. And that faculty is one of the essentials of all leaders of men, whether on the ball field or the battlefield.[65]

In April 1910, Sam attended the Tigers' opening game in April with Charley Bennett, and there reunited with Jim McGuire, a teammate on the 1885 Indianapolis minor league team, who was now coaching for Tigers manager Hughie Jennings. McGuire recalled, "with much laughter, a trick that Thompson worked on the Indianapolis fans"[66] (when Thompson was with Detroit and when Indianapolis had a team in the National League). One day, four of Sam's brothers showed up in Indianapolis to see him play.

In those days Thompson was hitting a home run almost daily, and before he went to the game he arranged with the brothers to throw money at him if he hit a home run. Sam was meeting them on the nose that day, and, if I am not mistaken, he made three home runs. Every time he trotted home his brothers stood up and threw silver dollars at him, yelling like Indians. It worked all right, for the fans fell in with the scheme and showered money on Sam, who gathered up a handkerchief full before the game ended. "I'll try to make a sneak [sneak away] with the money and my brothers will worry for fear they won't get theirs back." But he didn't get far, for those brothers were right on his heels, and they not only got back their $12 dollars [four brothers attended, and each threw three silver dollars on the field] but enough more to pay their expenses for the round trip [home to Danville].[67]

Sam Thompson at Navin Field, home of the Detroit Tigers, circa 1910 (courtesy Keith Thompson).

These stories by and about Big Sam, which were published in the years following his brief curtain call in big league ball with the Tigers, reveal dimensions of his personality and an understanding and appreciation for the game that remained unspoken during his career, thanks to his naturally quiet and retiring nature. It is perhaps not surprising that many of the great slugger's observations deal with those players on the diamond who were his natural adversaries—the pitchers.

As the years passed, Thompson's feats on the diamond faded from the public's memory, although occasionally, when the nation's thoughts turned to baseball in the spring, stories about him resurfaced. A March 1913 article in the *Indianapolis Sun*, for example, revived the legend of his alleged "discovery" by Dan O'Leary.[68] Another story reported that "Thompson is now selling real estate in Detroit, and as the Michigan metropolis is in the throes of growing pains, Sam is piling up the dollars."[69]

In October 1913, Sam and Ida "quietly celebrated their silver wedding anniversary"[70] with a small party for friends and family at their home on Ash Street in Detroit. A local news item noted that "the years tend to sit lightly on both their heads, and the joy of living is theirs in enviable measure."[71]

Back in 1890, Thompson briefly was the teammate of Billy Sunday, the speedy, light-hitting outfielder who in August of that year was traded to the Phillies from the Pirates. Sunday, an Ames, Iowa, native, had spent the early years of his career with the Chicago White Stockings, many of whose players, like George Gore and Mike Kelly, were famous for their habitual boozing and carous-

Sam and Ida Thompson's 25th wedding anniversary photograph, 1913 (courtesy Keith Thompson).

ing. The impressionable young Sunday became a regular member of that group until one Sunday. In Billy Sunday's words,

> It was Sunday afternoon and we got tanked up and then went and sat down on a corner ... across the street a company of men and women were playing instruments ... and others were singing the Gospel hymns that I used to hear my mother sing ... I sobbed and sobbed, and a young man stepped out and said, "We are going to the Pacific Garden Mission; won't you come down to the mission too?" ... I arose and said to the boys [his fellow teammates], "I'm through.... We've come to a parting of the ways."[72]

Sunday eventually became an evangelical preacher, and never returned to his earlier wayward life.

In 1890, Sunday came to a crossroad in his life. His outfield work and speed on the bases were valued by the Phillies, and the team was ready to offer him a contract through the 1893 season. However, he had also received an offer to become national secretary for the Young Men's Christian Association. After much deliberation, he made the decision to retire from baseball and take the job at the YMCA. By the early years of the 20th century, he had become a well-known preacher whose revivalist sermons attracted thousands across the country. Sunday frequently drew on his years as a professional baseball player to add a unique element to his sermons.

> One oddity of Sunday's rhetorical style was his frequent use of baseball imagery. In his sermons, Christ throws fastballs at temptation and calls the devil out; sinners are left on base; and those who repent their sins slide— Billy Sunday would slide headfirst across the stage to emphasize this point— into salvation. Billy Sunday never entirely severed his connection to baseball; he frequently was a spectator at major-league parks, and loved to serve as a volunteer umpire in the minor-league games.[73]

At the conclusion of his sermons, Sunday would ask those in the audience to "hit the sawdust trail," that is, to walk to the front of the meeting place and either become a Christian or re-affirm their faith. Sunday's unusual expression to describe this action was symbolic, and had originated during one of his revivals held in Bellingham, Washington. It derived from the practice that lumbermen had of depositing a trail of sawdust in dense forest in order to be able to find their way home.[74]

At one of Sunday's religious rallies in Detroit in November 1916, Sam Thompson and Charley Bennett went down the "sawdust trail." "Sam Thompson, veteran outfielder of big league balldom, 'hit the trail'"

Charley Bennett, left, Billy Sunday, center, and Sam Thompson, share a happy moment, circa 1920. After retiring from baseball, Sunday became a nationally known evangelical preacher. During one of Sunday's crusades in Detroit in 1916, both Charley Bennett and Sam Thompson reaffirmed their faith (courtesy Don Thompson).

and professed the Christian faith at the last meeting of Billy Sunday's revival, which closed at Detroit Sunday night. Charlie Bennett, another star player, a catcher, also went forward."[75] Details of the scene were offered by the *Detroit Times*.

> While Bill [Billy Sunday] was busy grasping the hands of the trail hitters, a tall, gray man came along the line. Billy threw his arms about his neck, embraced him and cried, "Hello, Sam. God bless you." Presently in a lull of trail hitters, Billy dashed suddenly from the pulpit and ran into the audience. Dropping before another gray-haired man, he began to pray. Soon he pulled the man down on the floor beside him and together they prayed. And then an usher assisted the crippled man up to the platform. He was Charlie Bennett. Sam Thompson also was ushered to the platform and Billy, with his arms around his two old comrades, introduced them and told how overjoyed he was that they had found their Savior through his efforts. Then, as a sort of extra climax, Mrs. Sunday ushered Mrs. Bennett and Mrs. Thompson to the platform. "We are wives of the three old ball players," she called, "and we were the wives of them when they were playing a quarter of a century ago, which I think is going some in these days of rapid divorce."[76]

During World War I, Sam served as a U.S. Deputy Marshal in Detroit. While American troops were fighting in Europe, U.S. marshals were assigned the task of protecting the home front from enemy aliens, spies and saboteurs. One of Thompson's primary tasks was registering alien women who were crossing the U.S.-Canadian border in Detroit. During the world influenza pandemic of 1918, ever-cautious Sam made headlines by wearing a protective gauze mask to ward off flu germs while performing his duties. Nearly 700,000 Americans died in the flu pandemic, ten times the number of U.S. losses in the war. Under the headline "Ex-Baseball Star Takes No Chances," one report noted that "Mr. Thompson sits in a room in the federal building that is inadequate to accommodate the crowds of women who are seeking alien war-plant zone permits. Saturday he donned a mask at Marshal Behrendt's suggestion, and while the women looked a bit miffed and his co-workers smiled, Sam sticks to his mask."[77]

Deputy Marshal Sam Thompson stayed on in the Detroit Federal Building after the war ended, serving as a crier (bailiff) in United States Judge Arthur Tuttle's court. During this period, a creative and thoughtful gesture on Sam's part once again brought the old ballplayer's name to the forefront in Detroit.

A bit of the rolling pin his mother used to roll out the crust for his pies and the dough for his cookies is now the gavel of United States Judge Arthur J. Tuttle. It was presented to him yesterday by Sam Thompson, ballplayer, who, after serving the Tigers faithfully for many years, took his post at the side of the court and has sounded "Hear ye, hear ye!" for many moons. It was faithful Sam who thought of the … rolling pin [as a substitute gavel] when the old one [gavel] was stolen some months back. The deputy Marshal wrote to … the judge's only sister…. And [she] sent down two relics of the Leslie home. One was a bone, once the foreleg of a horse the judge's father used to ride. The other was the rolling pin. One handle was off the pin. "'Twas worn off in loyal service," explained Judge Tuttle. "I remember watching her [his mother] hold the one remaining handle and roll out the cakes." And yesterday afternoon the intimates of the court assembled in the dignified court room. Miss Julia M. Baldwin was there. She helped Sam locate the sister and secure the emblem. She's been the judge's private secretary since long before he entered the federal court…. "What is this all about?" queried Judge Tuttle as the *Times* photographer prepared the flash. Then Sam told him. Tears came to Judge Tuttle's eyes. Lucky the prisoner who would have stood there at that moment awaiting sentence. "It was once the emblem of my mother's service—'tis now the symbol of mine."[78]

During his years of service with the Judge, Sam apparently gave Tuttle another, less tangible gift—an interest in baseball. "The old ball player … rarely missed a [Tigers] ball game and converted many public officials to fans. Among them was Judge Arthur J. Tuttle."[79]

Despite Sam's active lifestyle and full-time job, his close friend Charley Bennett revealed that in the early 1920s, the Danville slugger was experiencing unspecified health problems.[80] Nevertheless, Thompson remained adamant about continuing to work. "I have enough money not to work anymore … but I am going to stay on my job as long as I can stand on two feet and Uncle Sam will have me. When a man quits working, he might as well die."[81]

True to his word, Sam was busy working on the day he died. Tuesday, November 7, 1922, was Election Day in Detroit, and Sam was working that morning as an election board member at the McKinley School on Hamilton Avenue when he was stricken with a heart attack. A doctor was called, and after treatment, "Mr. Thompson was able, with the assistance of two police officers, to go to his home. He then undressed himself and went to bed, but within a few minutes suffered another heart attack which ended his life. Mr. Thompson for the last two weeks had been suffering from heart trouble. He was 62 years old."[82]

The subsequent outpouring of sympathy was unprecedented in the City of Straits.

> Far out on Trumball avenue in a block of little gray homes there stands a little gray home more tiny than even its neighbors, and on the pillars of the porch there still glows in the November air a green and vigorous vine.
>
> Friday afternoon there was gathered before this small cottage a group such as never before graced the street of little homes and may never again grace it. A group of millionaires, high officials in the government of city and state, judges and bankers and manufacturers. The group was so large that it filled the walks and overflowed into the well kept and tiny yard and into the yards of neighbors and the street was filled with a dull uproar as automobiles by the score drew up alongside the little gray home, deposited their loads and then purred on to stand as near as possible beside a curb that was lined with similar vehicles.
>
> An ambassador holding court or a famous diva making her last appearance might have brought such a line. But it was neither.... Within the cottage in the front room roses and lilies were piled until the ceilings touched with the bloom, and the voice of a minister who spoke beside the coffin was carried out to the listeners.... A bishop who had passed or the well beloved of a prince might have slept beside such flowers. And yet, all these men, all these flowers, all this honor was for a man who lived in humble circumstance— and who once had been a professional ball player.[83]

In addition to the six pallbearers for Sam's coffin, over 250 honorary pallbearers were present at the funeral service in his home. Their numbers included the sitting governor of Michigan, Alex J. Groesbeck, Detroit's Mayor, James J. Couzens, two bishops, a rabbi, a half-dozen ministers from different Christian denominations, Frank Navin, owner of the Tigers, Frederick K. Stearns, former owner of the Detroit Wolverines and past President of the Detroit Athletic Club, most of the surviving members of the Wolverines 1887 championship team, including Dan Brouthers, Hardy Richardson, Jim White, Charley Bennett and "Lady Baldwin," and eleven of Sam's former teammates from his years as player/manager for the DAC baseball team. It was a remarkable sendoff for the great Danville slugger, one that surprised and amazed his neighbors on his quiet block of Trumball Avenue.

As the crowd mingled about, both inside and outside the Thompson's house,

> The air was filled with names that once sent thrills down the spines of massed thousands gathered about the diamonds—"Cap" Anson and "Mike" Kelley [sic], old John Clarkson and Charlie Radbourne. The men in the crowd

before the little gray cottage had seen the day when they could call [recall] the record, batting and base running of every one of them ... the neighbors stared wonderingly out on the crowd and wonderingly at the thousands of flowers as they came pouring from the doors ready to take up the journey to Elmwood cemetery. "Old Mr. Thompson" they had known as a good neighbor, a quiet, unassuming man, who mowed his own lawn and carried home his own bundles, ever as they, and now that he was dead they were a little bewildered to know that the world was giving him a stately farewell.[84]

The man known as "Silent Sam," "the Danville Slugger," and "the Grand Old Man of the Game," was laid to rest in Ida Thompson's family plot at Elmwood Cemetery, in downtown Detroit.

Thompson tributes published in newspapers across the county praised both his baseball skills and his gentlemanly behavior on the diamond. Veteran syndicated sportswriter George Chadwick for example, related a humorous, but in all likelihood fanciful incident that took place between Sam and Giants catcher Buck Ewing.

Buck Ewing was behind the bat against Philadelphia in a game in 1889.... Ewing was something of a humorist and he counted on getting Sam Thompson's goat. As Big Sam walked to the plate, Ewing faced the stands, removed his cap, and said: "Gentlemen, you all know Mr. Thompson. He is about to bat. You can kiss the ball goodbye." Sam grinned, shifted his long legs around, dug in his spikes, let two go by and hit the third one. When last seen, the ball was headed for the next county. As Sam trailed the other three runners around the plate, he said to Ewing, "I make it a point never to disappoint an old pal, Buck."[85]

The story made great copy for sportswriter Chadwick, but may only be partially true, or perhaps not true at all. Sam did hit one home run against the Giants in 1889 (on July 24), but it was a two-run shot, and not a grand slam, as suggested by Chadwick ("Sam trailed the other three runners around the plate"). It was perhaps fitting that just as Sam's big league entry was described through the Dan O'Leary "discovery" myth, his departure from the earthly scene was accompanied by another story that is probably more myth than fact.

Of all the tributes published after Sam's death, none was more poignant nor had more chance of being accurate than that told his old friend and former teammate, Charley Bennett. Bennett's comments were introduced by sportswriter Charles Cameron of the *Detroit News*.

The longest comradeship of baseball teammates was broken forever Tuesday when "Charlie" Bennett, the first man to sign a contract with the old Detroit

National League team of the 80's learned of the sudden death of "Sam" Thompson, the "marvel" batsman and fielder of that team.... The career of Bennett and Thompson as "team mates" may be called the longest of record because of the unique ceremony by which it has been renewed every year. For more than 25 years at the first game in Detroit, the Mayor has pitched the first ball, Charlie Bennett has caught it, and Sam Thompson has umpired. Charlie Bennett was permanently injured in a railroad accident ... and it has always been a part of Sam's duty to take care of Charlie's cane when Bennett took his old position behind the plate.[86]

Following this introduction, Bennett spoke.

When anyone thinks of Sam Thompson, they think of his strength, his activity, of those phenomenal hits he made and those almost unbelievable one hand catches. You can't forget those things when you have seen them ... how he did run! He didn't seem to be moving so awfully fast, but he was reaching out so far with his feet like a race horse that he was covering ground much faster than some fellows who were more excited about it.... Sam took the breath away from the crowds, both in batting and fielding. I saw him once in Boston, chasing a fly which was apparently bound to hit the fence. The crowd was so big that day that they had seats right up against the fence. And Sam plunged right after that ball, right up against the fence at a dead run, and then reached up with that long right arm and pulled that ball down our of the air![87]

Charley Bennett concluded his tribute by reminding his audience of Thompson's fine personal traits.

But while we think of Sam as a wonderful player, don't ever forget other things about Sam. He was a wonderful friend. No one ever quarreled with Sam. No one ever knew him, with all his brutal strength, to be rough and brutal. He was always even tempered, and simple, and plain.... The last time I saw him ... I remarked to him casually: "Well, we're getting into the king row [getting old], Sam, and we're likely to go any time." He said, "That's right, Charlie." But after all we talk about death, we don't realize it, and so many of us have thought for years of Sam as a picture of strength and health and action—that we can't quite realize this, and it will be some time before we can.[88]

A year before Sam Thompson's death, his home run total was surpassed by Babe Ruth. With the passing years, all of Big Sam's contributions to the game were gradually forgotten. It would take another half century before the Danville slugger's diamond deeds would again briefly emerge from the dusty corridors of history.

CHAPTER SIX

The Long Road
to Cooperstown

"The younger generation, filled with admiration for the baseball
stars of today, are aware only in a vague way that there once was
a player of high renown known as Sam Thompson."—unsourced
newspaper clipping, Ida Thompson scrapbook

Playing in 11 full major league seasons (at least 60 percent of scheduled games), in three partial seasons, and in an eight-game cameo
appearance with the Detroit Tigers in 1906, Sam Thompson compiled
a .331 lifetime batting average, and is one of 30 players all-time with an
average over .330. His .415 mark in 1894 is the seventh-highest ever
recorded. Sam reached the 200-hit plateau three times, led the league
once in triples, extra base hits and batting average, twice in doubles,
home runs and total bases, and three times in hits. He scored over 100
runs in ten seasons and drove in over 100 runs in eight. His 1887 record
of 166 RBI, which was accomplished in just 127 games, stood for 34
years, until it was surpassed by Babe Ruth in 1921. Ruth, however, topped
Thompson's record by just two RBI, and did so while playing in 34 more
games. In addition to leading the league in RBI in 1887, Thompson took
league honors in hits, batting average, total bases and slugging—all while
facing a pitcher throwing to the plate from a distance of 55'6".

Sam's RBI ratio per-game was the league's best three times, and his
lifetime .923 RBI per-game is the highest in major league history. He was
the first player to hit 20 home runs and collect over 200 hits and 300 total
bases in a season. He is the only player to hit consecutive bases-loaded
triples in a game. In 1893, Sam collected 222 hits in just 131 games. Only
three players have ever recorded more hits in fewer games in a season.[1]

Although not considered swift on the bases, Thompson was a crafty, effective and at times aggressive base runner. He averaged 25 steals a year from 1889 to 1895, once stole five bases in an exhibition game, and at age 46, in the first game of his return to the diamond after a decade's absence, was thrown out trying to stretch a single into a double.

Defensively, Thompson led the league twice in fielding, assists and outfield double plays, and his total of 283 outfield assists ranks twelfth all time. Playing in just 63 games in his rookie season, he threw out 24 runners trying to advance. "Discounting three seasons when he was hurt and did not play much, Thompson averaged 24.8 assists a year ... on two occasions (1891 and 1895) Sam had over 30 assists."[2] By modern comparison, in their best seasons, Willie Mays had 23 assists, Joe DiMaggio, 22, and Roberto Clemente, 27. Depending on the reporting source, as we have seen, Sam in 1895 either became the first of four players in history to record three outfielder-to-catcher assists in a game or became the only player to record four such assists in a game.

Although all current records place Sam fifteenth all time in number of outfield double plays (61), research conducted for this study has uncovered another four assists. His new total of 65 is thirteenth all time.

Such all time rankings place Sam Thompson in an elite position in baseball history, and prompted historian Ed Koszarek to assert that "he is one of perhaps a dozen legitimate candidates for the title of greatest player in major league history."[3] Despite such praise, Big Sam's achievements on the diamond can only be fully appreciated by viewing them in their 19th-century baseball context.

> Comparing nineteenth-century ballplayers to players in later years is like equating peaches to nectarines. They are closely related, but they represent a different genre. The game Sam Thompson played had different rules, crude equipment, and awkwardly laid out playing fields. Each factor makes cross-generational comparisons difficult.... To fairly appreciate his greatness, researchers can only compare Sam with his peer players, who competed under similar conditions.[4]

Almost without exception, all-time record categories like hits, doubles, triples, runs scored and RBI are held by players who enjoyed long careers made up of long seasons. Sam Thompson, in contrast, had a moderately-long career in an era when seasons were much shorter. During his 11 full-time seasons, his team played 1447 games, and Sam played in 1329 of them, for an average of just 121 games per season.

In contrast, players who were active for a similar period in the 154-game era had the possibility of playing over 247 more games in that period of time compared to Thompson. Players over the same time span in the 162-game era have the possibility of playing almost 335 more games than Thompson did in his shorter 11 seasons. In his prime, as has been noted, Thompson played in as many as 185 league and exhibition games in a season. If he would have had the opportunity to play in more regulation games per season, there is little doubt that his records would be even more impressive.

Given the significant disparity between the length of modern major league seasons and their 19th-century counterparts, many of Sam Thompson's accomplishments on the diamond acquire greater significance. Collecting 200 hits and 100 RBI in a season, for example, is a singular accomplishment for a player in any era. It is even more noteworthy, however, when achieved in a shorter season. This is the case with many Thompson hitting records, including his 203 hits and 166 RBI in 127 games in 1887, his 211 hits and 165 RBI in 119 games in 1895, 222 hits in 131 games in 1893, and 147 RBI in just 102 games in his injury-shortened 1894 season.

Shorter seasons must also be taken into account when assessing Sam's career assist record. He ranks twelfth all-time in this category with 283. Ty Cobb ranks second on the all time assist list, with over 100 more than Thompson. Cobb, however, played in more than twice the number of games as Thompson. Of all outfield-assist leaders who have played at least 1,000 games, including Tris Speaker, baseball's all time leader, none has a higher assist rate than Thompson—one every 4.9 games.

Sam's double plays number 65. No player in the top twenty all-time in this category has reached this plateau in fewer games, and Sam's ratio of double plays per games played –one every 22 games, ranks third all-time behind Tom Brown (one every 21 games) and Tris Speaker (one every 19 games).

Significant differences exist between the 19th-century game and its modern equivalent in regard to both the quality of the baseballs that players fielded or tried to hit and the nature of the gloves they used in the field. Unless such differences in equipment are acknowledged, the performance of early-era players on the field or at bat cannot be properly assessed.

At first glance, for example, Sam Thompson's lifetime fielding average of .934 appears to be exceptionally low, until we recall the primitive type glove he used to field his position. In his 2004 autobiography, *Baseball Forever* former Pirate outfielder and Hall of Fame inductee Ralph Kiner reminds us that "other than training and medical improvements, the biggest refinements in the game have to do with on field equipment. The most revolutionary change had been the tremendous improvement of the glove. Yet nobody talks about this.... If you look at old timers' pancake gloves ... dating back to baseball's 19th-century origins, you wonder how fielders ever used them because they were so flat."[5] Using gloves without pockets or webbing between the thumb and index finger, early era players had to use both hands to make catches because "the bare hand was needed to keep the ball from popping out of the glove."[6]

Kiner further notes that "two-handed catches limit your range and ability to make the fantastic plays that are made today."[7] Despite such limitations, and despite the fact that in Philadelphia Sam Thompson played for nearly a decade in what was considered the most difficult sun field in the league, he was renowned, as we have seen, for his spectacular running and leaping catches, which frequently were followed by strong and accurate throws across the diamond or to home plate to catch runners attempting to advance.

Thanks in great part to fielding either barehanded or with primitive gloves, only six outfielders whose careers were completed before 1900 and who played at least 1,000 games registered a fielding average over .900. Of these, Sam Thompson's .934 average ranks first.

While Thompson's home run total of 126 is second to Roger Connor's 138 four-baggers among 19th century players, Connor had the advantage of playing in almost 600 more games than Thompson. Sam's home run average per year is slightly better than that of the great Giants slugger (8.0 versus 7.6). Although Thompson's and Connor's home run totals cannot compare with those of modern long-ball hitters, they were exceptional in the era, given the nature of the "dead ball" used in all games.

Until Sam's final full season, 1896, "a ball a game was the norm, and if batted out of the park, the game's continuance awaited the pleasure of some anonymous 'urchin.' It he chose to return it, he was given free admission. If not, the house reluctantly put a new one in play."[8] Softer than its modern counterpart, "the nineteenth-century ball was kept in play whether it became scratched, soiled or water-logged, or the seams broke, prompting some managers … to chose to bat first when playing at home in order to get a crack at a fresh, new ball. The longer a ball was in play, the more difficult it was to hit for distance."[9] It is significant, therefore, that 36 percent of Sam Thompson's home runs were hit in the seventh inning or later, and 10 percent were hit in the ninth inning, when the dead ball was hardest to hit for distance.

Sam Thompson's lifetime slugging average of .505 ranks 85th all time. Compared to some great modern players, like Mickey Mantle and Willie Mays (both .557 slugging) and Henry Aaron (.555), this is a good but not outstanding average. However, of the 84 players who precede Thompson on that list, only one other, fellow 19th-century slugger Dan Brouthers (.519, 62nd place) had to contend, as Thompson did during his career, with pitches thrown from a distance of 50' or 55'6", and only Thompson and Brouthers had to try to hit a "dead ball" for their entire career.

The outpouring of sympathy in Detroit over Sam Thompson's death in November 1922 soon subsided, and in baseball's new "lively ball" era, the diamond deeds of the greatest run producer in the game's history were quickly forgotten. When questioned about Thompson a week after his death, Babe Ruth, the new home run king, revealed that he had never heard of the Danville slugger.[10] In the last years of his life, Thompson himself joined in the general public's obsession with the new long-ball hitters, and in doing so, he ironically contributed to blurring the memory of his own slugging accomplishments in the minds of the game's fans.

Soon after Sam's death, sportswriter Al Spink published a story recounting the visit of former Western League catcher John Cavanaugh to Detroit. Cavanaugh, a fire chief from Chicago, had made the trip to the City of Straits to meet his old friend Charley Bennett and to measure the distance of a home run hit by Babe Ruth at Navin Field (formerly Bennett Field) the previous season. After reuniting with Bennett, Cavanaugh explained to him the purpose of his visit.

> I've come to see all that's left of the Big Four team … and to get their opinions as to who was the greatest batsman. I've heard that Ruth hit the ball harder and farther than any of the Big Four hit. I understand that Ruth made one hit on the Detroit grounds last summer that has never been beaten, and I'm

going to measure it tomorrow, and then I want you to tell me whether it was ever beaten by Dan Brouthers, Sam Thompson, or any of the other great sluggers on your old Big Four team.[11]

Early the next morning, Cavanaugh and Bennett called on Sam Thompson, and together the three old timers went to measure Babe Ruth's hit.

"Is the Babe a greater hitter than you were in your prime?" John asked Sam.
"Yes" was the prompt reply.
"A greater hitter than Brouthers?"
"Yes."
"A greater hitter than Buck Ewing or Roger Connor or any of our old gang?"
"Yes, greater than the best of them."[12]

Then Cavanaugh, tape measure in hand, "went out on the Detroit grounds to be shown. They crossed the long outer garden (outfield grass) to the right field fence, and then Big Sam said, 'No, the ball didn't stop here. It sailed high way over the fence and then over the brick house you see way off yonder.'"[13] Cavanaugh then went outside the grounds and "kept on measuring until he got to the brick house, and then he continued measuring even beyond there, and when he got to the spot where the ball had landed, he discovered that he had tolled off 656 feet. And then the three veterans admitted that this beat all long-hitting records, past and present."[14]

In 1936, four decades after Sam Thompson's last full major league season, the Baseball Hall of Fame was established at Cooperstown, New York, and its inaugural class of inductees, consisting of Babe Ruth, Ty Cobb, Honus Wagner, Walter Johnson and Christy Mathewson, was announced. Of this distinguished quintet, only Wagner had begun his career in the 19th century—its last three years. His remaining seventeen seasons were played in the 1900s. Two 19th century baseball men, George Wright and Connie Mack, were selected in 1937, although not for their playing careers, but for their managing and executive contributions to the game.

The first 19th century players to be inducted for their work on the field were named in 1939. First baseman Cap Anson, pitcher Candy Cummings (the putative inventor of the curve ball), catcher Buck Ewing and pitcher Hoss Radbourn earned the honor, and longtime Chicago

White Stockings owner Al Spalding also received the nod for his contributions as an administrator. No selections were made during World War II, but in 1945, seven pre–1900 players were named, including Dan Brouthers and Mike Kelly. However, voting records from Veterans Committee reveal that from the Hall of Fame's inception through 1945, Sam Thompson not only had not been selected in the balloting— he had not received even one vote.

Only three more 19th-century players gained admission to the Hall of Fame between 1946 and 1953, with Sam Thompson once again not considered in the balloting. In the aftermath of the 1953 election, Major League Baseball Commissioner and native Hoosier Ford Frick suggested a new plan for election to the Hall of Fame that would have resulted in the immediate selection of Sam Thompson for the honor. For Frick, "if a player hits .400 for a season, he should become a Hall of Famer at once. If a pitcher throws a perfect game, he should receive a similar recognition. No balloting necessary in either case."[15]

The *Indianapolis Times'* report of the proposal noted that "if Frick wins his point, the name of a second Hoosier will be inscribed in the Cooperstown shrine…. The name of the late Mordecai (Three Finger) Brown is already there…. But down through the years the batting record of Big Sam Thompson (born in Danville, Ind.) has been overlooked … Thompson starred before the turn of the century…. He wrecked the fences with his bat and is down in history as one of baseball's greatest sluggers."[16]

Frick's plan would also have resulted in the immediate selection of 17 men who had previously hit .400, including Ted Williams, who hit .406 for Boston in 1941, and who was still an active player. The idea gained no support, either from other Hall of Fame executives, the Baseball Writers' Association, or the Veterans Committee.

It took eight more years (until 1961), before another 19th-century player, Billy Hamilton, gained admission to the Hall of Fame, and once again, Sam Thompson received no consideration on the ballot. At this point, Indianapolis sportswriter Dick Mittman took up Sam's cause in a long article[17] that carefully outlined Sam's accomplishments, making reference to a similar argument made in 1925 by the distinguished sportswriter John B. Foster.

Mittman then put forward a theory to try to explain Thompson's failure to gain any attention or support from the Veterans Committee. "Sam Thompson was born 35 years too soon. That's why sluggers like Mickey Mantle and Frank Howard are shooting at Babe Ruth's home run record instead of Sam's. Sam was the premier long-ball clouter of baseball from 1885 to 1896, yet his talents at losing a baseball actually were derided by the game's proponents of that era. That's why Sam isn't in baseball's Hall of Fame today."[18]

To support his case, Mittman cited the 1896 *Spalding Baseball Guide*, which criticized Thompson because he belonged to "the rutty class of slugging batsmen, who think of nothing else when they go to the bat but that of gaining the applause of the "'groundlings' [fans] by the ... hit to the outfield for a 'homer,' one of the least difficult hits known to batting in baseball, as it needs only muscle and not brains to make it."[19]

Concluding his defense of Thompson, Mittman observed, "That was Big Sam's fate ... to be a slugger in the day of the single and sacrifice. Still he held the career homer record until The Babe came along and certainly deserves a spot in the Hall of Fame."[20] Mittman was not alone in his erroneous claim that Sam held the home record before Ruth, since it was not until the 1970s that investigators confirmed that Roger Connor was the true 19th century home run king, with Sam taking second place.

Mittman's impassioned plea met with deaf ears at Cooperstown, where between 1963 and 1973 the Veterans Committee selected five more 19th century players (pitchers John Clarkson, Tim Keefe, Jim Galvin and Mickey Welch, outfielder Willie Keeler, and multi-position player John Ward). In the balloting during these years, Sam Thompson once again did not receive a vote.

By the early 1970s however, someone was diligently working behind the scenes to promote Sam's cause. He was Victor B. Meyer, a chemical engineer and a decidedly feisty amateur baseball historian from Berkely Heights, New Jersey, who began his campaign in March 1970 by sending Charles Segar, then secretary-treasurer of Major League Baseball, an elaborate lifetime performance chart comparing Thompson's record to that of all other 19th-century players already inducted into the Hall of Fame.[21] Meyer's painstaking research, which was completed in the pre-internet era, remains today an impressive and comprehensive compilation.

Just prior to the 1971 Hall of Fame vote, Meyer revised and updated his performance charts to include a section comparing the number of Sam Thompson's individual league batting, running and fielding titles with those of his contemporaries who previously had been elected to the Hall of Fame. The data revealed that of the 18 players studied, Sam Thompson, the only player mentioned who was not yet a Hall of Famer, ranked extremely high in achieving league titles. In Meyer's words,

> If anything, the revised material makes his [Thompson's] claim even more compelling, if that is possible ... only three of the nineteen players [studied] ranked among the top third in every one of the ten categories [batting average, hits, doubles, triples home runs, etc.]: Brouthers, Delehanty, and Sam Thompson; and that in the most significant category of all, the production of runs—which is what offense in baseball is all about—Thompson stands alone at the very top.[22]

Meyer's final comments deal with Thompson's great defensive work in right field. They are noteworthy, since in previous expressions of support for his candidacy, his fielding and throwing had been completely overlooked. "Finally, his superb fielding, both on the statistics and according to eyewitness newspaper reports, can only enforce the conviction that this man was one of the very greatest outfielders that ever lived."[23]

In closing, Meyer declared that Thompson's "continued exclusion" from the Hall of Fame a was "historical omission of the first magnitude,"[24] stating that "with this material at hand, I cannot believe the Committee would permit any further delay in Sam Thompson's election to the Hall of Fame."[25]

Three months later, after the Veterans Committee had selected six players, all but one of whom, Joe Kelley, were from the post–1900 era, Meyer fired off a stinging letter to Hall of Fame president Paul S. Kerr in which he asserted that "it is no longer possible to claim that 'Big Sam' has been merely overlooked. His impressive credentials have been amply set forth *and made available* to the Veterans Committee by this writer, if not by others."[26] Meyer then suggested that Secretary-Treasurer Charles Seger had not made available to the Veterans Committee the copious documentation that he had supplied him. "I ... assumed that all members had indeed received them. It would seem that they did not, for it is hard to believe that with this information at hand they could, in all good conscience, have perpetuated the grave injustice to the memory of this great player."[27]

In a final plea, Meyer then recommended that an unusual step be taken to rectify the situation: "There is *still time to finally do the right thing*—though the inexplicable and inexcusable delay over thirty-five years in giving Sam Thompson his due can never be fully amended. Your own Committee rules do empower you to hold a *special election*, by mail if necessary. I sincerely urge you to do so."[28]

No special election followed, and, truth be told, the sincere but belligerent attitude expressed by Meyer in his communications with Major League and Hall of Fame representatives may have harmed, and not helped, his cause. His luck began to change, however, when he met Clifford Kachline, a writer for the *Sporting News* for more than two decades who assumed the role of Historian of the Baseball Hall of Fame on the death of Lee Allen in 1969, and who also was a founding member of the Society for American Baseball Research (1971). Unlike Charles Seger and Paul Kerr, the Major League Baseball and Hall of Fame representatives with whom Meyer had dealt with in the past, Kachline "was a stickler for the exactness of baseball records, and he doggedly worked to get records corrected."[29] Here finally, was a person who could appreciate Meyer's meticulous research on Sam Thompson, and over the next few years the New Jersey expert on Big Sam diligently supplied Kachline with every scrap of information, both biographical and statistical, that his research had uncovered.

In the meantime, the Veterans Committee had selected four more players, two in 1972 and two in 1973, only one of whom, Giants pitcher Mickey Welch, was from the pre–1900 era. Meyer, however had picked up another ally, *St. Louis Post-Dispatch* sportswriter Bob Broeg, in his quest to enshrine Thompson in the Hall of Fame. Broeg covered the Cardinals for forty years, and is credited with having invented Stan Musial's famous nickname, "the Man," as in "Stan the Man." More significantly for Meyer, however, was the fact that in 1972, Broeg was named to the Board of Directors of the Hall of Fame, and in September 1973, he published a column entitled "Sam Thompson—Forgotten Slugger"[30] that perhaps did more to further Thompson's cause than all the efforts that preceded it.

Broeg called Thompson "the slugger who was born too soon,"[31] echoing an idea expressed decades earlier by Mittman. He cited Victor Meyer's efforts on Big Sam's behalf, made reference to Charley Bennett's comments from his Thompson eulogy, and for good measure even included Dan O'Leary's tall tale about discovering Sam while he was repairing a roof in Danville.

Broeg closed his essay with a prescient observation: "When Thompson died at the age of 62, a baseball sentimentalist offered to buy his home-run bat. His widow refused to sell. Mrs. Thompson must have figured with feminine intuition that someday baseball would look more kindly on the early-day Babe Ruth who had used his brawn rather than brains to hit home runs instead of bunt singles."[32]

It did not take long for the Hall of Fame, in Broeg's words, to "look more kindly" on Thompson. On January 28, 1974, 78 years after his last full major league season, the Veterans committee named Samuel Luther Thompson to the Baseball Hall of Fame. He was joined by old-timers Jim Bottomly, first baseman for the St. Louis Cardinals, and umpire Jocko Conlan. The 1974 Negro League Committee selected Cool Papa Bell for induction, and the Baseball Writers chose Yankee greats Mickey Mantle and Whitey Ford.

In a follow-up column on the 1974 selection process, Bob Broeg revealed that the Veterans' Committee that had selected Big Sam had this time been provided with virtually all the information that Victor Meyer, Dick Mittman, and he himself had reviewed about Thompson. Of particular interest was the inclusion of the previously-mentioned reference to the 1896 *Spalding Baseball Guide*, which described the home run as "one of the least difficult hits known to batting in baseball": "When that paragraph was read to them, you should have seen the amused faces on the Hall of Fame's Veterans' Committee, men of the caliber of Bill Terry, Charley Gehringer, Joe Cronin, Waite Hoyt and Stan Musial. In light of present standards, it is laughable to think that a man [Thompson] could be penalized for using his brawn to hit homers rather than his brains to lay down bunt singles."[33]

Thanks to Broeg and Vincent Meyer, the Committee had also been supplied with a copy of Charley Bennett's eulogy for Sam, which, as discussed in Chapter Five, praised him as much for his defense as well as his offense.

> The Veterans' Committee seeks to avoid relying only on cold statistics, aware that figures do indeed lie at times or, at least, mislead, particularly when defense is called. And the truth is that even though the so-called Old Timers committee

does have some members well into their 80's, not even they are old enough to have first-hand knowledge of some ancient candidates for the Hall of Fame. So it is significant that when Sam Thompson died in 1922 ... former catcher Charley Bennett hailed him as much for his fielding as for his hitting.[34]

Although the Committee may have been aware of Sam's defensive prowess, newspaper accounts of Thompson's selection never mentioned it, and Baseball Commissioner Bowie Kuhn's remarks at the Induction Ceremony in Cooperstown followed suit.

> We now come to the dedication of the new plaques which will be placed in the Hall of Fame in 1974. I will simply read to you the words as they appear on these plaques, because the words tell more than anything I could add of the greatness of these men as baseball players.
> **Samuel Luther Thompson**, Detroit National League, Philadelphia National League, 1885–1898; Detroit American League, 1906. One of the foremost sluggers of his day. Lifetime batting average of .336 [actually, .331]. He batted better than .400 twice. A great clutch hitter[,] he collected 200 or more hits in a season three times. He topped the National League in home runs and runs batted in twice. Surely he was one of the greatest hitters in the history of our national game.[35]

Over the course of the twenty-year campaign to have Sam Thompson considered for election to the Hall of Fame, two claims about aspects of his play were made that require further clarification. The first, by sportswriters Mittman and Broeg, was that Big Sam invented the "bounce" or "one-hop" throw from the outfield to a base or to home plate.

A review of accounts of every game that Sam played during his career failed to produce any verification for this claim. The subsequent realization, however, that all or most of Thompson's outfield throws, regardless of their distance, arrived at their destination in the air and not after a bounce on the ground, is yet another indication of his strong and accurate throwing arm.

According to Thompson family tradition, that famous throwing arm may have been Sam's right one, and not his left. Nephew Lawrence Thompson recalled that when the great slugger would return to hunt and fish in the woods and streams near his native Danville, he handled his gun and rod as a right-hander would.

Although this study has cited descriptions of two incidents from Sam's career that might suggest that he may have thrown right-handed, Charley Bennett's previously-mentioned specific recollection of Thompson catching a ball with his right hand corroborates the accepted notion that Thompson threw left handed.

In his landmark study *The New Bill James Historical Baseball Abstract*[36] renowned baseball statistician Bill James ranks the 100 best players all-time at each position. He arrives at his conclusions by combining data gleaned from a complex statistical analysis (James' "Win Shares") and a series of subjective variables.[37]

In James' ranking system, Sam Thompson, a lifetime .331 hitter who has the highest assist-per-game ratio of any outfielder who played over 1,000 games, and the highest fielding average of any 19th century major league outfielder who played over 1,000 games, ranks just 37th all time among right fielders. While James' rating system is widely accepted today as a valued approach to rating players, some of the data he provides that affects his ranking of Sam Thompson requires review.

In establishing the framework for his study, James logically distinguishes between all outfielders by dividing them into three obvious categories—right fielders, center fielders and left fielders. Clearly then, James feels, as every manager does, that there are special aspects to playing each outfield position that require special skills.

Sam Thompson spent 1409 of his 1410 major league games in right field (he played first base in the other contest). In contrast, many players with whom he is compared in James' system, including many who are ranked higher as right fielders, played the position much less frequently over the course of their careers. In the information James provides for each player, however, this discrepancy is not noted. Instead, each player's total number of games *played*, not his total number of games *played in right field* is listed. When such a discrepancy is taken into consideration, obvious issues arise.

New York Yankee Bobby Murcer, for example, ranks 17th among right fielders on James' list. James lists Murcer's total number of games played (1908), but does not clarify that of this total, only 844 games (44.2 percent) were spent in right field. According to James, former Dodger, Reggie Smith ranks 20th among right fielders. However, Smith spent only 879 of his total of 1,987 games in right field (again, as in Murcer's case, 44.2 percent of his total games) José Canseco, who ranks 36th for James, one slot ahead of Sam Thompson, played just 47.5 percent (1011) of his total of 2124 games in right field.

Among the most egregious disparities between Thompson's playing history and right fielders who outrank him in James' system are the cases of Sam Crawford (ranked 20th) and Pedro Guerrero (ranked 25th). Over 15 seasons, Guerrero played less than half the time in the outfield, and spent only 21.5 percent of his games (240 games) in right field. In 2517 games, Hall of Famer Sam Crawford is known to have played just 395 times in right field (15.6 percent). By way of comparison, in 99.9 percent of Sam Thompson's major league games (1409 of 1410), he played right field. Such examples suggest the obvious: statistical comparison and ranking of players by position can only be meaningful if the players in question are indeed playing the same position.

Bill James also provides a narrative about each player who figures in his rankings. In this area, some clarification must likewise be made with regard to his comments on Sam Thompson. James states that Thompson ranks first in RBI per game among 10 outfielders whom he provides for comparison and contrast. While James is correct in this assertion, he fails to note the more important fact—that Thompson not only ranks first among these ten outfielders, but ranks first in RBI per game among *all* players who have ever played the game.

Additionally, in his only mention of Thompson's defense, James perpetuates an inaccurate impression of his ability by quoting an anonymous writer for the 1923 *Reach Guide*, who stated that "Sam was not such a fine outfielder."[38] In contrast, the results of this study, based on a review of every game Thompson ever played, demonstrate the opposite to be true. In the words of Victor B. Meyer, "this man was one of the very greatest outfielders that ever lived."[39]

In the four decades that have transpired since Sam Thompson's election to the Hall of Fame, his extended family, his native state and his home town have worked hard to keep his name and accomplishments alive. In 1979, Thompson was among a distinguished group of Hoosier major leaguers inducted into the first class of the Indiana Baseball Hall of Fame. Fellow inductees that year included Sam's contemporary, Giants pitcher Amos Rusie, whose nickname, "The Hoosier Thunderbolt," celebrated his Indiana heritage, as well as later-era players like Sam Rice, Gil Hodges and Carl Erskine.[40]

In June 1998, a family reunion in Danville for the descendants of Sam's parents, Jesse and Rebecca Thompson, culminated in a town cel-

Sam Thompson's grave, Elmwood Cemetery, Detroit. The small, original grave marker is in the foreground. In 2000, Thompson family members erected the large granite stone that commemorates Sam's career (courtesy Nathan Thompson).

ebration of Sam Thompson Day, during which a proclamation was read honoring the Danville slugger, a plaque laid near the local ball field, and the field itself dedicated in Thompson's name. Each year since, Danville High School presents the Sam Thompson Award to the local ball player who best emulates Sam's good sportsmanship on the field.

When Sam was buried in 1922, a simple marker containing his name and the year of his birth and death was erected at his grave. In 2000, members of the Thompson family met in Detroit to dedicate a large granite memorial at the grave that summarized Sam's achievements on the diamond and noted his Hall of Fame status. The monument also features a large likeness of a wolverine, the logo of Sam's first major league team. In 2006, through the efforts of the Thompson and the McPheeters families, an Indiana State Historical Marker dedicated to Sam was placed by the roadside on Main Street in Danville.

While there is unanimous consensus among baseball historians that Sam Thompson was one of the greatest hitters in the history of the game, his equally impressive skill as an outfielder who possessed a strong, accurate and reliable throwing arm continues to be overlooked. Three recent articles on the Danville slugger illustrate this point well.

The first, published in 1998, highlights both Sam's offensive and defensive skills.[41] A second, published in 2007, mentions Sam's fielding only in passing, and suggests that his high assist numbers were due to the short right field wall at the Huntingdon Street Grounds in Philadelphia.[42] This observation overlooks the fact that while playing right field in Detroit's spacious Recreation Park in his first three major league seasons, Thompson averaged almost 26 assists per year. A third essay, published in 2011, makes no mention at all of either Thompson's outstanding fielding or of his assist records.[43]

Despite the persistent modern notion that Big Sam Thompson's greatness lies only in his hitting ability, his contemporaries recognized him for who he was— an enormously talented "five skills" player who could hit both for power and average, steal a base, make spectacular outfield catches, and routinely throw out runners attempting to advance to any base on the diamond. Few from his generation would fail to concur with veteran player and sportswriter Tim Murnane's observation that "I never knew the equal of this man Thompson as a great fielding, hard hitting right fielder."[44]

Highlights of Sam Thompson's Career

(11 full and 3 partial seasons)
1410 Games, 5967 at-bats, 1259 runs, 1981 hits,
343 doubles, 160 triples, 126 home runs,
1305 RBI, 232 stolen bases

Offense

LEAGUE LEADER

Batting Average: .372, 1887
Slugging: .565, 1887; .696, 1894; .654, 1895
Hits: 203, 1887; 172, 1890; 222, 1893
Total Bases: 308, 1887; 352, 1895
Doubles: 41, 1890; 37, 1893
Triples: 23, 1887
Home Runs: 20, 1889; 18, 1895
RBI: 166, 1887; 147, 1894; 165, 1895
Extra-base Hits: 84, 1895
  - *Nine .300-plus seasons*
  - *One .400-plus season (.415 in 1894)*
  - *Eight 100-plus RBI seasons*
  - *Ten 100-plus Run seasons*
  - *Three 200-plus hit seasons*
  - *25 stolen bases per year average, 1889–1895*

TEAM LEADER

Hits: 1887, 1890, 1892, 1893, 1895

Runs: 1893
Doubles: 1890, 1893
Triples: 1887, 1891, 1894, 1895
Home Runs: 1891, 1895
RBI: 1885, 1887, 1890, 1891, 1892, 1894, 1895
Slugging: 1885, 1894, 1895

Defense

LEAGUE LEADER

Fielding: .972, 1894; .974, 1896
Assists: 32, 1891; 28, 1896
Double-Plays: 11, 1886; 11, 1896
  • *Six 20-plus outfield assist seasons*
  • *Two 30-plus outfield assist seasons*
  • *65 outfield double plays*

All Time Records

Highest RBI per game ratio (.923) in history
First player with 200 hits in a season (203) (1887) [127 games]
First player with 150-plus RBI (168) in a season (1887) [127 games]
Only player to hit consecutive bases-loaded triples in a game
First (of three players all time) with at least three hits in six successive games
Highest assist-per-game ratio (1 every 4.9 games) of any outfielder (1,000-plus games)
Highest fielding average (.934) among outfielders who completed their careers in the 19th century (1,000-plus games).
First player (of four all time) to record three outfielder-to-catcher assists in a game

Chapter Notes

Chapter One

1. *Indiana State Business Directory*, 1881–1882, 2.

2. *Paris Gazette*, quoted in the *Hendricks County Republican*, July 15, 1886.

3. *Hendricks County Republican*, April 30, 1925.

4. Ibid.

5. Ibid.

6. Ibid.

7. Ibid.

8. Ibid.

9. Ibid.

10. Ibid.

11. *Hendricks County Union*, April 3, 1873.

12. U.S. Census, Hendricks County, Indiana, June 11, 1880.

13. *Hendricks County Republican*, December 15, 1881.

14. Don Thompson, "Sam Thompson," sabr.org.bioproj/person/be0fab8.

15. *Indianapolis Journal*, May 13, 1837, quoted in James H. Madison's *The Indiana Way: A State History* (Bloomington: Indiana University Press, 1990), 104.

16. *Des Moines News*, January 5, 1913.

17. *Hartford Courant*, February 3, 1923.

18. *Indianapolis Journal*, May 28, 1885.

19. I express my deep appreciation to Steve DeHoff for providing me access to his research on Danville, Indiana, baseball and Sam Thompson's career.

20. *Hendricks County Republican*, July 12, 1883.

21. *Hendricks County Republican*, February 8, 1906.

22. *Hendricks County Republican*, July 5, 1883.

23. *Sporting Life*, April 8, 1893.

24. *Friday Caller* (Plainfield, Indiana), August 23, 1912.

25. Ibid.

26. Ibid.

27. Ibid.

28. Ibid.

29. Ibid.

30. Ibid.

31. Ibid.

32. *Hendricks County Republican*, July 26, 1883.

33. *Hendricks County Republican*, August 30, 1883.

34. *Indianapolis Times*, September 22, 1883.

35. *Evansville Daily Journal*, February 29, 1884.

36. David Nemec, *Major League Baseball Profiles, 1871–1900*, Vol. II (Lincoln: University of Nebraska Press, 2011), 362.

37. Paul Browne, "Dan O'Leary," sabr.org/bioproj/person/22dc582f.

38. *Sporting Life*, March 13, 1897.

39. *Indianapolis Sun*, July 5, 1897.

40. *Chicago Tribune*, December 10, 1905.

41. Ibid.

42. Ibid.

43. Ibid.

44. *Salt Lake Herald*, March 13, 1907.

45. *Washington Post*, December 25, 1910.

46. *Indianapolis Sun*, March 10, 1913.

47. *Washington Times*, January 23, 1922.

48. Norman Macht, "Samuel Luther Thompson," in *Baseball's First Stars*, Frederick Ivor-Campbell, Robert L. Tiemann and Mark Rucker, eds. (Cleveland: SABR, 1986), 165.

49. David L. Fleitz, *More Ghosts in the*

Gallery (Jefferson, NC: McFarland, 2007), 154.

50. *Lowell Sun*, October 2, 1948.

51. *Hendricks County Republican*, December 15, 1881.

52. *Evening Times* (Cumberland, Maryland), March 25, 1911.

53. *Ogden Standard*, March 30, 1918.

54. *The Bee* (Danville, Virginia), January 1, 1925.

55. Nemec, *Major League Baseball Profiles*, Vol. II, 66.

56. *Sporting Life*, March 13, 1887.

57. *El Paso Herald*, November 3, 1913.

58. *Sporting Life*, July 6, 1895.

59. *Kansas City Star*, February 26, 1927.

60. *The Sporting News*, July 14, 1907.

61. *The Sporting News*, July 16, 1899.

62. *Sporting Life*, September 12, 1896.

63. *Sporting Life*, July 8, 1895.

64. *The Decatur Review*, July 16, 1899.

65. *Sporting Life*, July 5, 1898.

66. Jeffrey Graf, "The Term *Hoosier*," www.indian.edu/~librcsd/internet/extra/**hoosier**.html.

67. Ibid.

68. Ibid.

69. *The Sporting News*, May 24, 1886.

70. *Washington Post*, December 25, 1910.

71. *Indianapolis Sun*, July 6, 1895,

72. *The Sporting News*, August 10, 1895.

73. David Quentin Voigt, *American Baseball*, Vol.1 (State College: Pennsylvania State University Press, 1992) 73–74.

74. *Evansville Daily Journal*, May 1, 1884.

75. *Louisville Courier Journal*, April 6, 1884.

76. Ibid.

77. *Evansville Daily Journal*, April 7, 1884.

78. *Sporting Life*, April 8, 1893.

79. *Evansville Daily Journal*, August 18, 1884.

80. Ibid.

81. *Evansville Daily Journal*, August 19, 1884.

82. Ibid.

83. *Evansville Daily Journal*, September 15, 1884.

84. *Evansville Daily Journal*, April 16, 1884.

85. *Evansville Daily Journal*, April 20, 1884.

86. *Evansville Daily Journal*, April 26, 1884.

87. *Evansville Daily Journal*, August 4, 1884.

88. *Evansville Daily Journal*, June 23, 1884.

89. *Evansville Daily Journal*, June 30, 1884.

90. *Evansville Daily Journal*, July 8, 1884.

91. Peter Morris, *Catcher* (Chicago: Ivan R. Dee, 2009), 205.

92. Nemec, *Major League Baseball Profiles*, Vol. II, 257.

93. *Evansville Daily Journal*, August 17, 1884.

94. *Evansville Argus*, quoted in the *Hendricks County Republican*, September 4, 1884.

95. *Sporting Life*, April 15, 1885.

96. *Indianapolis Daily Journal*, April 7, 1885.

97. *Indianapolis Daily Journal*, April 12, 1885.

98. *Indianapolis Daily Journal*, April 14, 1885.

99. *Indianapolis Daily Journal*, April 23, 1885.

100. *Sporting Life*, April 14, 1885.

101. *Indianapolis Daily Journal*, April 28, 1885.

102. *Indianapolis Daily Journal*, April 29, 1885.

103. *Indianapolis Daily Journal*, May 29, 1885.

104. *Indianapolis Daily Journal*, June 4, 1885.

105. *Indianapolis Daily Journal*, June 6, 1885.

106. Ibid.

107. *Indianapolis Daily Journal*, June 12, 1885.

108. Ibid.

109. *Indianapolis Daily Journal*, June 6, 1885.

110. *Indianapolis Daily Journal*, June 15, 1885.

Chapter Two

1. Peter Morris, et al., eds., *Base Ball Pioneers:1850–1870* (Jefferson, NC: McFarland, 2012) 169.
2. John William Leonard, *The Industries of Detroit* (Detroit: J.M. Elstner, 1887), 150.
3. *Successful Men of Michigan* (Detroit: SI. U. Collins, 1914), 6.
4. George W. Stark, "Detroit's Veteran Magnate Tells How He Kidnapped Ball Players," un-sourced newspaper article, no date, Don Thompson's Sam Thompson clipping file.
5. *Indianapolis Sunday Star*, June 16, 1929.
6. *Detroit Free Press*, July 3, 1885.
7. Ibid.
8. Bill Carle, "Eugene Moriarty Found," *SABR Biographic Research Committee Report* November/December 2013.
9. Don Thompson, "Sam Thompson," sabr.org.bioproj/person/be0fab8; and Richard Bak, *A Place for Summer: A Narrative History of Tiger Stadium I* (Detroit: Wayne State University Press, 1998), 33.
10. Sam Thompson player file, National Baseball Hall of Fame Library, Cooperstown, NY.
11. Stark, in Don Thompson's Sam Thompson clipping file.
12. *Detroit Free Press*, July 5, 1885.
13. *Detroit Free Press*, July 13, 1885.
14. *Detroit Free Press*, August 19, 1885.
15. *Detroit Evening News*, October 20, 1885.
16. *Detroit Free Press*, September 30, 1885.
17. *Detroit Free Press*, October 1, 1885.
18. *Sporting Life*, November 11, 1885.
19. *Sporting Life*, October 14, 1885.
20. *Detroit Free Press*, September 19, 1885.
21. Stark, in Don Thompson's Sam Thompson clipping file.
22. *Detroit Free Press*, September 22, 1885.
23. *Sporting Life*, September 23, 1885.
24. Roy Kerr, *Big Dan Brouthers* (Jefferson, NC: McFarland, 2013), 45–46.
25. Stark, in Don Thompson's Sam Thompson clipping file.
26. Nemec, *Major League Baseball Profiles*, Vol. II, 149.
27. David Nemec, *Major League Baseball Profiles*, Vol. I, (Lincoln: University of Nebraska Press, 2011), 9.
28. *Detroit Free Press*, April 30, 1886.
29. *Sporting Life*, May 12, 1886.
30. *Detroit Free Press*, June 15, 1886.
31. *Detroit Free Press*, June 30, 1886.
32. Nemec, *Major League Baseball Profiles*, Vol. 1, 237.
33. Ibid.
34. *Detroit Free Press*, July 18, 1886.
35. *Detroit Free Press*, July 2, 1886.
36. Ibid.
37. *Detroit Morning Times*, July 2, 1886.
38. *Detroit Free Press*, July 2, 1886.
39. *Detroit Free Press*, July 4, 1886.
40. *Detroit Free Press*, July 23, 1886.
41. *Detroit Morning Times*, July 10, 1886.
42. *Detroit Free Press*, July 18, 1886.
43. *Detroit Morning Times*, July 19, 1886.
44. *Detroit Free Press*, August 6, 1886.
45. *Boston Herald*, cited in the *Detroit Free Press*, August 8, 1886.
46. *Detroit Free Press*, August 13, 1886.
47. *Detroit Free Press*, August 15, 1886.
48. *Detroit Morning Times*, August 25, 1886.
49. *Detroit Free Press*, August 21, 1886.
50. *Detroit Free Press*, August 26, 1886.
51. Ibid.
52. *Detroit Free Press*, September 3, 1886.
53. Ibid.
54. Ibid.
55. *Detroit Free Press*, September 18, 1886.
56. *Detroit Free Press*, September 23, 1886.
57. *Detroit Free Press*, September 9, 1886.
58. *Detroit Free Press*, September 4, 1886.
59. Nemec, *Major League Baseball Profiles*, Vol. 1, 621.
60. *National Republican*, January 2, 1887.
61. *Sporting Life*, November 23, 1887.
62. *Detroit Free Press*, April 22, 1887.
63. *Detroit Free Press*, April 27, 1887.
64. *Detroit Free Press*, April 29, 1887.

65. Ibid.
66. *Detroit Free Press*, May 2, 1887.
67. *Detroit Free Press*, May 7, 1887.
68. *Detroit Free Press*, May 9, 1887.
69. *Sporting Life*, April 7, 1887.
70. *Detroit Free Press*, May 21, 1887.
71. Ibid.
72. *Detroit Free Press*, June 1, 1887.
73. Ibid.
74. Quoted in the *Detroit Free Press*, July 1, 1887.
75. *Detroit Free Press*, June 11, 1887.
76. *Detroit Free Press*, July 2, 1887.
77. *Detroit Free Press*, July 16, 1887.
78. *Detroit Free Press*, July 23, 1887.
79. *Detroit Free Press*, July 16, 1887.
80. *Sporting News*, July 23, 1887.
81. *Detroit Free Press*, July 20, 1887.
82. *Detroit Free Press*, July 21, 1887.
83. *Detroit Free Press*, July 26, 1887.
84. *Detroit Free Press*, July 28, 1887.
85. *Detroit Free Press*, August 2, 1887.
86. *Detroit Free Press*, August 17, 1887.
87. *Sporting News*, August 13, 1887.
88. *Detroit Free Press*, September 4, 1887.
89. *Detroit Free Press*, September 17, 1887.
90. *Detroit Free Press*, August 31, 1887.
91. *Detroit Free Press*, September 6, 1887.
92. Ibid.
93. *Detroit Free Press*, September 29, 1887.
94. *Detroit Free Press*, September 13, 1887.
95. Ibid.
96. *Detroit Free Press*, September 24, 1887.
97. *Detroit Free Press*, September 12, 1887.
98. *Boston Globe*, October 17, 1887.
99. Roy Kerr, *Buck Ewing: A Baseball Biography* (Jefferson, NC: McFarland, 2012), 93.
100. Dean A. Sullivan, ed., *Early Innings: A Documentary History of Baseball* (Lincoln: University of Nebraska Press, 1995), 39.
101. Ibid., 196.
102. *Detroit Free Press*, October 18, 1887.
103. *Detroit Free Press*, October 19, 1887.
104. Ibid.
105. Ibid.
106. *Detroit Free Press*, October 20, 1887.
107. *Detroit Free Press*, October 22, 1887.
108. Ibid.
109. *Detroit Free Press*, October 25, 1887.
110. *Detroit Morning Times*, December 30, 1887.
111. *Detroit Free Press*, April 21, 1888.
112. Ibid.
113. *Detroit Free Press*, April 1, 1888.
114. *Detroit Free Press*, April 2, 188.
115. *Detroit Morning Times*, March 30, 1887.
116. *Detroit Morning Times*, April 2, 1888.
117. *Sporting Life*, April 11, 1888.
118. *Detroit Free Press*, April 8, 1888.
119. Ibid.
120. *Detroit Free Press*, April 22, 1888.
121. *Detroit Morning Times*, May 5, 1888.
122. *Detroit Free Press*, July 7, 1888.
123. *Sporting News*, August 18, 1888.
124. *Sporting Life*, August 29, 1888.
125. *Sporting News*, June 2, 1888.
126. *Detroit Free Press*, June 29, 1888.
127. *Sporting News*, June 2, 1888.
128. *Detroit Free Press*, October 14, 1888.
129. Sam Thompson, letter to his parents, October 23, 1888, Keith Thompson's Sam Thompson clipping file.
130. *Detroit Free Press*, October 26, 1888.
131. *Sporting Life*, November 21, 1888.

Chapter Three

1. *Sporting Life*, December 31, 1885, cited in Block, *Baseball Before We Knew It* (Lincoln: University of Nebraska Press, 2005), 158.
2. John Shiffert, *Baseball in Philadelphia* (Jefferson, NC: McFarland, 2006), 114–15.
3. Harold Seymour, *Baseball: The Early Years* (New York: Oxford University Press, 1960), 269.
4. *Sporting Life*, September 12, 1888.

5. *Sporting Life*, March 5, 1892.
6. Ibid.
7. *Sporting Life*, January 23, 1889.
8. *Philadelphia Inquirer*, March 23, 1889.
9. *Sporting Life*, March 27, 1889.
10. *Philadelphia Record*, April 7, 1889.
11. *Philadelphia Inquirer*, April 8, 1889.
12. *Philadelphia Record*, April 1, 1889.
13. *Philadelphia Inquirer*, April 13, 1889.
14. *Philadelphia Press*, April 10, 1889.
15. *Sporting Life*, September 9, 1886.
16. *Philadelphia Press*, April 30, 1889.
17. *Philadelphia Inquirer*, May 6, 1889.
18. Shiffert, 121.
19. *City of Philadelphia Plat Book, Part of Ward 19, 18 & 37*, 1922, Bill Jenkinson's Sam Thompson player file.
20. *Philadelphia Press*, August 14, 1889.
21. *Philadelphia Press*, September 7, 1889.
22. *Philadelphia Record*, May 31, 1889.
23. *Philadelphia Press*, August 29, 1889.
24. *Philadelphia Inquirer*, August 29, 1889.
25. *New York Times*, August 29, 1889.
26. *Philadelphia Press*, May 17, 1889.
27. *Philadelphia Record*, July 30, 1889.
28. Ibid.
29. Quoted in the *Philadelphia Press*, August 3, 1889.
30. *Philadelphia Press*, June 8, 1889.
31. *Philadelphia Pres*, May 16, 1889.
32. Ibid.
33. Ibid.
34. *Philadelphia Press*, May 19, 1889.
35. *Philadelphia Press*, July 5, 1889.
36. *Philadelphia Inquirer*, August 22, 1889.
37. *Philadelphia Record*, September 15, 1889.
38. *Philadelphia Press*, August 20, 1889.
39. *Sporting Life*, July 28, 1889.
40. *Sporting Life*, June 26, 1889.
41. *Philadelphia Record*, May 20, 1889.
42. Tim Keefe, "The Brotherhood and Its Work," originally published in the 1890 *Players' League National Base Ball Guide*, reproduced in *Early Innings*, Benjamin J. Rader, ed., 196.

43. *Philadelphia Inquirer*, November 20, 1889.
44. *Sporting Life*, December 18, 1889.
45. *Philadelphia Inquirer*, December 28, 1889.
46. Ibid.
47. Ibid.
48. *Salem* [Ohio] *Daily News*, December 24, 1889.
49. *Sporting Life*, January 1, 1890.
50. Keefe, 196.
51. Jerrold Casway, *Ed Delehanty and the Emerald Age of Baseball* (Notre Dame: Notre Dame University Press, 2004), 56.
52. *Public Ledger* [Philadelphia], March 25, 1890.
53. Nemec, *Major League Baseball Profiles* Vol. I, 445.
54. *Philadelphia Press*, August 31, 1889.
55. *Philadelphia Press*, June 6, 1890.
56. *Philadelphia Press*, June 7, 1890.
57. *Philadelphia Press*, June 6, 1890.
58. *Philadelphia Press*, June 17, 1890.
59. *Philadelphia Press*, July 8, 1890.
60. Ibid.
61. *Philadelphia Press*, July 18,, 1890.
62. *Philadelphia Press*, September 11, 1890.
63. Shiffert, 158.
64. *Sporting Life*, May 28, 1891.
65. Shiffert, 158.
66. *Philadelphia Item*, February 24, 1890, cited in Casway, *Ed Delehanty*, 51.
67. Casway, *Ed Delehanty*, 66.
68. Ibid., 68.
69. *Philadelphia Inquirer*, April 24, 1891.
70. *Sporting Life*, May 23, 1891.
71. *Philadelphia Inquirer*, June 17, 1891.
72. *Philadelphia Inquirer*, June 30, 1891.
73. *Philadelphia Inquirer*, July 1, 1891.
74. *Philadelphia Inquirer*, May 21, 1891.
75. *Philadelphia Inquirer*, August 14, 1891.
76. *Philadelphia Inquirer*, May 31, 1891.
77. Nemec, *Major League Baseball Profiles*, Vol. II, 109.
78. *Sporting Life*, September 17, 1892
79. Nemec, *Major League Baseball Profiles*, Vol. II, 110–11.
80. Casway, *Ed Delehanty*, 73.

81. Ibid., 74.
82. Shiffert, 163.
83. *Philadelphia Inquirer*, March 21, 1892.
84. *Philadelphia Inquirer*, April 3, 1892.
85. *Sporting Life*, April 28, 1892.
86. *Philadelphia Inquirer*, May 30, 1892.
87. *Philadelphia Inquirer*, June 3, 1892.
88. *Philadelphia Inquirer*, June 4, 1892.
89. *Philadelphia Inquirer*, September 27, 1892.
90. *Sporting Life*, November 5, 1892.

Chapter Four

1. *Sporting Life*, March 18, 1893.
2. *Philadelphia Inquirer*, April 20, 1893.
3. *Philadelphia Inquirer*, August 10, 1893.
4. *Philadelphia Inquirer*, October 2, 1893.
5. *Philadelphia Inquirer*, July 21, 1893.
6. *Philadelphia Inquirer*, August 26, 1893.
7. *Weekly Notes of Cases Argued and Determined in the Supreme Court of Pennsylvania*, Vol. 44 (Philadelphia: Kay and Brother, 1899), 444.
8. *Philadelphia Inquirer*, October 2, 1893.
9. Shiffert, 163.
10. David Nemec, *The Great Encyclopedia of 19th Century Major League Baseball* (New York: Donald Fine, 1997), 496.
11. Frederick G. Lieb and Stan Baumgartner, *The Philadelphia Phillies*, 44, cited in Casway, 83.
12. Christopher Devine, *Harry Wright* (Jefferson, NC: McFarland: 2003), 165.
13. *The Sporting News*, October 12, 1895.
14. *Sporting Life*, October 7, 1893.
15. *Sporting Life*, October 14, 1893.
16. Casway, *Ed Delehanty*, 80.
17. *Sporting Life*, October 23, 1897.
18. Ibid.
19. Ibid.
20. Unsourced, undated newspaper article, Betty Jackson's Sam and Ida Thompson file.
21. *Sporting Life*, June 2, 1894.

22. Nemec, *The Great Encyclopedia of 19th Century Major League Baseball*, 541.
23. *Sporting Life*, January 13, 1894.
24. *Sporting Life*, March 18, 1894.
25. *The Sporting News*, March 24, 1894.
26. *Sporting Life*, March 18, 1894.
27. *Sporting Life*, January 27, 1894.
28. *Philadelphia Inquirer*, April 28, 1894.
29. *Sporting Life*, May 19, 1894.
30. *Sporting Life*, May 26, 1894.
31. Shiffert, 164.
32. *Philadelphia Inquirer*, August 18, 1894.
33. *Philadelphia Inquirer*, August 20, 1894.
34. Ibid.
35. *Philadelphia Inquirer*, September 7, 1894.
36. *Philadelphia Inquirer*, September 1, 1894.
37. *Sporting Life*, July 21, 1894.
38. *Sporting Life*, September 15, 1894.
39. Ibid.
40. *Sporting Life*, October 13, 1894.
41. Nemec, *Major League Baseball Profiles*, Vol. I, 146.
42. *Sporting Life*, April 27, 1895.
43. *Philadelphia Inquirer*, May 4, 1895.
44. *Philadelphia Inquirer*, September 20, 1895.
45. Ibid.
46. *Philadelphia Inquirer*, September 21, 1895.
47. *Philadelphia Inquirer*, June 4, 1895.
48. *Philadelphia Inquirer*, June 15, 1895.
49. *Philadelphia Inquirer*, August 7, 1895.
50. *Brooklyn Eagle*, August 2, 1895.
51. *Philadelphia Inquirer*, August 2, 1895.
52. *Brooklyn Eagle*, August 2, 1895.
53. Ibid.
54. *Philadelphia Inquirer*, August 2, 1895.
55. www.baseball-almanac.com/rb_ofas.shtml.
56. *Sporting Life*, July 13, 1895.
57. *Sporting Life*, June 29, 1895.
58. *Sporting Life*, May 18, 1895.
59. *Sporting Life*, November 16, 1895.
60. *The Sporting News*, October 5, 1895.
61. *Sporting Life*, November 16, 1895.

62. Joseph M. Overfield, "James Joseph Collins," in *Baseball's First Stars*, Frederick Ivor-Campbell et al., eds. (Cleveland: SABR, 1996), 35.

63. Jerrold Casway, "The Best Outfield Ever?" *The Baseball Research Journal*, 27 (1998), 6.

64. Ibid.

65. Ibid., 5.

66. Ibid., 6.

67. Nemec, *Major League Baseball Profiles*, Vol. I., 521.

68. Ibid., 464.

69. Casway, *Ed*, 114.

70. Shiffert, 169.

71. *Sporting Life*, August 8, 1896.

72. *Sporting Life*, November 14, 1896.

73. Casway, *Ed Delehanty*, 111.

74. *Sporting Life*, December 12, 1896, cited in Casway, *Ed Delehanty*, 119–20.

75. www.baseball-reference.com/players/t/thompsa01.shtml.

76. *Philadelphia Inquirer*, July 24, 1896.

77. *Sporting Life*, October 31, 1896.

78. *Philadelphia Inquirer*, August 18, 1896.

79. *Philadelphia Inquirer*, August 27, 1896.

80. *Philadelphia Inquirer*, June 18, 1896.

81. *Philadelphia Inquirer*, April 29, 1896.

82. *Philadelphia Inquirer*, May 3, 1896.

83. *Philadelphia Inquirer*, May 7, 1896.

84. *Philadelphia Inquirer*, June 2, 1896.

85. *Philadelphia Inquirer*, June 24, 1896.

86. *Sporting Life*, October 31, 1896.

87. *Sporting Life*, February 6, 1897.

88. Casway, *Ed Delehanty*, 131.

89. *Sporting Life*, May 1, 1897.

90. *Sporting Life*, April 3, 1897.

91. *Philadelphia Inquirer*, April 8, 1897.

92. *Sporting Life*, April 24, 1897.

93. *Sporting Life*, May 22, 1897.

94. *Sporting Life*, August 7, 1897.

95. *Sporting Life*, October 2, 1897.

96. *Sporting Life*, December 25, 1897.

97. *Sporting Life*, February 4, 1898.

98. *Sporting Life*, February 12, 1898.

99. Ibid.

100. *Sporting Life*, April 2, 1898.

101. *Sporting Life*, March 26, 1898.

102. *Sporting Life*, April 9, 1898.

103. Ibid.

104. *Philadelphia Inquirer*, April 23, 1898.

105. *Sporting Life*, April 30, 1898.

106. *Philadelphia Inquirer*, April 25, 1898.

107. *Sporting Life*, April 30, 1898.

108. *Philadelphia Inquirer*, May 14, 1898.

109. *Philadelphia Inquirer*, May 15, 1898.

110. *Sporting Life*, June 11, 1898.

111. *Sporting Life*, June 4, 1898.

112. Ibid.

Chapter Five

1. Thomas Gilbert, *Dead Ball* (New York: Franklin Watts, 1996), 10.

2. Ibid., 12.

3. Seymour, 304.

4. Ibid., 302.

5. Ibid., 289.

6. Roy Kerr, *Buck Ewing: A Baseball Biography* (Jefferson, NC: McFarland, 2012), 165.

7. Franz Lidz, "More Than the Phils," portfolio.com.

8. John Shiffert, "A History of Cheating in Baseball," ziskonline.com.

9. Ibid.

10. sportencyclopedia.ocm/mlb/al/bjohnson.html.

11. Ibid.

12. Fred Lieb, *The Detroit Tigers* (Kent, OH: Kent State University Press, 2008), 22.

13. Dan O'Brien, "Rube Waddell," sabr.org/bioproj/person/a5b2cb4.

14. Ibid.

15. *Washington Post*, November 28, 1898.

16. *Sporting Life*, December 10, 1898.

17. *Sporting Life*, March 11, 1898.

18. *Sporting Life*, April 15, 1898.

19. *Sporting Life*, May 29, 1898.

20. *Sporting Life*, October 7, 1898.

21. Thomas Schlereth, *Victorian America* (New York: HarperCollins, 1991), 218.

22. *The Detroit Athletic Club News* 97, Issue 10 (October 2012), 28.

23. *Sporting Life*, October 14, 1899.
24. *Sporting Life*, November 18, 1899.
25. *Sporting Life*, April 12, 1902.
26. *Houston Daily Post*, May 2, 1898.
27. *Sporting Life*, January 6, 1900.
28. *Sporting Life*, March 10, 1900.
29. *Danville Republican*, August 30, 1900.
30. *Sporting Life*, January 5, 1901.
31. *Sporting Life*, March 30, 1901.
32. *The Republican* (Hendricks County, Indiana), April 10, 1902.
33. *Sporting Life*, May 9, 1903.
34. Unsourced, undated newspaper article, Ida Thompson scrapbook.
35. *Detroit Athletic Club News* 97, Issue 10 (October 2012), 94.
36. Al Stump, *Cobb* (Chapel Hill: Algonquin Books, 1994), 127.
37. *The Detroit Athletic Club News* 97, Issue 10 (October 2012), 87–88.
38. *Sporting Life*, September 8, 1906.
39. Ibid.
40. *Sporting News*, September 8, 1906.
41. Ibid.
42. *Washington Post*, September 16, 1906.
43. *Sporting News*, September 8, 1906.
44. *Hartford Courant*, September 1, 1906.
45. *Sporting Life*, September 8, 1906,
46. *Washington Post*, September 16, 1906.
47. *Evening Star* (Washington, D.C.), September 12, 1906.
48. *Washington Post*, September 2, 1906.
49. *Evening Star*, September 12, 1906.
50. *St. Louis Post-Dispatch*, October 8, 1973.
51. Unsourced, undated newspaper article, Sam Thompson player file, National Baseball Hall of Fame Library, Cooperstown, NY.
52. *Washington Post*, September 16, 1906.
53. Kerr, *Buck Ewing*, 62.
54. *Indianapolis Sun*, November 9, 1906.
55. Ibid.
56. *Spokane Press*, December 29, 1906.
57. Ibid.
58. Ibid.
59. Ibid.
60. *Logansport Daily Reporter*, January 23, 1908.
61. Ibid.

62. Ibid.
63. *Sporting Life*, April 25, 1908.
64. *Indianapolis Sun*, March 9, 1909.
65. Unsourced, undated newspaper article, Betty Jackson's Sam and Ida Thompson file.
66. *Tacoma Times*, April 25, 1910.
67. Ibid.
68. *Indianapolis Sun*, March 10, 1913.
69. *Seattle Star*, January 9, 1914.
70. Unsourced, undated newspaper article, Ida Thompson scrapbook.
71. Ibid.
72. *Boston Herald*, December 3, 1916.
73. Thomas Gilbert, *Superstars and Monopoly Wars* (New York: Franklin Watts, 1995), 47
74. William T. Ellis, *Billy Sunday: The Man and His Message* (Swarthmore, PA: L.T. Myers, 1914), 158.
75. *The Republican*, November 9, 1916.
76. *Detroit Times*, cited in *The Republican*, November 9, 1916.
77. Unsourced, undated newspaper article, Ida Thompson scrapbook.
78. Ibid.
79. *Detroit News*, November 7, 1922.
80. Unsourced, undated newspaper article, Ida Thompson scrapbook.
81. *Detroit News*, November 7, 1922.
82. Ibid.
83. *Detroit News*, n.d., Ida Thompson scrapbook.
84. Ibid.
85. *San Antonio Light*, November 12, 1922.
86. Unsourced, undated newspaper article, Ida Thompson scrapbook.
87. Ibid.
88. Ibid.

Chapter Six

1. These players are Tip O'Neill (225 hits in 124 games in 1887); Hugh Duffy (237 hits in 125 games in 1894), and Willie Keeler (239 hits in 129 games in 1897).
2. Jerrold Casway, "How About Big Sam Thompson?" *Nineteenth Century Notes*, Spring, 2008, 6.

3. Ed Koszarek, *The Players League* (Jefferson, NC: McFarland, 2006), 339.

4. Casway, "How About Big Sam Thompson?" 6.

5. Ralph Kiner, *Baseball Forever* (Chicago: Triumph Books, 2004), 37.

6. Ibid.

7. Ibid.

8. David Voigt, *American Baseball* (State College, PA: Penn State U Press, 1983), 289.

9. Roy Kerr, *Big Dan Brouthers* (Jefferson, NC: McFarland, 2013), 127.

10. *The Ogden Standard Examiner*, November 12, 1922.

11. *Reno Evening Gazette*, November 14, 1922.

12. Ibid.

13. Ibid.

14. Ibid.

15. *Indianapolis Times*, February 2, 1953.

16. Ibid.

17. *Indianapolis Sun*, March 26, 1961.

18. Ibid.

19. Ibid.

20. Ibid.

21. Victor B. Meyer, letter to Charles M. Seger, March 13, 1970, Sam Thompson Player File, National Baseball Hall of Fame Library, Cooperstown, NY.

22. Victor B. Meyer, letter to Charles M. Seger, January 3, 1971, Sam Thompson Player File, National Baseball Hall of Fame Library, Cooperstown, NY.

23. Ibid.

24. Ibid.

25. Ibid.

26. Victor B. Meyer, letter to Paul S. Kerr, April 27, 1971. Sam Thompson Player File, National Baseball Hall of Fame Library, Cooperstown, NY.

27. Ibid.

28. Ibid.

29. sabr.org/about/clifford-s-kachline.

30. Bob Broeg, "Sam Thompson-Forgotten Slugger," unsourced newspaper clipping, September 8, 1973, Sam Thompson Player File, National Baseball Hall of Fame Library, Cooperstown, NY.

31. Ibid.

32. Ibid.

33. Bob Broeg, unsourced newspaper clipping, February 16, 1974, Sam Thompson Player File, National Baseball Hall of Fame Library, Cooperstown, NY.

34. Ibid.

35. Bowie Kuhn, "1974 Hall of Fame Induction Ceremony Remarks," Sam Thompson Player File, National Baseball Hall of Fame Library, Cooperstown, NY.

36. Bill James, *The New Bill James Historical Baseball Abstract*, rev. ed. (New York: The Free Press, 2001).

37. Ibid., 331–369.

38. Ibid., 812.

39. Victor B. Meyer, letter to Charles M. Seger, January 3, 1971, Sam Thompson Player File, National Baseball Hall of Fame Library, Cooperstown, NY.

40. http:www.indbaseballhalloffame.org/inductees/Thompson.html.

41. Casway, "How About Big Sam Thompson?" 6.

42. David Fleitz, "Sam Thompson," in *More Ghosts in the Gallery* (Jefferson, NC: McFarland, 2007), 157; 161.

43. Nemec, "Sam Thompson," *Major League Baseball Profiles*, Vol. II, 66–67.

44. *Sporting Life*, October 15, 1904.

Bibliography

Articles

Broeg, Bob. "Sam Thompson-Forgotten Slugger." Unsourced newspaper clipping, September 8, 1973, Sam Thompson Player File, National Baseball Hall of Fame Library, Cooperstown, NY.

Browne, Paul. "Dan O'Leary." sabr.org/bioproj/person/22dc582f.

Carle, Bill. "Eugene Moriarty Found." *SABR Biographic Research Committee Report*, November/December 2013.

Casway, Jerrold. "How About Big Sam Thompson?" *Nineteenth Century Notes*, 27 (1998).

_____. "The Best Outfield Ever?" *The Baseball Research Journal*, 27 (1998).

Fleitz, David L. "Sam Thompson." *More Ghosts in the Gallery*. Jefferson, NC: McFarland, 2007.

Graf, Jeffrey. "The Term *Hoosier*." www.indian.edu/librcsd/internet/extra/hoosier.html.

Keefe, Tim. "The Brotherhood and Its Work." In *Early Innings*, Dean A. Sullivan, ed. Lincoln: University of Nebraska Press, 1995.

Lidz, Franz. "More that the Phils." portfolio.com.

Macht, Norman. "Samuel Luther Thompson." in *Baseball's First Stars*, Frederick Ivor-Campbell et al., eds. Cleveland: SABR, 1996.

Overfield, Joseph M. "James Joseph Collins." In *Baseball's First Stars*, Frederick Ivor-Campbell et al., eds. Cleveland: SABR, 1996.

O'Brien, Dan. "Rube Waddell." sabr.org/bioproj/person/a5b2cb4.

Stark, George W. "Detroit's Veteran Magnate Tells How He Kidnapped Ball Players." Unsourced newspaper article, no date, Don Thompson's Sam Thompson Clipping File.

Thompson, Don. "Sam Thompson." sabr.org.bioproj/person/be0fab8.

Books

Bak, Richard. *A Place for Summer: A Narrative History of Tiger Stadium.* Detroit: Wayne State U Press, 1998.

Block, David. *Baseball Before We Knew It: A Search for the Roots of the Game.* Lincoln: University of Nebraska Press, 2005.

Casway, Jerrold. *Ed Delehanty and the Emerald Age of Baseball.* Notre Dame: Notre Dame University Press, 2004.

Devine, Christopher. *Harry Wright: The Father of Professional Baseball.* Jefferson, NC: McFarland, 2003.

Ellis, William T. *Billy Sunday: The Man and His Message.* Swarthmore, PA: L.T. Myers, 1914. Online version at https//archive.org/details/billysundaymanhi00sundia2.

Fleitz, David. *More Ghosts in the Gallery.* Jefferson, NC: McFarland, 2007.

Gilbert, Thomas. *Deadball.* New York: Franklin Watts, 1996.

_____. *Superstars and Monopoly Wars.* New York: Franklin Watts, 1995.

Ivor-Campbell, Frederick, et al., eds.

Baseball's First Stars. Cleveland: SABR, 1986.

James, Bill. *The New Bill James Historical Baseball Abstract*, rev. ed. New York: The Free Press, 2001.

Kerr, Roy. *Big Dan Brouthers: Baseball's First Great Slugger*. Jefferson, NC: McFarland, 2013.

_____. *Buck Ewing: A Baseball Biography*. Jefferson, NC: McFarland, 2012.

Kiner, Ralph. *Baseball Forever: Reflections on 60 Years in the Game*. Chicago: Triumph Books, 2004.

Koszarek, Ed. *The Players League: History, Clubs, Ballplayers and Statistics*. Jefferson, NC: McFarland, 2006.

Leonard, John William. *The Industries of Detroit: Historical, Descriptive and Statistical*. Detroit: J. M. Elstner, 1887.

Lieb, Frederick G. *The Detroit Tigers*. Kent, OH: Kent State University Press, 2008.

Madison, James H. *The Indiana Way: A State History*. Bloomington: Indiana University Press, 1990.

Morris, Peter. *Catcher*. Chicago: Ivan R. Dee, 2009.

_____ et al., eds. *Base Ball Pioneers: 1850–1870*. Jefferson, NC: McFarland, 2012.

Nemec, David. *The Great Encyclopedia of 19th Century Major League Baseball*. New York: Donald Fine, 1997.

_____. *Major League Baseball Profiles: 1871–1900. Volume I: The Ballplayers Who Built the Game*. Lincoln: University of Nebraska Press, 2011.

_____. *Major League Baseball Profiles: 1871–1900. Volume II: The Hall of Famers and Memorable Personalities Who Shaped the Game*. Lincoln: University of Nebraska Press, 2011.

Schlereth, Thomas. *Victorian America: Transformations in Everyday Life*. New York: HarperCollins, 1991.

Seymour, Harold. *Baseball: The Early Years*. New York: Oxford University Press, 1960.

Shiffert, John. *Baseball in Philadelphia: A History of the Early Game, 1831–1900*. Jefferson, NC: McFarland, 2006.

Sowell, Mike. *July 2, 1903: The Mysterious Death of Hall-of-Famer Big Ed Delehanty*. New York: Macmillan, 1992.

Spatz, Lyle, ed. *The SABR Baseball List & Record Book*. New York: Scribner, 2007.

Stump, Al. *Cobb*. Chapel Hill: Algonquin Books, 1994.

Successful Men of Michigan: A Compilation of Useful Biographical Sketches of Prominent Men. Detroit: SI. U. Collins, 1914.

Sullivan, Dean A., ed. *Early Innings: A Documentary History of Baseball, 1825–1908*. Lincoln: University of Nebraska Press, 1995.

Voigt, David Quentin. *American Baseball: From the Gentleman's Sport to the Commissioner System*. State College: Pennsylvania State University Press, 1983.

Weekly Notes of Cases Argued in the Supreme Court of Pennsylvania, Vol. 44. Philadelphia: Kay and Brother, 1899.

Westcott, Rich. *Philadelphia's Old Ballparks*. Philadelphia: Temple University Press, 1996.

Newspapers

The Bee [Danville, Virginia]
Boston Herald
Brooklyn Eagle
Chicago Tribune
Decatur Review
Des Moines News
Detroit Evening News
Detroit Free Press
Detroit Morning Times
Detroit News
El Paso Herald
Evansville Argus
Evansville Daily Journal
Evening Star [*Washington, D.C.*]
Evening Times [Cumberland, Maryland]
Friday Caller [Plainfield, Indiana]

Hartford Courant
Hendricks County Republican
Houston Daily Post
Indianapolis Daily Journal
Indianapolis Journal
Indianapolis Sun
Indianapolis Sunday Star
Indianapolis Times
Kansas City Star
Logansport Daily Reporter
Louisville Courier Journal
Lowell Sun
National Republican [*Washington, D.C.*]
New York Times
Ogden Standard Examiner
Paris Gazette [Paris, Indiana]
Philadelphia Inquirer
Philadelphia Press
Philadelphia Record
Public Ledger [Philadelphia]
Reno Evening Gazette
The Republican [Hendricks County, Indiana]
St. Louis Post-Dispatch
Salem Daily News [Ohio]
Salt Lake Herald
San Antonio Light
Seattle Star
Spokane Press
Tacoma Times
Washington Post
Washington Times

Miscellaneous

City of Philadelphia Plat Book, Part of Ward 19, 18 & 37, 1922.
The Detroit Athletic Club News, 125th Anniversary Issue, Volume 97, Issue 10, October 2012.
Indiana State Business Directory, 1881–82.
U.S. Census, Hendricks County, Indiana, 1880.

Online Sources

www.baseball-almanac.com/rb_ofas.shtml.
www.baseball-reference.com/players/t/thompsa01.shtml.

http://www.indbaseballhalloffame.org/inductees/Thompson.html.
sportencyclopedia.ocm/mlb/al/bjohnson.html.
sabr.org/about/clifford-s-kachline
sabr.org/bioproj.

Baseball Periodicals

Sporting Life
The Sporting News

Unpublished Sources

Betty Jarabek Jackson, Sam and Ida Thompson file, Huxley, Iowa.
Bill Jenkinson, Sam Thompson player file, Willow Grove, Pennsylvania.
Bowie Kuhn, "1974 Hall of Fame Induction Ceremony Remarks," Sam Thompson player file, National Baseball Hall of Fame Library, Cooperstown, NY.
Don Thompson, Sam Thompson player file, Mesa, AZ.
Ida Thompson, Sam Thompson Scrapbook (fragments).
Keith Thompson, Sam Thompson player file, Bellport, New York.
Sam Thompson, letter to his parents, October 23, 1888, in Keith Thompson's Sam Thompson clipping file.
Sam Thompson Player File, National Baseball Hall of Fame Library, Cooperstown, NY.
Victor B. Meyer, letter to Charles M. Seger, March 13, 1970. Sam Thompson player file, National Baseball Hall of Fame Library, Cooperstown, NY.
Victor B. Meyer, letter to Charles M. Seger, January 3, 1971. Sam Thompson player file, National Baseball Hall of Fame Library, Cooperstown, NY.
Victor B. Meyer, Letter to Paul S. Kerr, April 27, 1971. Sam Thompson Player file, National Baseball Hall of Fame Library, Cooperstown, NY.

Index

Index

Index